The publisher gratefully acknowledges the generous support of the Ahmanson Foundation Humanities Endowment Fund of the University of California Press Foundation.

CALIFORNIA STUDIES IN FOOD AND CULTURE

Darra Goldstein, Editor

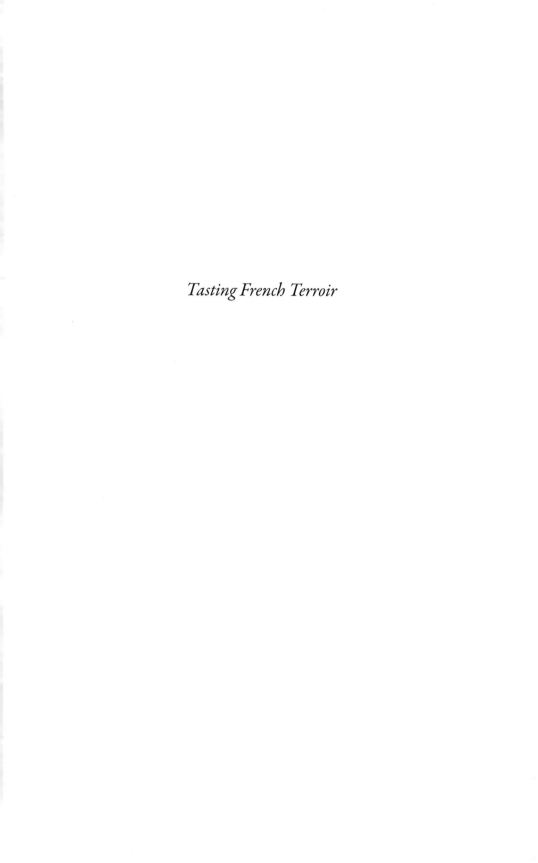

Tasting French Terroir

Tasting French Terroir

THE HISTORY OF AN IDEA

Thomas Parker

UNIVERSITY OF CALIFORNIA PRESS

University of California Press, one of the most distinguished university presses in the United States, enriches lives around the world by advancing scholarship in the humanities, social sciences, and natural sciences. Its activities are supported by the UC Press Foundation and by philanthropic contributions from individuals and institutions. For more information, visit www.ucpress.edu.

University of California Press
Oakland, California

Library of Congress Cataloging-in-Publication Data
Parker, Thomas, 1969– author.
    Tasting French terroir : the history of an idea / Thomas Parker.
        p.   cm.—(California studies in food and culture ; 54)
    Includes bibliographical references and index.
    ISBN 978-0-520-27750-2 (cloth : alk. paper)
    ISBN 978-0-520-27751-9 (pbk. : alk. paper)
    ISBN 978-0-520-96133-3 (ebook)
    1. Terroir—France—History.   I. Title.   II. Series: California studies in food and culture ; 54.
    SB387.8.F8P36   2015
    634.80944—dc23

                                                    2014039227

Manufactured in the United States of America

24   23   22   21   20   19   18   17   16   15
10   9   8   7   6   5   4   3   2   1

In keeping with a commitment to support environmentally responsible and sustainable printing practices, UC Press has printed this book on Natures Natural, a fiber that contains 30% post-consumer waste and meets the minimum requirements of ANSI/NISO Z39.48–1992 (R 1997) (*Permanence of Paper*).

This book is dedicated to all of the friends who have joined me on this prolonged quest to uncover the origin of terroir. May you all continue to boire bon et frais . . .

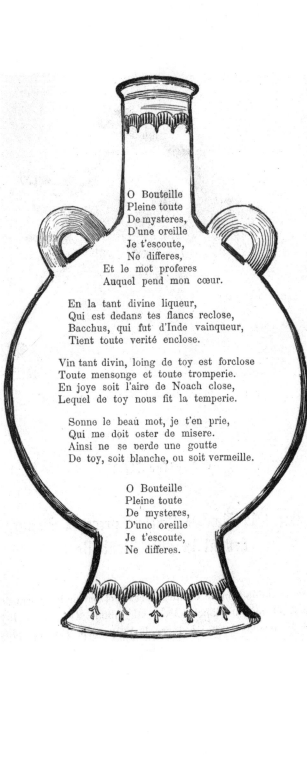

O Bouteille
Pleine toute
De mysteres,
D'une oreille
Je t'escoute,
Ne differes,
Et le mot proferes
Auquel pend mon cœur.

En la tant divine liqueur,
Qui est dedans tes flancs reclose,
Bacchus, qui fut d'Inde vainqueur,
Tient toute verité enclose.

Vin tant divin, loing de toy est forclose
Toute mensonge et toute tromperie.
En joye soit l'aire de Noach close,
Lequel de toy nous fit la temperie.

Sonne le beaù mot, je t'en prie,
Qui me doit oster de misere.
Ainsi ne se verde une goutte
De toy, soit blanche, ou soit vermeille.

O Bouteille
Pleine toute
De mysteres,
D'uno oreille
Je t'escoute,
Ne differes.

CONTENTS

ILLUSTRATIONS

ACKNOWLEDGMENTS

From conversations over glasses of wine to those over late-night lamp oil, many friends, acquaintances, and colleagues inside and outside academia were essential in bringing this project to fruition. They range from Pierre Brigandat, who offered me my first job in Champagne, France, in the late 1980s, to Bob Wesley, who taught me to drink and understand Burgundy, and Mark Whitmore, who gave me the chance to work in the wine-importing business in the 1990s. These individuals provided me with my first taste of terroir.

Many people were as generous with their knowledge and time in helping to shape the intellectual side of my project. At Vassar, I would like to thank Susan Hiner and Cindy Kerr, who read and commented on portions of the manuscript. Pierre Force and the Columbia University Early Modern Salon provided enthusiasm, inspiration, and direction by reading and commenting on an early chapter. I owe a particular debt of gratitude to François Rigolot, who was an enormous help in the Renaissance portion of the book, reading, making suggestions, and developing my working bibliography as the manuscript began to take shape. Colleagues at the North American Society for Seventeenth-Century French Literature, the Society for Interdisciplinary French Seventeenth-Century Studies, the Kentucky Foreign Language Conference, Atlantic World Foodways, and the Université de Bourgogne have listened to and commented on oral versions of many of this book's chapters. I could not have completed the project without their advice. Later, Michael Garval and Priscilla Ferguson were central in providing help as I selected artwork and a cover image. Most of all, Pauline LeVen was there throughout the writing process to provide thoughtful feedback and help me develop ideas.

The work of several scholars had a particular impact on my work. These individuals include Françoise Argod-Dutard, Julia Csergo, Jennifer Davis, Kolleen Guy, Timothy Hampton, Chandra Mukerji, Susan Pinkard, Florent Quellier, Timothy Tomasik, and Amy Trubek. Duke University and the Mellon Humanities Writ Large program were generous in providing me with a fellowship and the time to finish the book, as were the members of the French History and Cultural Seminar at the National Humanities Center, who read and commented on a chapter of the manuscript.

The people at the University of California Press have been incredible. I would like to thank Darra Goldstein, Kate Marshall, and Stacy Eisenstark for giving me the chance to work with such an incredible operation. Above all, the UC Press readers, including Jennifer Davis and Priscilla Ferguson, were instrumental. No measure of the success this work may enjoy would have been possible without their superb remarks and suggestions.

Introduction

TERROIR AND THE CULINARY ROOTS
OF FRENCH IDENTITY

IN 1962, IN A BOOK ENTITLED *Les Mots du Général de Gaulle,* Ernest Mignon sketched the personality of the first president of France's Fifth Republic with a variety of anecdotes. One illuminating quotation conjured an image of de Gaulle in a comparatively humble light, asking, "How can you be expected to govern a country that has 246 kinds of cheese?"[1] The phrase not only resonated among the French, who must have nodded their heads knowingly, thinking about the intractability of their regional neighbors, but also captured an international audience (*Newsweek* republished the same quote later in the year, disseminating the idea widely to its middle-class readers).[2] Since then, though the number of cheeses invariably changes with each retelling, the quote has become a well-worn cliché, representing a sort of truism in France and abroad: the French are finicky and opinionated about their food. Moreover, that culinary persnicketiness is iconic of the very character of a people who possess at least as many different ideas about what is "right" in politics as they do about tastes in cheese. Ironically, although the assertion is that the French are as locally varied in tastes as Babel was in tongues, France's food-centric diversity is the one thing that the nation seems to agree on unanimously, paradoxically carving out a sort of national unity through its culinary multiplicity.

While still good for a chuckle today, the sentiment that gave rise to de Gaulle's quip was far from novel when it was published by Mignon. The tradition in France of linking the food each person consumes to his or her character dates back to theories on the humors popular throughout Europe in the Middle Ages. The practice became all the more common when Renaissance France began to construct a part of the country's cultural identity by evoking the causal power of land to create differences in food, language, and people.

How and why the phenomenon resonated so strongly in France is a complicated question, but a lot can be understood by examining the nation's notion of *terroir*. That unique concept and word have served for hundreds of years in France to describe how flavor and personality in a product are determined according to its specific region or origin. This book sets out to examine the idea of terroir, demonstrating how its early evolution reveals something about the construction of a specifically French identity, the birth of culinary distinction and connoisseurship, and the sorts of regionalist and nationalist sentiments that appear above in the quote from de Gaulle.

The word *terroir* is today most prevalent among culinary enthusiasts, who use it to map a food or wine to its specific place of origin. The taste of terroir *(goût du terroir)* is understood as the spectrum of appreciable flavors or fragrances created by the unique physiographic constitution of the plot of land where a given product was grown and produced. Various rudimentary definitions existed already in the seventeenth century, when the *Dictionnaire de l'Académie française* defined terroir as "earth considered with respect to agriculture," specifying that one who indicates that a wine has a *"goût du terroir"* means that the wine has "a certain smell, a certain taste that comes from the quality of the terroir."[3] This description in turn evolved from a set of precedents and values that the following pages set out to unpack, revealing how the notion has become central to the French culinary experience. Indeed, France became so convinced of the reliability of place-based eating that the country began making regional quality control laws in the early twentieth century, staking out boundaries, articulating intrinsic characteristics, and rigorously defining agricultural products according to terroir.[4]

These efforts culminated in 1935 with the inception of the French Institut National des Appellations d'Origine (INAO), a governing organization that regulates foods and wines according to their terroir. Since then, the number of products marketed, conceived, and appreciated according to their origin has grown into a list baffling for those unacquainted with the notion. It includes wine, cheese, salt, prunes, olive oil, ham, honey, and red pepper, to name a few, but also anchovies, oysters, and mussels (whose characteristics are influenced by different areas of the sea or the *"merroir"*). In each case, specific environmental factors in tandem with a set of agricultural practices and a culturally determined method of perceiving flavor profiles allow the informed taster to trace a product to its provenance.

The INAO has physically delimited the growing area of each of these products with the designation *appellation d'origine contrôlée* (AOC) or *indication géographique protégée* (IGP). Such designations ensure, for example, that the AOC Comté cheese of the Jura is produced from the milk of Montbéliarde or French Simmental cows free-ranging on the flora from the mountain meadows of the Jura massif in the summer and on hay cut from the same fields in the winter, thus granting it flavors that cannot be imitated elsewhere. The connoisseur uses these guidelines to add an intellectual framework to gustatory and sensorial experience, formalizing the culinary moment by means of a judgment about geographic authenticity. Indeed, no small part of the enjoyment of such a product lies in the taster's determination as to how its taste corresponds to the taster's mental construct of the region in question.[5]

That a food's taste may be determined and appreciated according to its origin is easy enough to understand, but historically the French took it further. They posited that terroir affects not only the cheese *but also* the cheese-maker, not only the produce but also the farmer. This phenomenon is what the following pages set out to investigate, submitting that terroir's genesis and evolution can be used to reveal something about France's changing political, cultural, and philosophical identity. Quite simply, in many ways the French approached tasting their food in the same way that they went about perceiving people, using climatic determinism to depict normative behavior in both categories. Instead of considering itself a melting pot where flavors come together to add seamless dimension to the "plate" as a whole, France has historically found its unifying aspect in its diversity, characterized by starkly different, sometimes contrasting regional ingredients. The French consciousness of this diversity manifests itself not only in material food culture, but also in reflections on language, literature, and philosophy, reminding people of who they are (or who they *think* they are) on a daily basis.

Terroir's broad applicability in French culture allows it to function as a unique measuring stick by which to judge questions of taste and identity in relation to the influence exercised by origin. This concept is so characteristically French that other countries do not possess equivalent terms for "terroir" and resort to using the French word untranslated.[6] Indeed, no other nation in the world's history has developed the notion to the degree the French have. The results of an inquiry into the concept are both important and surprising. They tell the story of a wide-ranging essentialist relationship between humans and the earth in France. Adherents embracing terroir as a model for people included within it modalities for understanding such varied "objects" as the work of an author, an artist's painting, and even a woman's beauty. Early iterations attempted to conceptualize nations, classify languages, and make laws using

FIGURE 1. This early twentieth-century advertisement for a cocoa and chocolate product depicts the regional specialties of the Loir-et-Cher *département* with caricatures that are half people, half food or wine. The patriotic overtones are summed up by the title: *"La France Gastronomique."*

the earth's influence as a gauge for normalcy and authenticity. Ironically, these nonculinary reflections evolved back into new expectations in the connoisseurship of wine and food, in a dialogic relationship with the world of cuisine.

As the layers of terroir's history are peeled back they reveal a longstanding ambivalence toward the concept. That is, despite a trend to equate both human beings and their agricultural products with terroir, the French have demonstrated a steady counterpressure to "liberate" people, their thoughts, their physical attributes, and even their foods from the influence of the earth. At certain times, this has led segments of the culture to redefine how they perceive foods and characterize flavors in a *negative* relation to terroir. Still, even as aspects of terroir were held in low regard, the concept was paradoxically reinforced through pejorative uses. Indeed, it gained as much definition from being cast into opprobrium as it did from being held in esteem, and this tension entrenched it all the deeper in the French imagination.

FROM EARLY ORIGINS AND DEFINITIONS TO RECENT STUDIES

The concept known today as terroir derived from a variety of terms and influences, and the notion's complex genesis explains this book's approach. First, the word's own origin extends beyond agriculture strictly defined. Terroir evolved from a way of thinking about land that dates to antiquity, and derives from the Latin *territorium,* signifying the land round a town, that is, a domain, district, or territory.[7] In other words, it combines the social construction of space (town, district, etc.) with the agricultural role of land. Although some authors from antiquity, including Varro and Columella, focused on *territorium* in a more limited agricultural context, others, such as Virgil, employed the concept with greater emphasis on social space.[8] The French, from the Renaissance poets to the early modern writers of agricultural treatises, incorporated both of these senses into the country's ever-expanding development of the notion.

Among the several plausible reasons why the concept of terroir found such fertile ground in the French imagination, three stand out. First, France has historically been Europe's most developed agricultural and wine-producing country, providing ample opportunity for terroir to expand in importance literally and metaphorically in the course of being evoked in everyday life.[9] Second, both royalty and religious groups such as the Cistercian monks in Burgundy in the twelfth century and the popes in Chateauneuf-du-Pape during the Avignon papacy made certain wine regions famous, creating an association among specific vineyards, power, and social prestige. To take another early example, the *Battle of Wines* (1224) by Henri Andeli recounts in verse the legendary contest held by King Philip-Augustus, in which French and Mediterranean white wines were judged by an English priest. Those held in esteem were retained, while those deemed inferior were "excommunicated" and henceforth were received in the public mind as inferior.[10] Even at this early moment, terroirs were judged and circumscribed by the country's royal and religious authorities, a trend that would only intensify as both the king and the Church garnered increasing power in the early modern era.

Finally, although the historian Florent Quellier has shown that vendors of food used the region of origin as a selling point for fruits and vegetables as early as the thirteenth century, a confluence of factors caused a rapid evolution in the relationship between food, place, and identity in the Renaissance.[11] France's particular cultural and social evolution engaged with the agricultural paradigm in several unexpected ways. One of the most important of these includes the construction of a specifically "French" literary identity during the Renaissance. The invention of the printing press and a proliferation of books in French (instead of Latin) coincided with a moment in which writers sought ways to depict themselves as possessing a separate French linguistic individuality. Using ideas about the determining influence of the French land became a modality for understanding the identity of French language, just as such ideas were beginning to organize how wine and food were categorized.

All of this does not undermine the validity of terroir as an actual causal force, but rather underscores its perception as such. To take up once again the de Gaulle quote, what he is rumored to have said does not primarily concern the history of cheese in France, nor does it make a case for hierarchies of cheese flavors and origins. Instead, it provides a commentary on the ways the French have defined themselves with respect to food and place. By focusing on this optic and the resulting questions of identity, my approach differs from that of other methodologies and studies invoking terroir. The anthropologist Amy Trubek's excellent book *The Taste of Place: A Cultural Journey into Terroir,* for example, examines mostly modern food-centric themes of terroir in France and America. For my part, though an account of food culture occurs to some degree in every chapter of the following pages, I take up food in conjunction with terroir only insofar as it is useful in allowing us to understand a specific history of ideas and an early framing of the French nation. The historian Kolleen Guy's approach, also referred to in the pages to follow, takes aim at a series of cultural angles that interest me as well, but unlike me, she mostly concentrated on the modern evolution of the idea of terroir. My goal is not to displace the work of such scholars, but to complement it with a premodern literary, cultural, and philosophical perspective essential to the comprehension of the phenomenon. Other accounts, such as those found in the historian Susan Pinkard's book *A Revolution in Taste: The Rise of French Cuisine,* the geographer Jean-Robert Pitte's *Gastronomie française,* and the essays in Jean-Louis Flandrin and Massimo Montanari's edited volume *Food: A Culinary History,* query the history of food and culture in early modern France, but do not focus on terroir.[12] Again, the history of cuisine is not my main concern here: I am tracing a history of ideas in which food culture is often the yardstick, but not the object.

Finally, a vast array of more purely geographic and geological inquiries into the notion of terroir seek to explain how it physically alters flavors of foods and wines, including works by Emmanuelle Vaudour, more known in France, and by James Wilson and, more recently, Jancis Robinson, Hugh Johnson, and Percy Dougherty, who are better known in England and the United States.[13] Although it is common for such approaches to include a cultural dimension, these scholars too are ultimately interested in what we can know about terroir in an agricultural and food-centered analysis, this time with a more scientific perspective. Such scholars, along with others from adjoining disciplines, will, I hope, discover a new piece of terroir's history in the following pages.

SEEING TERROIR

The chapters below are organized chronologically from the Renaissance on, but I have taken care not to oversimplify by presenting a linear progression of food and identity without contradiction. In fact, there are many contradictions and much ambivalence in the evolution presented and I try to draw attention to both as they arise. Far from presenting an obstacle, these contradictions help strengthen the thesis that terroir was in fact reinforced as a concept by its divisive nature.

More important than the axis of time is that of space. The chapters below reflect on the literal and metaphorical distance that separates phenomena qualified as being influenced by terroir (food flavors, language, social mores, artistic tastes, etc.) and posit that circumstances of conflict have most readily contributed to the concept's evolution. That is, the most instructive points occur where there is friction between qualities being framed geographically. This often arises from a binary essentialism in which one set of attributes is defined negatively in opposition to another set: the qualities of the product of one terroir are known not by what they are, but by what they *are not*. The transition from one set of characteristics to another, the space where this occurs, and the reasons motivating the change ultimately best reveal the concept's nature.

Such a model is easily clarified with the tangible example of wine. The common qualification that one wine has "cherry flavors" magnifies the perceived difference between it and another wine from an adjacent terroir, where the wine taste is, say, "gamey." The way of speaking itself, the term invented to qualify the difference, replaces vaguely perceived sensorial qualities in the taster's mind to create solid, discernible, contrasting identities: "cherries" versus "game." Tasters, through these manners of speaking, suggest and create for themselves, and for others, a greater dissimilarity than might otherwise be perceived if the difference in smells were not qualified by disjunctive words and images. In a circular movement, these descriptors skew sensorial perceptions, eliciting broader perceived differences than would have been possible without them. Moving from this concrete example to the larger implications of the idea, when the French "taste their nation every day" (or taste a region of the nation), they are also enhancing the mental framework of terroir, further parsing it, and defining it in relation to *other* regions and nations in a way that reifies and reinforces both identity and differences.

It is within these parameters of identity and difference that the metric of taste is relevant. As Pierre Bourdieu famously indicated in *La Distinction* (1979), tastes (both literal and metaphorical) serve as a way of distinguishing individuals within societal hierarchies. Bourdieu's famous categorization in the culinary realm is between the *goût de nécessité* and the *goût de luxe,* with the former, the "taste of necessity," belonging to those who choose their preferences chiefly in terms of the foods that will physically sustain them. Generally speaking, the *goût de nécessité* gravitates toward foods that are heavier, heartier, and more caloric.[14] The "taste of luxury" prefers foods that are lighter, more elegant, and finally less nutritive. By demonstrating the prerequisite "cultural capital" to know about these foods and the financial capital to afford them, discriminating eaters can frame themselves as belonging to a higher economic and intellectual class. When it comes to the cultural construction of terroir, eaters in early modern France made food choices with consideration to how those choices might allow access to higher levels of social standing. Indeed, as the pages of this book will reveal, the birth of geographical connoisseurship in the seventeenth century was predicated on eating for class and distinction.

In order to query adequately the questions raised above, an expanded terminology is necessary. Along with terroir, I examine a small lexicon that functioned as synonyms, near synonyms, and closely related concepts, all of them part of the overarching development of place-based identity. These include most prominently the terms *climat* (climate), *terrain, canton, sol* (soil), and, in several more generalized contexts, *pays* (country), *territoire,* and *province.* In some situations, after terroir had acquired decidedly negative connotations, other terms or circumlocutions appeared in order to express the effect of place without emphasizing the phenomenon in a pejorative way. In other contexts, similar notions were used to describe climatic determinism on the macro-level, accounting for the effect of the general climate on a region's inhabitants. *Climat* in those contexts most often pertains to the qualities of the air (whose effect on people is often detailed only in a vague way) or to the sun and heat (which are typically ascribed as encouraging laziness and libido). I analyze *climat* in its larger sense because it provides an important model, one more often attributed to people than to plants or flavors, in which the developing notion of terroir as a multidisciplinary concept found a parallel, reinforcing application. Indeed, as Bruno Latour has argued, it is in understanding the mediation between different discourses and realms of thought that systems of meaning are created. Science is not "pure" and objectively constructed without the influence of social forces, nor are social phenomena understandable without grasping the role science has played, either explicitly or behind the scenes. All actors must be accounted for. Expanding my lexicon in parallel with my optic has allowed me to paint a more compelling, accurate, and, I hope, intriguing account of the interplay of factors behind terroir's origin.[15]

Lastly, although terroir is often defined as the flavor of "origin," it is important to draw attention to the fact that a first origin or birthplace is not always what users have in mind when they employ the word. A person or plant can be *transplanted* after birth and the power of the new terroir will take hold. Thus, terroir is sometimes, but not always, synonymous with original provenance.

Other theoretical constructs have been central in informing my treatment of terroir, nation, and identity, ranging from Mary Douglas's work *Purity and Danger*, a perceptive analysis of social wariness toward dirt and disorder that helps me to account for how terroir-based identities fell out of favor, to Norbert Elias's account of the construction of social hierarchy and power in the seventeenth century in *The Court Society*. Lastly, David Bell's *The Cult of the Nation in France: Inventing Nationalism, 1680–1800* has provided a series of distinctions separating the category of "national sentiment," which occurs in the accounts detailed below, from "nationalism," which is a modern construct dating from the years leading up to the French Revolution.

AN OVERVIEW OF TERROIR AND FRENCH IDENTITY

To reveal the relationship between French cuisine and cultural identity in the Renaissance, there is no better place to begin than François Rabelais, one of France's most iconic authors when it comes to carousing and merriment, whose works are the Holy Grail for French literary gastronauts. Chapter 1 explores how the footprint left by Rabelais's fictional giants still pervades

France's culinary identity. Through reinvigorated bacchic myth, the giants illustrate Rabelais's broader humanistic vision, foregrounding a tension that has historically been part of the French use of food and territory to qualify people. That is, terroir today speaks of sobriety, a means of lucidly framing and defining the intrinsic qualities of land according to the outward, aesthetic roadmap it projects on its products. Rabelais on the other hand, for all his attention to food, drink, and Loire Valley landmarks, centers his work on the drunken disregard of borders and boundaries in wine, language, and class. He inaugurated a French wine culture that was centered on place almost in spite of himself.

Bacchic images were polyvalent in the Renaissance, and the period also saw the rise of a naturalistic trend toward terroir in the group of contemporaneous poets known as the Pléiade. In their verse, Bacchus appears both as an inebriation that obviates borders of time and space, and also as its contrary, a georgic fascination with the power of the soil to define human character according to place. The evolution and establishment of terroir in the French imagination at this point occurred primarily not in respect to wine, but rather in respect to regional pride and poetry. This poetry and prose together created an ethos around wine that would influence agricultural manuals of the time and endure to the present day.

As Renaissance France began to frame itself as a country, anthropological considerations of the influence of place on human behavior become frequent outside the culinary context. Authors such as Michel de Montaigne, France's most prominent essayist, and Jean Bodin, often referred to as France's first major political theorist, illustrate this trend clearly at the end of the sixteenth century. Chapter 2 demonstrates how these considerations, along with the literary influences examined in chapter 1, rival in importance more strictly agricultural reflections on the influence of the earth. After being normalized with respect to humans, meditations on the still inchoate concept of terroir returned to the world of plants at the end of the century in Olivier de Serres's *Théâtre d'agriculture,* France's most famous agricultural manual.

Chapter 3 reports on the much different trajectory of terroir in the seventeenth century, where it was once again central to questions of identity. Examining the influence of important language theorists, such as Vaugelas and Bellegarde, demonstrates that as much as language helped give rise to the concept of terroir in the sixteenth century, it also spurred great ambivalence toward it in the seventeenth century. The very identification with terroir that the poets of the Renaissance had glorified was now widely debased. That shift has much to tell us about societal values at a time when France was reaching its historical apogee of prestige and world influence. During that moment, anything described as "tasting of the terroir" became a sign of rusticity and impurity. That is not to say that origins were not important markers of prestige at the time. Indeed, the very factors that served to make terroir a dubious attribute were also instrumental in cementing the concept in a French society that cleaved to hierarchies. Those who were not rustic *needed* others to "smell of the terroir" in order to distinguish themselves as pure and unblemished. Modern connoisseurship, born at this point, did not arise as much from a love of food and wine as from a need for social distinction.

During this recalibration, considerations of the role of terroir spread from language to the aesthetics of the garden, with Versailles as its epitome. The new emphasis on rationality bolstered an urge not to coexist with but to *control* nature through science, and reinforced a trend in taste in which the "natural" was broken into two categories: "high nature," or nature as it should exist, and nature as it actually existed, riddled with imperfection and altered by the contingencies of life on earth. Chapter 4 examines how nature was "denatured" as individuals sought to perfect it, notably in the gardens of Versailles, where the machinations concerning plant life were foils for the lives of human beings.

Chapter 5 outlines how seventeenth-century French society helped reinforce food and class identity at a socially charged moment in its historical evolution. The practice of connoisseurship was indelibly shaped by Saint-Évremond, the most famous food snob of the seventeenth century. His proclivity for the wines from Champagne hinged on many factors, including new iterations of Hippocratic and Galenic understandings of health and humors. The medical discourse on humors was already mostly obsolete in late seventeenth-century science, yet remained central when it came to social debates and the politics of class.

Chapter 6 bridges the divide between social class and political identity, explaining how circumstances combined to bring terroir to center stage in an attempt to save France's bourgeoning concept of national unity in a debate early in the eighteenth century between proponents of the *thèse nobiliaire* (advocating the legitimacy of the nobles as a ruling class) and those of the *thèse absolutiste* (supporting absolute rule by the monarch). Led by the writings of the Count de Boulainvilliers, disenfranchised nobles questioned the unchecked absolutist jurisdiction of Louis XIV and Louis XV, arguing that as nobles they had hereditary rights to power and higher social standing.

The response to this threat came from one of the eighteenth century's most respected aesthetic theorists, the Abbot Du Bos, who, using terroir as a tool, dismantled the exclusionary ideology brought to the fore by Boulainvilliers.

Chapter 7 reflects on how, in the years leading up to the Revolution, terroir came to be a part of what made a French person French. In other words, terroir returned to fashion in certain circles just in time to redefine and cement French roots, through a definition that framed nationhood. This novel turn in terroir's evolution was born out of considerations removed from food mores, but, as the chapter brings to light, terroir soon made its entrance back into wine and food. Here, in what one might describe as the rebirth of a terrestrial nation, it is possible to underscore the pre- and immediate post-Revolutionary consequences that this development would have in the food world and the world at large.

The conclusion provides a short account of how this complex and polyvalent history exercises influence on modern ideas about terroir. To this end, I offer a reflection that begins in the early years of the twentieth century when terroir became highly visible in the French public eye. I present a panoramic perspective of the concept's use through two optics: terroir as it radiates from the land toward expectations concerning its produce, and terroir as it is perceived from the outside inward, allowing tasters to experience and *live* the land indirectly through its fruits. This demonstration will, I hope, incite my readers to conclude with me that twentieth-century practices of tasting terroir began hundreds of years ago and were shaped as much by considerations in the realm of literature, language, and national identity as by a priori "scientific" discourses. In the end, I submit that, just as the French appreciate the diverse fragrances of a wine by knowing a little something about its origin, we will better understand French culture itself if we grasp terroir by its historical roots.

ONE

Rabelais's Table and the Poets
of the Pléiade

BOTH FRANÇOIS RABELAIS'S sixteenth-century mock epic in prose and
the writings of the group of poets known as the Pléiade provide great insight
into how fictional representations of food and wine linked origins to identity.[1] Consider the two influences in juxtaposition: on the one hand, Rabelais
presents depictions of regional, cultural, linguistic, and culinary boundaries
in order to transgress them, building walls only to break them down and
create harmony among readers. On the other hand, the poets of the Pléiade
use language on wine to reaffirm territorial distinctions, establishing identity
and harmony by forming communities *within* regional walls. These influences in the realm of fiction created an important dialogue that dovetailed
later in the century with a burgeoning corpus of wisdom texts on wine, farming, and food to mark the beginning of terroir's modern evolution. This chapter details that phenomenon, elucidating the literary contributions behind a
specifically French brand of culinary aesthetics and regional identity in the
Renaissance.

RABELAIS: TRANSGRESSING BORDERS IN BODY,
LANGUAGE, AND SPACE

There is no better place to begin a discussion on the role of food in France's
cultural imagination than Rabelais, who remains widely known for the extravagant culinary exploits depicted in his writing. Besides recounting epic culinary
consumption, his five-volume complete works invite readers into a bawdy and
biting satire of religion, a criticism of unjust war, and a hilarious yet profound
representation of humanist values initially centered around the adventures of

two giants: Gargantua and his son Pantagruel. The second book of the series, which I examine closely below, *The Very Horrific Life of the Great Gargantua, Father of Pantagruel* (1534), precedes the first in terms of the narrative's chronology, and begins with the birth of Gargantua to his parents Grandgousier and Gargamelle.[2] Even though the term *terroir* appears only once in the work (in chapter 49 of the third volume of the series), Rabelais succeeds in taking food, place, and identity center stage throughout his opus.

Ironically, Rabelaisian food descriptions construct place in the opposite way from what one would expect: just as often as he uses geographical features to create individual identities, Rabelais elides distinctions by conflating food and people from different areas. Far from causing the significance of the provenance to disappear, this tactic has just the opposite effect, reaffirming the importance of origin as an object of transgression. Nowhere is this more evident, as I will show immediately below, than when initially stark representations of place and cuisine are challenged by linguistic tropes and depictions, blotting out the credibility of regional connoisseurship through comical images of an indiscriminate, all-consuming body.

From the beginning of *The Very Horrific Life,* even before the birth of Gargantua, Rabelais brings these strategies to bear, providing an example of the importance of food in a "bodily" description of the giant's father, Grandgousier (the name signifies "big throat"), that doubles as a characterization of France's culinary wealth:

> Grandgousier was a great joker in his time, loving to drink hearty as well as any man who was then in the world, and fond of eating salty. To this end, he ordinarily had on hand a good supply of Mainz and Bayonne hams, plenty of smoked ox tongues, an abundance of andouilles in season and mustard salted beef. Backed up by botargo, a provision of sausages (not those of Bologna, for he feared Lombard mouthfuls), but of Bigorre, of Longaulnay, of La Brenne, and of La Rouergue.[3]

The accumulation of meats and sausages suggests geographic diversity humorously in the fatty, intestinal offerings from the four corners of the country (roughly speaking, Mainz or "Mayence," though now in Germany, was historically one of these corners, Bayonne another, Brittany and Provence, represented in the list of sausages, the two others). These copious preparations speak to the variety of France's offerings and terroirs, while casting Grandgousier as an icon of France as he symbolically incarnates the country's collective wares by enthusiastically ingesting them. Yet, though the passage constructs terroirs in the reader's imagination, it also breaks them down, as the regional specialties are assimilated indifferently in Grandgousier's belly.

The same phenomenon occurs linguistically: the passage reflects culinary variety in the food catalogued, mixing common French vernacular terms with strange names and places (e.g., the un-French sounding word *botargo,* a Mediterranean caviar preparation made from red mullet, and the Breton place-name Longaulnay).[4] Just as with foods, the names serve as often to destabilize identity as to frame it. As the Rabelaisian narrator himself later points out, the name of one of the primary characters, the giant Pantagruel, unites two linguistic groups and two lands: *panta* means all in Greek and *gruel* signifies thirst in Arabic.[5] Gargantua, for his part, is baptized both for his enormous throat (*garganta* means throat in both Spanish and Portuguese) and for the name's resemblance to the bodily function *gargouiller* (to gurgle), a noise that in medieval French mixes connotations of ingestion and excretion, since it can just as easily apply to the throat as to the intestines. Finally Gargamelle, Gargantua's mother, has a Langdocien name signifying throat (*gargamello)* that originally derives from the Arabic for the same word.[6] Like the meat items above, specific countries, regions, and linguistic heritages are summarily evoked only to be immediately subsumed in the all-assimilating umbrella of Rabelais's prose, inviting readers to leave pretensions about their own geographic identity behind in favor of collective merriment.

This breaking of boundaries is mirrored in the stories' fascination with the excess of physical quantities and the overstepping of limits. Although the giants' prodigious anatomies and unerring drive for culinary satisfaction make them convincing gourmands (Gargantua is born shouting an imperative, "Drink, drink, drink"), they are less credible as gourmets. Indeed, Grandgousier, Gargamelle, and other characters, such as Panurge and Frère Jean, who appear in the later volumes, tend toward indiscriminate eating, pleasure, and song. This bacchanalian atmosphere is constantly recalled by the language play of the passages, which seems to suggest the importance of excessive drinking over measured enjoyment: the text is peppered with maxims such as "it is to me an eternity of boozing and boozing for eternity," "always drinking," "forever watering," and "keep drinking, you'll never die."[7] Each quote accentuates excess by omitting any mention of chronological borders or physical limits, implying the triumph of an all-encompassing gluttonous, corporal inebriation over mindful consumption.

FIGURE 2. This 1950s postcard features the "Keep drinking, you'll never die" quote from *Gargantua*. The design both reaffirms the individual identities of the wine-producing towns, in the separate photos and map, and elides them, in the excessive hedonism suggested by the quote and in the visual blending between the palpable bunches of grapes, the woman's curvaceous breasts, and the similarly curvy glass of wine.

Nowhere is Rabelais's excess presented more clearly than when the narrator describes Gargantua's table manners in the first book. The studied appreciation of foods and origins through moderation and refinement could not be further removed from this graphic, bodily depiction:

> Meanwhile four of his men threw into his mouth, one after the other continuously, mustard by the pailful. Then he drank a horrific draft of white wine to relieve his kidneys. Afterward, he ate according to the season, food to suit his appetite, and he stopped eating when his belly was dilated. For drinking he had no end nor rule, for he said that the bounds and limits of drinking were when, as the person drank, the cork in his slippers swelled upward a half a foot.[8]

Between the doses of mustard, the images of kidneys and bellies (the choicest cuts always get less emphasis than the entrails in Rabelais), the gulps of wine, and the distended midsections, the reader realizes readily that these exploits at the table hardly symbolize culinary refinement. The real key lies in the last sentence: *For drinking he had no end nor rule.* The rest of this book will show that connoisseurship, as it took shape in France, consisted in drawing limits and cataloguing flavors according to the specificity of alimentary origins in a discerning and mindful way. The Rabelaisian character doles out counterexamples: he exists in a world of excess where the bounds and limits evoked are most often the ones his unrestrained ingestion breaks.

One of the most bawdy—and *bodily*—moments of the five books illustrates this point perfectly. The scene in question is one where Rabelais evokes wine in the context of excretion rather than of discriminating culinary appreciation. As Gargantua and Grandgousier are discussing the merits of various swabs for wiping behinds (the suggestions range from goose necks, to cats, to velvet), Gargantua's father praises and encourages his son for his prodigious findings and rewards him with the promise of wine: "Oh," said Grandgousier, "[. . .] go on with your ass-wipative discourse, I pray you. And, by my beard! For one puncheon you shall have sixty casks, I mean of good Breton wine, which does not grow in Brittany, but in that good Véron region."[9] The humor lies not only in the excessive amounts of wine given in recompense but also in its specificity, and the emphasis on its goodness in the unpalatable scatological context. More importantly, the misnomer *vin breton* constitutes a telling sign of the territorial ambivalence and language games that run throughout Rabelais's work: there is a disjunction between the name of the wine and its origin. The wine is from Véron, a very small place-specific viticultural town close to Chinon, but it is here named for the Bretons, who were known for their excessive consumption of Loire wine, shipped upriver for their personal use.[10]

Such transgression of borders (both geographical borders and the social borders of good taste) ultimately reaffirms the existence of the identities those borders frame. This is apparent in Rabelais's modern legacy in the Loire Valley, where most of the fictional exploits take place. That association is a source of pride in the Touraine region, where a recent festival sponsored by the local *Maison des vins* and tourist office offered a conference about Rabelais's imprint on the collective local imagination.[11] To give a particularly compelling example, despite the ambiguity and the "ass-wipative" context in which the reference to *vin breton* occurs, the tourist board of Véron continues to cite that passage today in its website documentation of the region, using Rabelais's cultural capital to bolster Véron as a perennial wine-producing terroir distinct from other regions.[12]

RENAISSANCE BACCHUS AND THE LITERARY
CONSTRUCTION OF WINE CULTURE

When it comes to framing French Renaissance wine culture in both prose and poetry, there is no element quite so central as the mythological character Bacchus. Half man and half god (his Greek analogue, Dionysos, is the son of the mortal Semele and of Zeus), Bacchus was the protector of vines, overseeing viticulture in a rational, naturalized context. He was also the god of drunken revelry and excess. Renaissance literature inscribed these multiple aspects of the myth into its pages and, in so doing, created a broader meaning for wine that continues to endure in French culture. Indeed, literary fiction helped reinforce images of wine as a beverage with a purpose beyond either mere sustenance or the medicinal ends that otherwise preoccupied the period's wine writing.

In the pages of Rabelais, Bacchus is a force not only of inebriation and folly, but also of conviviality, universality, and great wisdom. In the group of sixteenth-century Renaissance poets known as the Pléiade, Bacchus often connotes enjoying friendship and maximizing the pleasure of daily life. But there is another element at play. Through representations borrowed from the Virgilian tradition of didactic poetry, Bacchus appears in a naturalistic register of farming and place-specific wines, deployed not to celebrate culinary culture in itself, but to create linguistic identity and foster poetic inspiration. Instead of standing for a force of inebriation, he represents lucidity; instead of defining terroir in negative terms, he circumscribes it positively in a discourse on place and the origin of language. Renaissance French bacchic culture at once transcends and frames terroir as a trope for literary and culinary identity.

In *Gargantua,* bacchic references, specifically to Silenus, traditionally the tutor of Bacchus, and the donkey that almost always accompanies him, appear in the opening lines of the prologue. There, the narrator invokes Bacchus by way of the passage in Plato's *Symposium* where Alcibiades likens Socrates to Silenus.[13] Glossing Plato, Rabelais invites readers to "consume" the pages that follow, assimilating the reading with the practice of having a cool drink. In other words, the consumption in question is not the highfalutin stuff of pompous literary pronouncements, nor of highly discerning culinary choices for that matter, but a refreshment that comes easily and naturally in a sort of literary inebriation that Rabelais invites his readers to share.

In fact, after the first pages, one might conclude that in order to read Rabelais seriously, one must paradoxically read him for fun, as if enjoying a glass or two of wine.

> Most illustrious drinkers, and you, most precious poxies—for you, not to others my writings are dedicated—Alcibiades, in Plato's dialogue entitled *The Symposium,* praising his master Socrates, incontrovertibly the prince of philosophers, among other things says he is like the Sileni. Sileni were in olden times little boxes, such as we see nowadays in apothecaries' shops, painted on the outside with merry frivolous pictures [. . .] but inside they preserved fine drugs [. . .] and other valuables.[14]

In Greco-Roman mythology, Sileni are half-man and half-goat followers and companions to Bacchus. That mix of human and animal forms foreshadows Rabelais's overstepping of linguistic, terrestrial, and social borders, but it also offers another, more important lesson. As the prologue explains, Alcibiades makes the comparison because Socrates, though ugly on the outside, contained infinite wisdom on the inside. This representation offers one of many contradictions that will endure throughout the work: drunken excess on the exterior ultimately leads to wisdom, virtue, and sobriety on the interior.[15] As Rabelais points out, the boxes of pharmaceuticals are a metaphor for the book itself. The work is like a vessel holding great wisdom that the reader taps into through enjoyment. Laughter leads to an epiphany and to "superhuman understanding." For Rabelais, the understanding in question is not to be found in the end, but in the joyous means of the investigation. As the author hastens to add, borrowing and reversing the sense of an adage Erasmus applied to Demosthenes, his pages were composed with "more wine than oil." In other words, bacchic inspiration from wine contributed to the work's genesis more than labored travails completed with late-night lamp oil. Accordingly, readers are enjoined to consume the pages with joy.

This ethos pervades the five books of the series and provides a clear example of how a Rabelaisian ideal seeped into French culinary culture. In France today, there is a class of wines that are for easy drinking, referred to as *vins de soif,* or "wines for thirst." These wines hold no pretensions toward being the object of "serious" analysis and are intended to create flowing conversation and conviviality. To take one relevant example, the Loire Valley wine producers Catherine and Pierre Breton offer a "Cuvée Trinch," a direct reference, the label explains, to Rabelais. They bill it as fruity wine made with young vines, to drink without compunction or afterthought during a spontaneous lunch, in contrast with their more serious, contemplative "terroir" wines that need to be aged. The focus for the Trinch wine is on social communion rather than connoisseurship.

But there is far more to Bacchus in Rabelais. True to the prologue, the reader's journey is filled with lavish eating and carnivalesque depictions whose topical signification quickly gives way to a more sustained philosophical or social meaning. This is the case throughout the five-volume series, but it is the last volume that offers some of the most compelling scenarios concerning wine and identity.[16] Diverse images of Bacchus emphatically suggest wine as a panacea when Pantagruel, joined by Panurge and Frère Jean, nears the completion of his journey to find the oracular Divine Bottle *(la Dive bouteille)*. This bottle, for all of the pomp associated with it, is destined to foretell only whether or not Panurge will be cuckolded if he marries. Despite its triviality, the quest for the bottle gives rise to several instances where representations of Bacchus and Silenus simultaneously reinforce and undermine wine's specific terrestrial identity.

The first important moment occurs as the trio make their way to the doors of the subterranean temple where the Divine Bottle lies and discover, inscribed in gold letters in Greek, the sentence "In wine is truth." The maxim, originally attributed to the Greek poet Alcaeus, greets the travelers as they proceed. Since it was a common Renaissance theme to suggest that the truth dwells beneath the earth, the oracular placement of the Greek adage seems all the more plausible.[17] A further auspicious sign combines wine, truth, and the specificity of place: the text indicates that the Divine Bottle lies buried beneath the soil of the Loire Valley wine town Chinon, which is also Rabelais's birthplace. The prestige of the place and the "realness" of it in terms of the author's biological origins suggest that great truths should be around the next corner.

The jocular image of Bacchus, however, quickly reemerges and drowns out any serious analytic ponderings about telluric verities. Instead of accentuating the notion of terroir or of a specific origin for the Divine Bottle, the text evokes origin and identity only to trample over it. Notwithstanding the place-specificity of Chinon, the temple entrance lies beyond a mixed vineyard whose heterogeneous vines hail from diverse regions, countries, and even different time periods: "Approaching the temple of the Dive Bouteille, we had to pass through a great vineyard formed of all kinds of wines, such as Falernian, Malmsey, Muscadine, Tabbia, Beaune, Mirevaux, Orléans, Picardent, Arbois, Coussy, Anjou, Graves, Corsica, Véron, Nérac, and others.

The vineyard was planted long ago by Bacchus, with such a benediction that in every season it bore leaves, flowers, and fruits like the orange trees of San Remo."[18] This description both reinforces the oenological identity of these places by naming them and dismantles them, in the same sort of hodgepodge of diversity that characterized the sausages in Grandgousier's belly. The famous wines of the Renaissance world confuse culinary identity in a senseless communal vineyard where northern latitudes mix with southern, wet with dry, cold with warm, old with new, and prestigious with mundane. The description collapses wine's natural boundaries and, instead of valorizing the qualities of the earth, accentuates the occult influence of Bacchus by transgressing geography and chronology alike: the physical medley of appellations bear fruit from every place in every season.

The ongoing abrogation of limits appears with the most resonance when Panurge finally drinks from the Divine Bottle near the end of the last book. The group is confronted with the oracular bottle, which cracks in the fountain waters in which it is immersed and begins to boil. As it rends, there is a gasp, "Then was heard this word: *Trinch*."[19] Panurge is called upon to gloss the wine as he drinks it, and as he is invited to combine textual interpretation and wine consumption, the situation seems propitious at last for the analytic experience to take precedent over hedonistic revelry. The Divine Bottle *ought* to yield through rational analysis a concrete message of wisdom. Yet when the opened bottle finally reveals itself from the fountain as a mythical Falernian wine shaped like a book, it does something different.[20]

Instead of volumes of insight pouring forth, the bottle rewards the band with just a droplet of a word: *trinch*. The sound is inauspicious, but the result is more meaningful than it would first appear. Bacbuc, the group's initiatress and guardian of the bottle (her name derives from the Hebrew word for bottle), explains: "*Trinch* is a panomphaen word celebrated and understood by all nations, and it means 'Drink' [*Beuvez*]. Therefore we maintain that not by laughing but by drinking does man distinguish himself. I don't say drinking simply and absolutely in the strictest sense, for beasts drink as well as man, but I mean drinking cool delicious wine. Take note, friends, that from wine we incline to the divine [*de vin divin on devient*] [. . .] for power it has to fill the soul with all truth, all knowledge, and philosophy."[21] The oracle thus utters a universally understood word for conviviality, further distancing the imagery from any sort of geographical precision in order to affirm an all-inclusive humanist truth. The awareness of each individual as part of a pan-geographic togetherness continues to hold sway through an inebriated sort of poetic ecstasy, as Panurge launches into the peroration of gibberish in senseless rimes and verse that closes the book. The entire scene colorfully reenacts the message the Rabelaisian narrator had already summed up perfectly in the *Quart livre:* "By the aid of Bacchus (that's the good tasty delicious wine) are the spirits of humans raised high, their bodies evidently lightened, and what was terrestrial in them is made supple."[22] Bacchus both represents the earth and acts as a conveyance for transcending earth's physical holds in placeless, universal joy.

FRENCH VERSE AND THE VINE: FROM SKY TO EARTH IN THE POETRY OF THE PLÉIADE

Variations on Rabelaisian themes that promoted Bacchus as a force paving over difference in favor of unity made their way into French poetry of the 1540s and 1550s, while other images did just the opposite.[23] Both aspects of the poetic testimony in question came from the Renaissance poets of the Pléiade, which included most notably Pierre de Ronsard, Joachim du Bellay, Jacques Peletier du Mans, Remy Belleau, and Jean-Antoine de Baïf. The Pléiade made use of images of wine and the vine as it endeavored to accentuate the distinctiveness of the French language, using the latter as a base on which to build an entire national identity. Most prominent in this mission was du Bellay's *Defense and Illustration of the French Language,* which appeared in 1549.

The significance of this work from du Bellay with respect to agriculture and identity is unmistakable, but the transition to wine as building boundaries through language, instead of breaking down barriers, is not as abrupt, and the poetry of the Pléiade conveys both messages. Similar to Rabelais's depiction in the *Quart livre,* several poetic representations of wine positioned it as working to deliver earth to the heavens and heavens to the earth in the form of inspiration and communion with the gods.[24] In Pierre de Ronsard's *Hymne de Bacchus,* wine initiates the drinker to a repast in the heavens that dissolves earthly differences and invites mortals to rub elbows with immortals:

> With you, Father, replete with your sweet ambrosia
> We lift human fancy to the sky
> Carried in your chariot, and of vicious men

Purged from your liquor, we dare rise to the heavens
And sit at the great Jupiter's table.[25]

Along with harmony and communion, the poets of the Pléiade offered even more fundamental reasons to partake: the abstemious person is "mired in sadness," while those who tipple are united in good health, joy, and dance. Such representations are not far from the depictions of wine in Rabelais, but they also derive from the advent of new elements nuancing bacchic representation.

The source of one such nuance was Henri Estienne's rediscovery of pseudo-Anacreontic poetry, which Estienne mistakenly thought dated to Greece's Archaic period, in the fifth or sixth century BCE.[26] Estienne had, in fact, discovered third century BCE imitations of Anacreontic verse (later called Anacreonta). He and the Pléiade construed the work, which included a large series of bacchic songs, to be from the earliest reaches of classical Greek civilization and thus to incarnate pure human expression and naturalness before it had been "corrupted" by time and successive layers of cultural patina. This supposed naturalness in verse was thought to be one of the greatest gifts antiquity could bestow upon the Renaissance poetic endeavor, and the Pléiade, likening it to unadulterated agricultural produce, sought to appropriate it as a linguistic model for the bourgeoning French language, which the poets valued for its relative youth and purity.

Pseudo-Anacreontic verse lacked the prodigious excess of Rabelais, but was explicit in promoting themes of good company, abundance, and corporal gratification. Perhaps the most important notion associated with it was that of *carpe diem,* a theme that came about in large part from the influence of Horace, but which the Pléiade poets also viewed as having been a central component of wine and writing in Anacreon.[27] Happiness was not hopelessly mediated away from the "here and now," relegated to the vagaries of the afterlife, but known instantly—and naturally—through writing, drinking, and other terrestrial pleasures. One poem by Ronsard reunites these features strikingly, expressing the amicable spirit of wine and the ambiance sought in the poetic endeavor. Evoking *carpe diem* in addressing Corydon, the stock poetic name for a shepherd, Ronsard depicts Bacchus as whiling away the summer under the shade of a trellis. The verse encourages readers to live day by day, enjoying rural life, friendship, and the fruits of the earth, but also equates drinking to literary production, suggesting that the two are joined in an organic process:

Man after his ultimate death
No longer drinks or eats over there,
And his barn that he left
Full of wheat before his demise,
And his cellar full of wine
No longer enter his mind.
Hey, what benefits does anxiety bring?
[...] Pour and repour some more
Into this great golden goblet.
I am going to drink to Henri Estienne,
Who gave us from the underworld
The sweet Teian lyre
Lost by old Anacreon.
To you, graceful Anacreon,
The cup owes its pleasure,
And Bacchus owes to you his bottles;
Venus owes to you her companion, Love,
And Silenus owes to you to drink away
The summer under the shade of the trellis.[28]

Everything in this poem mediated by Anacreontic verse lends itself to portraying the friendship and conviviality that went with French Renaissance wine culture. The georgic images of a barn and wine cellar, the invocation of familiar names, and the informal verb in the second person imperative bring the gods to the ground in a natural register.

More than drinking is going on here, though. In addition to the invocation of a lyre, the instrument of poetic inspiration, from the Ionian city Teos, the birthplace of Anacreon, the language unites words and wine. Specifically, the "pour and repour some more"—*verse et reverse encore*—doubles as a word game in French, with the imperative *verse* reminiscent of the verb *versifier,* to compose verse. Moreover, *vers* both means verse in French and also would have suggested its homonym *verre,* or drinking glass. The repetitive drinking (*reverse* meaning repour) and the successive lines of poetry go hand in hand, inviting the reader into the happy world of wine consumption and joyous literary creation.

Most importantly, although the representation is not place specific, it *is* specific in linking literary inspiration to the ground and to a summer day under a trellis, evoking a natural relationship between the poet, the earth, its produce, and its seasons. Instead of blurring the latter, as Rabelais had done, the author brings time and place into sharp focus. Such changes were soon to combine with another important evolution as the Pléiade began to present a rationalized depiction of Bacchus with a personal and poetic identity defined by specific places. Once again, the impetus for the characterization came from antiquity: not from Plato as was the case in Rabelais, but from Virgil.

VIRGIL'S INFLUENCE ON FRENCH RENAISSANCE LAND, AGRICULTURE, AND LANGUAGE

In 1636, when the English poet John Dryden purportedly referred to Virgil's *Georgics* as "the best poem by the best poet," he reaffirmed what many in France already believed. Ninety years earlier, members of the Pléiade such as Peletier du Mans and Ronsard, deeply inspired by Virgil's didactic style and thematic content, had roundly heralded his poetry for its perfection.[29] Virgil's *Georgics*, divided into four books that mimic the natural cycle of the seasons, bills itself as an educational poem on agriculture and working the land. Yet despite the apparent simplicity of its subject, the *Georgics* is often termed the most inscrutable of Virgil's works, clearly destined for educated audiences with little experience getting their hands dirty farming.[30] Readers perceived early on that the *Georgics* doubled as a parable on social and political life, employing agricultural metaphors to convey far-reaching messages.[31] Virgil's poem encourages the reader on both practical and ethical grounds to toil in order to survive and to benefit from nature, which could be either a positive or a hostile force. To prevail and find solutions, Virgil posits, his reader needs to think logically and find the determining causes of natural phenomena. In the *Georgics,* those causes and the resulting solutions are often located in the soil.

Book 2 of the *Georgics,* summarily titled *On Trees,* delivers a detailed account of viticulture that captivated the imagination of French Renaissance writers in particular. Its proem begins by spotlighting fields and stars and ends with Bacchus not drunk but diligently working in the winemaker's vat:

> Thus far the tillage of the fields and the stars of heaven:
> now you, Bacchus, will I sing [...]. Come hither, Lenaean
> sire, strip off your buskins and with me plunge your naked
> legs in the new must.[32]

Bacchus is heralded as a king ("sire," translated from the Latin *pater*), and there is an oblique reference to his theatrical tradition through his buskins and the epithet "Lenaean" (the Lenaia was a classical Greek festival celebrating Dionysos and included the production of plays).[33] In stripping off his shoes, however, the actor also strips his façade and is reborn without pretension in the "new" must of the wine. Indeed, the reader is astounded to see Bacchus joining in physical labor, slogging barelegged in the vat to crush grapes. Rather than communicating boundless silliness or endowing the poet with wings and sending his creative spirit aloft, Bacchus exalts the toils of the earth. "Nature lies under the soil" *(solo natura subest),* exclaims Virgil several lines later, and we are given to conclude that an explanation of the working of the world will come from an understanding of and communion with the earth's soils, not from the mysteries of the gods.[34]

Jacques Peletier du Mans, one of the early members of the Pléiade, owes a tangible debt to Virgil in his poem *L'Automne.* There he contradicts the whimsical insouciance of Rabelais's representation of wine, borrowing directly the image of Bacchus descending from the skies to help in the vat. As the name suggests, the poem is based within the framework of the natural cycle of the earth. This time, however, Bacchus's role is even further "grounded" than in Virgil, in a celebration that unites humans, nature, and technique:

> Winey Bacchus readies his hoops,
> Prepares wine presses, and repairs vessels.
> The harvester has his feet completely soiled
> From stamping and squashing the grapes.
> And this first run *(mère goutte)* taste
> That the pressed grape gives,
> In an undulating torrent
> Flows into the vat,
> And the large barrel works hard, and groans
> In a torturous embracing of the must.[35]

The poem expands Bacchus's role in its technical representation of presses, barrels, and grape must. The lexicon of labor is central, complete with the sounds of groaning. Bacchus thus finds himself on the human side of things, wrapped up in the nitty-gritty of winemaking. Not only will he stomp grapes, but he will also be involved in the specialized procedures of readying the winemaker's equipment for the process. The poem in French evokes the *mère goutte* not merely as specialized wine vocabulary meaning free-run juice, but as an image of the "earth mother." We are unequivocally in the context of naturalized mythology, in a celebration based on the Virgilian model. This fact is further confirmed when Peletier du Mans takes up a conversation on grafting roots several lines later, integrating yet another of the defining characteristics of the *Georgics.*[36]

Virgil's reception by the Pléiade reveals an evolution of thought in which perceptions of Bacchus remained poeticized, but also became progressively more rationalized, with wine and the vine taking hold of the French imagination as a science in which elements of divine inspiration joined rational labor. The trend of mythology being rationalized and naturalized in Virgil's *Georgics* is here distilled into a French vision of wine, language, and identity vastly different from that of Rabelais. It blends references to the god into a lengthy discussion on soils and microclimates in an ordered, rational discourse on the culture of vines and wine. Even more importantly, members of the Pléiade used the rationalized vision of wine provided by Virgil to describe how poetic language could be created, not as a product of drunken inspiration, but as a regional, agricultural product with an identity determined by the poet working in harmony with a specific place.

Joachim du Bellay explains in his *Défense et illustration de la langue française* (1549) that France, like Virgil's Rome, provides an auspicious climate to produce a rich harvest in both words and agriculture. Du Bellay elegizes France by borrowing directly from book 2 of the *Georgics,* in a depiction that first seems to be praising agricultural abundance only, but that in fact uses a discourse on the richness of the countryside to describe the potential of the French language. The text shows how the Pléiade used the *Georgics* metaphorically to assimilate agricultural and linguistic production. Du Bellay writes, "I will not speak here of the temperateness of the air, of the fertility of the earth, of the abundance of all sorts of fruits necessary for the comfort and upkeep of human life, and of innumerable other commodities [. . . .] I will not speak of all the large rivers, the many beautiful forests, towns no less opulent than strong, equipped with many weapons for war [. . .]. What is more, the enraged tiger, the cruel brood of lions, poisonous grasses and all of the other plagues of humanity are far from here."[37] This passage, which pertains France's potential to develop its own language on par with Latin, is taken directly from Virgil and appropriates explicitly the metaphor of the "cruel brood of lions."[38] France, like Virgil's Rome, is unencumbered by savage beasts and provides an auspicious climate to produce a rich linguistic harvest. Shifting seamlessly from agricultural bounty to linguistic richness, du Bellay uses an extended comparison of plants, fruits, and roots to explain how the Latin language became so rich in the first place, reminding his readers that cultivation goes hand in hand with abundance when it comes to culling the maximum either from fruits or from a language.[39] The agricultural metaphor from Virgil attests to a practice and a nationalistic set of aesthetics that the Renaissance would apply to both language and the vine, reinforcing agricultural standards through linguistic ideals.

In fact, du Bellay goes on to remind his readers that abundance comes only from diligent cultivation in fruits and words alike.[40] Using the Romans as a model, he refers to wordsmiths as "agriculturalists," who carefully use reason to choose a civilized terrain in order to give rise to a healthy plant, acculturating what was formerly a wild product: "But they [the Romans], acting as good agriculturalists, first transferred language from a wild place to a domestic one; then so that it would bear better fruit sooner, they cut from around it the useless sprigs, and put in their stead native cultivated sprigs, masterfully taken from the Greek language, which were so well grafted and integrated into the trunk that they henceforth no longer seemed adopted but natural."[41] Using pruning, grafting, and other agricultural techniques allows the writer to interact with, tame, and domesticate nature, integrating the characteristics of the land (nature) and the work of the poet (culture) into the final linguistic product.[42]

Ronsard took the use of Bacchus and agricultural metaphors one step further in *Les Plaisirs rustiques, à Maurice de la Porte* (1554). Again, allowing pastoral images to take on a specifically georgic thematic, he appropriates and localizes the god, casting him as watching over a specific geography, lending verisimilitude and naturalism to the representation by including physical landmarks from the shores of the Marne river in the French town of Meaux. Here, Bacchus is no longer a distant image casting a general regard, but rather looks benevolently upon specific vines, which are favorably compared to those of Ay, one of the most prestigious wine-producing towns in the Champagne region of the time:

> Meaux that a caring Bacchus has taken watch over
> And whose slopes he surveys with a friendly eye,
> Slopes rich in a wine whose succulent bounty
> Is not surpassed by the wines of Ay.
> Bacchus is not the only one to favor them,
> But also his female companion and the pastor of Amphrysus,
> The former turning his stalks blond,
> The latter turning the abundance of grasses green.[43]

Even if several elements of the depiction are owed directly to Virgil (Amphrysus, for example, is an epithet for Apollo taken directly from the *Georgics*), there is an important difference between Ronsard's work and most bacchic poetry predating the Pléiade.[44] Bacchus, transplanted from the ancient context, is not only naturalized here, but precisely *localized* in Renaissance France, with references to specific places in the French countryside.

In other words, for Ronsard and du Bellay, localizing the French language became an aesthetic construct, as both poets emphasized the specific "flavor" that came from the communion between the poet and his home terrain. In *À sa muse,* Ronsard explains how his fields inspire and shape his language, an influence he in turn cultivates in his writing. The poet, immortalized by his verse, then flies from the earth, conveying to the world his Vendômois origin:

> I will fly spritely through the universe,
> Eternalizing the fields where I reside,
> Covered and honored by my glory
> Gained from having joined the two different harpers
> With the soft twittering of my ivory lyre,
> Which became Vendômois through my verse.[45]

Although Ronsard takes inspiration from Horace's Ode 2.20 in invoking the winged poetic bird, the connection with the earth and the mark of the terroir are original to the French vision, representing a proclamation of the power of land to determine and "flavor" the poet's language or verse. As Peletier du Mans had put it several years earlier, summing up the relationship between landscape and language: "A mountain, a river, and just a bit of distance / Make the language of neighbors completely different."[46] To put it simply, the poets of the Pléiade shaped the French imagination of regional wine culture by using vines as a metaphor for language production. Words, like wine, are initially shaped by the terroir and subsequently cultivated by the labor of the writer or vineyardist.

FROM FICTION TO NATIONAL "TRUTHS": PLACE AND IDENTITY IN RENAISSANCE WINE WRITINGS

The attitudes of Rabelais and the Pléiade quickly left the pages of literature to inform early French agricultural writings, ultimately further assimilating place, agriculture, and identity. The wine culture that appeared in Rabelais makes its influence felt as early as Jacques Gohory's 1549 *Dissertation on the*

Vine, Wine, and the Harvest, the first technical book on wine written in the French language. The work, published under the pseudonym Orlando de Suave, appears as a mix between a practical manual on viticulture and wine-making, an apology for wine itself, and a joyous fictional foray of consumption.[47] As one scholar puts it, "the preface [...] owes entirely to Rabelais, and especially to his prologues."[48] Along with Rabelaisian-like word games (the phrase *envie d'envie en vie*—"craving to crave in life"—is inscribed in the frontispiece with Bacchus serving wine freely to an impish nude), other direct borrowings include inviting the reader to "consume" the manual instead of simply reading it, and a reference to wine being as important as oil in the writing process. But it is the prolonged accent on the pleasures of drinking that rings most clearly of Rabelais's fiction. Indeed the book, comprising a fictional dialogue between the author and two other characters (Perdrix and Plance), offers a convivial picaresque journey with wine and food along the way. Things are lively from the start as the characters banter about wine, acknowledging its dangers and (mostly) praising its merits. Along with themes from Rabelais, there is also much recourse to influences that shaped the Pléiade's wine writing. Not only are there many passages in verse exalting the benefits of wine, but Perdrix refers to wine as a gift from Mother Nature, including references to Virgil and Hesiod, while charging, as Horace had in Epistle 1.9, that no good poetry was ever written by water drinkers.[49]

What is striking is the degree to which Gohory romanticizes wine, positioning it as a vehicle that connects the drinker to a natural world whose hidden qualities are as powerful as they are marvelous. Perdrix, the protagonist and wine's chief apologist, describes the good smells of the vine in flower as more fetching than those of violets, roses, carnations, and jasmine. They are so alluring that "venomous snakes cannot stand the sweetness." These smells are transmitted into the wine and provide such powerful corporal sustenance that they not only protect the drinker against evil, but hold the soul in the body a little longer at the end of life, keeping it from leaving through death's door.[50] Dithyrambic exclamations aside, Gohory also provides pragmatic information in a place-specific optic, as the characters walk from the outskirts of Paris to a vineyard in Issy-les-Moulineaux (where the Gohory family had vine holdings). All the while, the author bolsters wine's reputability by bringing to the fore scientific and philosophical underpinnings from the likes of Hippocrates, Galen, Aristotle, and Plato. In other words, rather than merely inculcating general humanist truths in an inebriated Rabelaisian romp through the countryside, the work pointedly gives occasion for the reader to learn, for example, which is the best grape (*Morillon,* a regional word for Chardonnay) or where to plant vines for the most success (in drier areas with good drainage).

More importantly, great attention is paid to the vines of France, and the nascent national and regional pride that would appear in the Pléiade is clearly perceptible and framed in terms of wine, as Gohory provides the linguistic tools and specialized vocabulary in French that one needs to understand working vines and making wine. In so doing, the author demonstrates that the French language is capable of treating the science of the vine, and that one need not have recourse to the technical precision of Latin.[51] In fact, one could say that through the fictional dialogue the author translates and *transplants* both ancient culture and terminology into Renaissance France, not only glossing wine linguistically, but also painstakingly providing a modern interpretation of antiquity's parables, ethics, and philosophy on wine. Although antiquity is not bereft of its authority in this schema, Gohory lends to France and the French language a linguistic and technical autonomy, in terms both of wine and of the science of producing it.

In fact, Gohory's publication of France's first French wine manual appeared in the same year as du Bellay's *Défense et illustration de la langue française,* where, as demonstrated above, an analogy with wine and the vine framed the natural potential of the French language to attain excellence. (It is worth noting here that du Bellay knew Gohory at least as early as the 1550s, and there is evidence that the two discussed in depth the potential greatness of French as a language.)[52] Although Gohory does not explicitly invoke imbibing the wines of a specific place as an aesthetic experience that promotes a sense of identity, he measures France favorably in comparison to Italy. Instead of referring to the French language specifically, as the poets of the Pléiade had, Gohory uses the metrics of regional produce to portray France's superiority, explaining where one finds the best vines (Lagny sur Marne), wheat (Beauce), fruit trees (Touraine), beef (Auge), lamb (Berry), and horses (Brittany, Gascony).[53]

In other words, the first manual written in French appears in French not only for reasons of accessibility to a specific readership, but also as a testimonial to the value of France as a land with its own identity and vast terrestrial riches.[54] The litany of examples, as far flung as Grandgousier's meat passage— but *not* mixed indiscriminately—comes to a crescendo with Perdrix switching from the land's agricultural production to that of its men. He asks God to protect "noble France," whose earth gave rise to war heroes as remarkable as it crops. Gohory provides several examples, including the successful campaign of Brennus against Rome, reaffirming France's prestige and identity in comparison to the Romans not only in terms of language and agriculture, but also in the art of war.

Although Gohory's nationalistic tone and debt to literary sources did much to set the precedent for the way cuisine would come to be tied to identity in France, one cannot conclude that this dialectical vision of French glory welling up from a mix between exquisite regional produce and its burgeoning language was the only impetus for the establishment of terroir as a construct in the country's collective imagination. The poetic and patriotic element in Gohory was far from France's most influential Renaissance agricultural writing: sixteenth-century medical science also had a primary role in underscoring the notion of terroir. The physician Charles Estienne, in particular, published in Latin in 1554 a volume that was translated into French a decade later as *L'Agriculture et la maison rustique*. This French edition, supplemented by writing from Estienne's son in-law, Jean Liébault, was popular enough to be reedited five times during the sixteenth century alone.[55] In it, Estienne and Liébault draw out in great detail wines from various regions in France and, to a much lesser extent, certain other parts of Europe, commenting on their longevity, force of character, and potential impact on health. Although Estienne and Liébault paraphrase Homer and Plato regarding the virtue of wine taken in moderation for its capacity to expel worries and inspire the soul to virtue and honesty, the prose is largely clinical and completely at odds with the style of Gohory.[56] For the most part, wines in *L'Agriculture et la maison rustique* are simply listed according to their suitability for various health concerns and different human constitutions.

It is nevertheless of great relevance that the foremost factor in understanding and determining the constitution of any given wine is not the grape variety, which is rarely mentioned, but the region of origin and the terroir. Estienne and Liébault are clear about the effect of the earth: terroir affects taste. They recommend, following a method espoused by Virgil and Columella, putting the soil of a prospective grape planting site in water and then tasting the water. If the smell and taste of the water is agreeable, the wine from the site will be palatable. As the authors elaborate on origins, they explain how different wine colors make them appropriate for different human constitutions, with specific recourse to the notion of terroir. The categorization of terroirs and wine-growing regions is sometimes quite broad, incorporating what we would today consider as appellations (e.g., Beaune), communes (e.g., Arbois), provinces, or regions (e.g., Anjou). Yet, despite this prevailing lack of specificity, Estienne and Liébault also mention certain sites with much more precision, naming villages, burgs, and the very small locales presently known as *lieux-dits* (said-locations). The authors offer a number of other remarks, considering wine according to its age-worthiness, the changing qualities of different vintages, the moment in their evolution when they are best consumed, and so forth.

Each aspect of these descriptions, from the terroir or soils of the origin, to the color and maturity, has little to do with pleasure and a great deal to do with the effect that wines have on bodily health. Drinking a wine too young, they explain, is likely to stop up the circulation. Drinking a wine that is too aromatic, they advise, will bring excessive drunkenness. Drinking a wine that is too acidic will likely cause gout, and so on. The descriptors are employed in the context of health, while the aspects of excess, conviviality, or rapture that enliven the pages of Rabelais, the Pléiade, and Gohory are entirely missing. Still, place constitutes identity insofar as earthly humors and an individual's physical constitution are both defined according to the terroir. Estienne and Liébault frame a wine's desirability according to the class, health, and vocation in life of its ideal drinker. They explain that the lighter wines from Paris and the surrounding regions (which the authors single out as the best and most properly "French") are preferable for urbanites, the studious, and those living quiet, idle, and sedentary lives. Wines coming from warmer climates *(païs),* such as Gascony or Spain, on the other hand, burn the entrails and encumber the minds of those who drink them.

The most enduring message here is that humans are what they drink, or at least, they should drink what they are. In other words, according to the Hippocratic paradigm, people share intrinsic qualities with the foods they consume because the two originate from the same terroirs. Infelicitous matches can only bring danger. Unlike Rabelais's humanistic mixing of culinary wares, the authors circumscribe wine in xenophobic terms, warning consumers to distrust foreign wine in spite of any outwardly flattering aromas: "Now, although foreign wines that we have brought from warm regions seem to us flattering on the palate, they must be consumed with as much prudence as possible, so much is the case that in addition to their obvious qualities, they have hidden properties that can truthfully be known and trusted through a sympathy with the inhabitants of the terroir where such wines grow, but to us they are enemies through an antipathy they have with us, who are from a dissimilar land and terroir."[57] This strong relationship between one's origin and one's physical constitution inaugurates a different brand of French regional patriotism. It explains the emotional connection between people and the wines from their home regions, providing a physiological correlate for the affective predilection suggested in the Pléiade's poetry between the poet and vines from his native terroir.

Two other Renaissance medical volumes are of note. The first, *De Re Cibaria,* was written in Latin by Jean Bruyérin-Champier, François 1er's physician, and published in 1560 (it went untranslated in French until 1998).[58] The work goes to great lengths detailing all categories of food, providing their history, and explaining where the best produce originates, both in France and elsewhere.[59] Most of all, the pages make the case for France's culinary richness and agricultural superiority. When it comes to wine, Bruyérin-Champier pointedly dethrones Italy and praises France's temperate climate and soil. He allows that, as physicians and philosophers had indicated, the taste of fruits varies and develops according to the "the variety and nature of the juices of the terroir."[60] France's wines are the most agreeable, healthful, and so forth because of the greatness of it soils. Moreover, vines that have produced inferior grapes abroad lose their unappealing qualities when they are transplanted in France. In fact, the only way it is possible for France to fail in terms of wine is to follow the advice of the ignorant and not intensively cultivate and care for vines, a practice that will surely make for a botched crop under any circumstance.

De Re Cibaria is not marked by a clear debt to the literary depictions of Rabelais or the poets of the Pléiade, but shares with the latter group and Gohory the palpable influence of Virgil. Bruyérin-Champier quotes robustly from the *Georgics* and considers its author the foremost of authorities concerning wine and the vine. Like Gohory, he strips Italy of the superiority Virgil depicts in the *Georgics.* According to Bruyérin-Champier, Italy only knew the vine because the Romans robbed it from elsewhere and transplanted it to their own country.[61] The bit of patriotism hidden in the slight against Italy notwithstanding, he catalogues France's agricultural greatness without extensively focusing on the aesthetic experience. In other words, he does not wax with the paroxysms of gustatory joy seen in Gohory, nor promote wine as the romanticized encapsulation of the homeland as did Ronsard with his Vendômois fields. The work advances terroir as a concept that explains wines' goodness, and draws on many of the same sources as above, but Bruyérin-Champier does not *taste* French identity through the terroir in the same way that some of his more literary predecessors do.

A third volume of note is that of the Norman doctor Julien Le Paulmier, whose *Treatise on Wine and Cider* was translated from Latin into French in 1589. The work was less popular and original than the *Maison rustique* (many of its observations and some of its entire sentences are taken verbatim from Estienne and Liébault), but it is remarkable in that it contains a nuanced depiction of terroir in a work that specifically addresses wine and cider instead of pertaining to agriculture in general.[62] Although it is packaged under the auspices of a utilitarian guide to good health (Le Paulmier justifies the project to the king by suggesting that it will help his royal eminence live longer), there is a hint that the reader will find pleasure too.[63]

In fact, Le Paulmier provides the century's most modern-sounding description of a "gourmet" appreciation of wine. He describes terroir as one of the governing forces of a wine's merits or defects in flavor and constitution: "The nature of the terroir is a partial cause of the force and generosity or of the weakness and insipidness of wines."[64] Continuing, Le Paulmier indicates that the *"bon gourmet"* is able to discern all of the qualities and defects of a wine or cider, its terroir of origin, as well as its age.[65] Yet despite this relatively modern characterization, the "taste of terroir" itself is presented as a defect.[66] Le Paulmier, like other scientific authors, suggests that while the terroir is responsible for producing wine's different flavors, anything described as "tasting of terroir" in the sense of earth or minerals should be deemed defective, since such elements are dirty, unpleasantly earthy, or lacking in elegance.

Despite the less impassioned treatment of food, origin, and identity in the agricultural and viticultural writings of the physicians Estienne and Liébault, Bruyérin-Champier, and Le Paulmier, by the end of the sixteenth century the correlation between food and wine flavors and their place of origin appeared frequently as a way of staking a claim on the nation's richness and identity. There were some clear crossovers between the values associating place and identity in terms of wine and of the French language. And the literary influence of Rabelais is made clear in the first properly French technical manual. There was, however, a marked difference between the more matter-of-fact clinical statements of the scientific literature and the impassioned literary constructions. Both drew often enough from the same sources—the omnipresence of Virgil's *Georgics* is the common element binding the two genres together—but the differences are notable. Simply put, the literary sources used wine and food as a signifier for a more palpable aesthetic experience metaphorically extended to language and poetry, while terroir and identity remained more coldly clinical in the technical writings. In other words, terroir as an aesthetic construct conveying a specific regional identity was savored more directly through words and poetry than through wine and food in the sixteenth century.

TWO

The Plantification of People

CHAPTER 1 DEMONSTRATED HOW MEMBERS of the Pléiade helped romanticize a cerebral brand of "poetic terroir" that mixed the metaphors of wine, agricultural bounty, and theories concerning the genesis of the French language. It also showed how agricultural writing in Renaissance science pegged human bodily constitutions to terroir through wine.

In the last part of the sixteenth century, a new, third discourse bridged the gap between mind and body, attributing both physical and intellectual characteristics in humans to terroir by comparing them to plants. The comparison became a philosophical and literary leitmotif that remained popular into the twentieth century. Beyond its chronological longevity, it is important because it demonstrates how the evolving food and wine aesthetic in France was tethered to the broader relationship that the French carved out between people, their actions, and what they perceived as the determining power of the earth.

Michel de Montaigne, who remains today sixteenth-century France's most well-known writer, incorporated ancient theories on environmental determinism into his essays to portray behavior and moral sanctity as dependent on an individual's relationships with nature, environment, and terroir.[1] At the same time, one of Renaissance France's most important political theorists, Jean Bodin, classified the influence of climate on humans as common, but also as negative, upholding that the physical imprint of the earth and regional differences could adversely affect language and character. Together, Montaigne's and Bodin's visions perpetuated a model for the rational explanation of behavior according to the environment that, together with the authors adduced in chapter 1, helped set the stage for Olivier de Serre's *Théâtre d'agriculture,* France's most renowned and enduring agricultural manual.

FROM TERROIR IN WOMEN AND WRITING TO
UNADULTERATED TASTE IN SAVAGES

Montaigne's depiction of the relationship between people, nature, and earth provides valuable clues when it comes to explaining terroir's evolution. He wrote two essays in particular that offer insight into a set of values that became widely held in the sixteenth century. In the lesser known of the essays, "Of Smells" (1580), Montaigne evokes terroir in the scope of fragrances as he muses about what constitutes an ideal aroma.[2] Pondering the agreeability of smells in general while linking fragrance to ethics and the health of the body, the essayist observes that strong smells usually indicate an underlying disguised infirmity. At the opposite end of the spectrum, children have a neutral smell on their breath that correlates with their health and purity.[3] Montaigne applies the consideration to women and opines that the most exquisite fragrance is to smell of absolutely nothing, intimating that neutral-smelling women are as olfactorily innocent as children.[4]

The essay continues its extended metaphor conflating smell and ethics with a passage that assimilates human beings and the earth, prizing the same values of simplicity, naturalness, and authenticity that appeared in the pseudo-Anacreontic poetry of the Pléiade. It is in this context that Montaigne celebrates the bathing process of Scythian women by referring to a scrub native to their "terroir": "The simpler more natural smells seem to me the most agreeable. A concern for smells is chiefly a matter for the ladies. In deepest Barbary the Scythian women powder themselves after washing and smother whole face and body with a certain sweet-smelling unguent, native to their terroir; when they take off this cosmetic they find themselves smooth and nice-smelling for an approach to their menfolk."[5] Although the precise identity of the balm is unclear, the dichotomy between nature and artifice immediately jumps to the fore as Montaigne equates terroirs, smells, and people. The Scythians were widely represented as the epitome of barbarism in the sixteenth century, so it is implied that the beautifying technique in question is of the most primitive kind.[6] On the other hand, like Anacreontic verse, the technique is praised for being close to nature, translating its wholesome values in a gesture of artful artlessness and uncorrupted ingenuity. Here then, in the Scythian equivalent of a mud mask spread over the entire naked body, the "seasonings" are considered normal, guileless, and truthful precisely because they come from the Scythian earth. Montaigne accentuates the "smooth" and "sweet-smelling" outcome of the measure, but the terroir's perfume is equated in an oxymoronic way to an "anti-perfume" because it is simple and natural as opposed to contrived and artificial.[7]

Although it is at first surprising that the same aesthetic register should be used to define the best fragrance for women and the purity of writing sought after by the poets of the Pléiade, Montaigne uses similar descriptors to qualify his own literary production. In 1580, in the preface to his readers at the beginning of the *Essays,* he writes: "Here I want to be seen in my simple, natural, everyday fashion, without study or artifice; for it is my own self that I am painting. Here, drawn from life, you will read of my defects and my native form so far as respect for social convention allows: for had I found myself among those peoples who are said still to live under the sweet liberty of Nature's primal laws, I can assure you that I would most willingly have portrayed myself whole, and wholly naked."[8] Montaigne signals that though social conventions will ultimately limit the limpidity of his prose, the model of "naked" veracity he idealizes in writing is the same he extolls with respect to the Scythian women. This depiction of organic simplicity also recalls the naturalized mythology that the poets of the Pléiade used to qualify the genesis of their own verse, invoking the cultivation of their art in harmony with the natural tendencies of regional agriculture. We are left to conclude that these writers applied certain rhetorical topoi valorizing nature with respect to women, words, and wine with little difference; this commensurability of values would seem to explain how terroir early acquired a dialogic relationship inside and outside the domain of agriculture.

One finds evidence to support this claim in Montaigne's most famous essay, "Of the Cannibals," where the desirability of simplicity, naturalness, and purity in people is reinforced through a comparison to food. One of the essay's major themes is how human beings should inform their ethical principles by direct recourse to unspoiled nature. Good moral values, Montaigne explains through plant metaphors and references to antiquity, are consonant with the natural attributes of humanity's origin, before people were corrupted by the influence of society. Having once acknowledged the primacy of nature, he explains, quoting book 2 of the *Georgics,* we could construct a society that would surpass in perfection any that Plato could have imagined for his republic, since its inhabitants would be "fresh from the Gods" and would live according to ways "taught by nature."[9]

In a series of arguments centered on primitivism and cultural relativism, Montaigne describes how Europeans, who consider themselves more "civilized" than the native peoples of the New World, are actually denatured by their societies: they have degenerated from a state of natural purity to become *more* barbaric than the inhabitants of the New World. The latter, explains Montaigne, comparing humans to plants, are closer to nature precisely because they are like unadulterated fruits: "Those 'savages' are only wild in the sense that we call fruits wild when they are produced by Nature in her ordinary course; whereas it is fruit which we have artificially perverted and misled from the common order which we ought to call savage."[10] Montaigne advocates not only for preserving the human version of wild (as opposed to cultivated) fruit but, as the passage continues, also for preventing the distortion of nature by forcing it to conform to corrupted European tastes.[11]

Praising the true and natural qualities of the cannibals, Montaigne points out that even though our society encourages artifice and cultivation, natural flavors remain compelling when we experience them: "It is in the first kind [the New World inhabitant] that we find their true, vigorous, living, most natural and most useful properties and virtues, which we have bastardized in the other kind [the European] by merely adapting them to our corrupt tastes. Moreover, there is a delicious savour which even our taste finds excellent in a variety of fruits produced in those countries without cultivation: they rival our own. It is not sensible that artifice should be reverenced more than Nature, our great and powerful Mother."[12] Here, pristine "Mother Nature" is heralded as decisively superior to all else, an objective benchmark of goodness with respect to both the taste of fruits and the behavior of people. We imagine not only that conformity with nature constitutes the greatest measure of an honorable moral identity, but also that cultivating tastes according to mercurial fashions and predilections is simply "not sensible." Thus, even if Montaigne sometimes invokes the ideal of nature in a tongue-in-cheek way (his own writing is riddled with artifice), he measures truth and beauty according to a naturalistic register. It is in accordance with that register that Montaigne spells out a more concrete philosophical mapping of terroir, creating a model of normalcy by equating flavor, comportment, and origin.

THE NORMATIVE EFFECT OF TERROIR

Montaigne most clearly depicts the effect of climate and terroir on human beings in another high-profile essay, "Apology for Raymond Sebond." It is not altogether surprising to find a representation of the earth's power over people included here, since the essay constitutes an apology for natural theology, connecting the heavens to the physical laws of life on earth. The essay also offers a skeptical vision of human knowledge and moral values as Montaigne attempts to destabilize his readers, causing them to reconsider what they *think* they know about their own existence and question the sovereignty of their own reason. In the midst of his reflection, a key paragraph places humankind smack in the middle of a world determined by terroir.

The passage in question quotes the Latin authors Cicero and Vegetius, substituting "terroir" for the Latin *terra* ("earth" or "soil"), to reveal the effect that environment has on our appearance, outward behavior, and even reason. Montaigne explains that "the very form of our being—not only our colour, build, complexion and behavior, but our mental faculties as well—depends upon our native air, climate and terroir."[13] Here, Montaigne depicts terroir as more than just a particular plot of countryside, land, or dirt. Rather, he describes it, along with air and climate, as having the power to determine the shape and character of human beings. This recognition of the land's determining power also leads readers into the skeptical aspects of the essay. Montaigne's stance on terroir jeopardizes our belief that we act with complete autonomy: in reality, he says, environmental factors determine not only our physical constitutions but also the nonphysical attributes we associate with the mind and soul.

Yet not all autonomy is lost to the vagaries of the earth. Montaigne's matter-of-fact tone corresponds to a rationalized, Renaissance conception of nature itself that would have offered the reader some solace. Acknowledging nature's laws and admitting that they act upon us was, in this view, not a wholly constraining factor. Instead, since unraveling nature's mysteries and their relationship to human beings was considered to be the source of human enlightenment, merely *understanding* the natural cycle and defining how we are determined constituted a sort of freedom. Human agents, no longer hanging on blindly to destiny, could thus reexamine and redirect their reason according to the rules of the natural cycle.[14] It is not too extreme to say that Montaigne and other thinkers like him believed that humans *ought* naturally to be marked by climate and terroir. It was only when nature's mark became excessive that one would need to seek, through cultivation and education, to remove the patina of rusticity.

The depiction of human agency as a product of the natural order remained nevertheless ambivalent. The implications of climatic determinism appear more clearly as the passage in the "Apology" continues, with Montaigne alluding to both the positive and negative effects of the environment. This passage is significant because it reinforces what would become a popular French construct, one that differs from many ancient iterations of climatic determinism insofar as it compares humans to plants directly: "then men must vary as flora and fauna do: whether they are more warlike, just, equable, clever or dull, depends on where they were born. Here they are addicted to wine; there, to robbery and lechery; here they are inclined towards superstition; there to belief; here to freedom; there, to slavery [...] all depending on inclinations arising from their physical environment. Change their location, and, like trees, they take on a new character."[15] At first glance, Montaigne's approach may appear debasing, since it asserts that entire populations are determined by their origin, leaving no place for free will. On the other hand, the absence of free will casts humans as victims of the climate: those who are bellicose or inclined toward thievery, for example, are not inherently immoral, but simply come from a climate that rendered them so.

Leaving aside for the moment Montaigne's rhetorical strategy in creating a climatically determined representation of humanity, what is most striking here is the dangerous potential of remapping and essentializing entire populations according to qualities of the earth. Yet at the very moment when Montaigne seems closest to transforming climate and terroir into an exclusionary or even discriminatory construct, he alters the model to allow for an important detail: people, like plants, adapt when they are moved to conform to the environment surrounding them. What is ultimately important is not where humans are born, a scenario that would preclude human evolution and create fixed and limited societies (the kind that Rabelais's prose attempted to break down), but where they ultimately choose to live, a structure that permits adaptation and provides for the existence of community bonds. Transplanting human beings to a new environment encourages them to develop the characteristics of the surrounding climate or terroir. This process is similar to the grafting du Bellay suggested that the French perform with their language, splicing French shoots onto Latin rootstocks and planting them in French fields to sprout contemporary language that is both uniquely French, due to the soil it grows in, and indelibly marked by the prestigious stock of antiquity. Montaigne is not specific about whether the relocated person will retain any original characteristics as he or she takes on a new disposition, but the transplantation metaphor fed into a nascent vision of French immigration theory in which newcomers to a country eventually shed their old ways, adapting their mores to the new environment.

BODIN, CLIMATIC THEORY, AND
GEOGENOUS RACISM

When it came to discussing people from different countries, France's eminent sixteenth-century political philosopher Jean Bodin did not equate neutral smells with innocence, nor represent simplicity and naturalness as positive qualities, nor even encourage the self-reflectiveness implicit in Montaigne's cultural relativism. Yet, Montaigne's position conflating climate and identity seems almost anecdotal when compared to the stance of Bodin, and the latter was far more influential in inspiring explicit intellectual dialogues that crystallized climatic determinism in the French mind.[16] Specifically, Bodin's reflections on climate were shaped by influences ranging from ancient Greek medical theories on humors to the Roman architect Vitruvius and the historiographer Tacitus, who used climate to explain the evolution of Germanic civilization.[17]

Bodin provides a panoply of sources to support his argument, but like many Renaissance and early modern thinkers in this domain, he relies most heavily on ancient materialist medical theories such as those of Hippocrates and Galen. (See chapter 5 for more on the medical angle.) Bodin paraphrases both Galen and Hippocrates in book 5 of his *Six Livres de la République* in order to explain human identity according to shifts in geographic latitude.[18] In doing so, Bodin stakes his own theory on a clear, authoritative precedent, since Hippocrates had cast in no uncertain terms the climate's importance in determining character and values. In *Airs, Waters, and Places,* Hippocrates explains that the seasons "are the most important factors that create differences in men's constitutions; next come the land in which a man is reared, and the water. For in general you will find assimilated to the nature of land both the physique and the mental characteristics of the inhabitants."[19]

Along with what would have been the compelling authority of such ancient sources, Bodin's theory that the earth shaped the qualities of people, plants, and food was undoubtedly mediated by the quest to find a model of harmonious living in a country destabilized by the religious wars of the sixteenth century. Although *Les Six Livres de la République* (1576) is Bodin's most famous work, an earlier text, *Methodus ad facilem historiarum cognitionem* (Method for the Easy Knowledge of History) (1566), is in many ways more enlightening when it comes to linking the intricacies of environmental determinism to the contemporary political context. In a chapter entitled "By

Which Method to Know the Origins of the Distinctions between Human Beings," Bodin explains that the origin of human beings is one of the most challenging questions posed by historians. He enumerates the ways that races and groups have historically used origin, both biological and geographical, to claim superiority over others. For some, the sentiment of superiority comes from what they believe to be the heroic exploits of their ancestors and the transmission of this heroism through blood. Others give more far-fetched reasons. Julius Caesar, Bodin scornfully relates, believed himself descended from mortal royalty on his mother's side and the immortal gods on his father's side.

The crowning theory, which Bodin fervently sets out to disprove despite his belief in climatic determinism, supersedes such theories of class and heroism and had the most potential for widespread application. It is the theory of autochthony, the notion that races are born directly from the earth, with the region of its origin setting each race apart. Bodin gives his own origin story for this theory: "Those who didn't know their initial origin or who dissimulated it from the eyes of a hated foreigner declared themselves born from mother earth, autochthonous or geogenous. It is in this way that Aristides in the *Panathenaicus* theorized to the Athenians that they derived their origin from the earth herself, mother of all gods."[20] Bodin explains that, far from being merely an aberration left over from the follies of antiquity, the idea of autochthonous superiority persisted in his own time, with the Bretons convinced that they were superior because they were completely unadulterated by foreign influences.[21]

For Bodin, such reasoning constitutes not only an affront to Christianity, but also a significant threat to human relations, given that it results in groups of people closing themselves off to others. In other words, instead of viewing origin as a construct that builds community, Bodin perceives it as a threat to the civility of human relations, a force that destroys friendship and society: "And I am willing, up until a certain point, to excuse the ancients for it, but it can only come in our time from a serious error or a sacrilegious intention [...] in not recognizing any other origin in these nations but that of the native soil, [one separates] people from the society and friendship of others."[22] Warriors have often put down their weapons in battle, Bodin writes, when they realize that they share the same parents and ancestors, whereas those who boast of being autochthonous "break the bounds of human community" with a vocabulary that replaces the word "foreigner" with "enemy."[23] Bodin conveys a message similar to the one that Rabelais implicitly diffused through the characters of Gargantua and Grandgousier five decades earlier: using political theory rather than fiction, Bodin combats the practice of using physical limits and borders to define certain communities and shut others out.

Yet instead of subverting regionalism and borders through an ethos of drunken transgression and the lexicon of the commonly shared digestive body, Bodin's strategy paradoxically uses climatic determinism to sap power from those who would argue for the existence of exclusive identities based on autochthony. His argument opposes original autochthonous origins to adopted origins, using one brand of environmental determinism to combat another in a metaphor comparing people to plants. In order to do this, Bodin begins by upholding that people are *not* defined by autochthonous origins and that, despite regional differences, one can tell that there is kinship between people whose ancestors hailed from different countries because one can see similarities in the patterns and roots of disparate languages. Adducing several examples of words from a variety of ancient and contemporary languages that bear notable resemblances, he points out how different languages have evolved from a common lineage, thereby maintaining that the origins of diverse populations are indeed shared, despite regional differences. It is in the defense of this greater human community that Bodin deploys what would develop into his personal brand of climate theory.

In spite of the evidence for a once-common tongue, he maintains, we cannot deny that there are differences between languages in contemporary societies. There are three reasons for this. First, time in itself causes languages to change, and an old language eventually takes on nuances during its natural, organic evolution. A second reason for difference is the mixing of people from different colonies and from countries whose language has already undergone temporal alteration. For example, the Scythians in remixing their speech with that of the Romans compromised the homogeneity of the Latin language and caused the latter to forgo its purity. "Nature," as Bodin terms it, constitutes the third and most pertinent factor. Bodin explains that geographical influences cause language differences, asserting that the people of "the north" speak with hard consonants, pay little attention to vowels, and communicate with "frequent deep aspirations" because the climate and geography have given them violent temperaments and bestowed within them an "impetuous heat."[24] In other words, although he sees the dangers of supporting a theory of autochthony, Bodin is far from dismissive of the effects of soil and climate. In fact, for Bodin, climate becomes a way of reaffirming the intrinsic existence of a broadly shared human community. Though we sound different on the exterior, we all hail from the same roots.

In contrast to Montaigne, however, Bodin describes the effects of environment as *corruptions* from the norm, not the norm itself. Perfect language, in his view, was at some early point compromised by the adulteration caused not only by time but also by the environment. Bodin develops these nuances in a prolonged metaphor that appears both in *Methodus* and in the *République*, and explains human actions according to the nature of plants.[25] In it, Bodin warns that we must legislate to keep humans from "growing wild," since the climate will soon get the better of them in the absence of a civilizing force: "It is true that if the laws and customs are not maintained, people will quickly return to their nature: and if they are transported from one country to another, they will not change as quickly as plants that draw their sap from the earth, but they will change in the end."[26] Along with Montaigne, Bodin allows that people adapt to environments as do trees, albeit more slowly. More importantly, Bodin advocates, to a much greater extent than does Montaigne, that society should create a legislative structure to mitigate the earth's influence.

It is hardly surprising that Bodin's methodology, although politically motivated, dovetails with Hippocratic and Galenic medical sources. More unexpected, however, is the debt that Bodin's theories owe to diverse disciplines one would hardly expect to be associated with the genesis of climate theory or terroir. One illuminating example is that of the ancient Roman architect Vitruvius. In his *De Architectura,* translated from Latin into French as *Architecture ou Art de bien bâtir* in 1547, Vitruvius makes the case that precise geographical origins influence human behavior. It is worth quoting a lengthy passage from the author's eighth book because, though it is an ancient source, it constitutes one of the most modern-sounding and influential theories on terroir in the Renaissance. In it, Vitruvius explains that water varies as much as do fruits and wine, according to its origins. Using the exact metaphor of the soil and the sap that Bodin would later apply to human beings, Vitruvius writes:

> These things, different in taste, originate in the nature of the earth, and it is just so for the sap of fruit trees: if the roots, as with vines [...], did not take on qualities according to the virtue of territories, and the fruits did not take on fragrances in the same way, the flavors of everything would in each country be the same [...]. Sicily boasts Mamertine wine, which is a wine from Messina, and rivals all of the best wines of Italy, Campania from Naples provides Falernian wine and Terracina and Fundi produce Caecuban wine, which derives its name from a terroir not far from Gayette [...]. [I]t's the

same thing in other provinces where there is an innumerable multitude of wines, all different in qualities and virtues. [This] would be impossible if the property of the terrestrial humor did not infuse its flavors in the roots, and did not nourish a matter which, rising to the extremities of objects, engenders a sap proper for the place and the species.[27]

Aside from its relatively contemporary-sounding depiction of terroir, the example is important because it occurs in a text that does not evoke origins for the sake of appreciating food or wine. Rather, Vitruvius references wine and viticulture in order to convey to us how the earth, through the water its springs provide, can affect human health, beauty, and even the quality of the voice in song.

In other words, a discourse today known almost exclusively in the context of food appreciation was first motivated and shaped by the desire to understand human behavior, so that architects could plan accordingly for the future sourcing of water for states and cities. Even more curious is that no rough Latin equivalent of the word *terroir* occurs in Vitruvius's original text. The entire passage containing it ("which derives its name from a *terroir* not far from Gayette") is a gloss by the French translator, adapting Latin meaning to the French lexicon and retrojecting the Renaissance French term *terroir* into his translation of the ancient text. That is, although the concept's most modern textual articulation in the sixteenth century originates from ancient Italy, not Renaissance France, the word *terroir* itself is here a purely French construction.

Bodin makes no specific reference to this passage, but it is certain that he would have known it. He quotes *De Architectura,* Vitruvius's only surviving work, several times in his *Methodus,* always in the context of climatic determinism.[28] Elsewhere, putting this discourse to use and expanding on ideas he first propounded in the *Methodus,* Bodin adduces a practical application of architecture and law in the context of climate theory. In *Les Six Livres de la République,* he stipulates that any potential legislator must take into account the predominant terrestrial humors of the region to be governed. There is no use in trying to accommodate people to legislation that is completely in conflict with the predominating condition of the soil: "It is thus necessary that the wise governor of a people know well the humor of that people and its natural condition, before attempting something that will change its state or laws [...]. [O]ne must diversify the state of the republic according to the diversity of places, following the example of the good architect who fashions his building according to the style he finds in the place."[29]

Notwithstanding their shared rational calculus about the effect of the earth on its produce, the differences between Bodin and other Renaissance writers cannot be stressed enough. For Montaigne, the natural origin or terroir dictates customs and physical laws in a normative fashion, which Montaigne romanticizes, along the same lines as the poets of the Pléiade, as an ideal that humans should strive to cultivate and preserve. Bodin, on the other hand, represents the influence of climate and terroir as a corrupting force on society. He suggests that, in parallel with the biblical downfall, humans have degenerated from a pure state, and been corrupted by the march of time and the influence of different places. Or, to put it another way, terroir and climatic determinism for Montaigne produce the sweetest, most natural fruit, whereas for Bodin they constitute a stain on the human condition and a vice to be curbed as much as possible with the judicious application of laws. Both of these perspectives would be important going forward in terroir's evolution, which started to develop rapidly in the context of food and agriculture at the end of the sixteenth century in the work of Olivier de Serres.

TERROIR AT CENTER STAGE: OLIVIER DE SERRES AND THE *THÉÂTRE D'AGRICULTURE*

The gamut of sixteenth-century writings on terroir, agriculture, and identity discussed above prepared contemporary French readers for what remains known as the country's greatest work on farming: *The Agricultural Theater and The Management of Fields* (*Le Théâtre d'agriculture et ménage des champs*), published in 1600 by Olivier de Serres. We know that the manual was important from its inception, since sixteen thousand copies were produced in the first edition alone and sent to all of the parishes in France, with eight other editions to follow in the first years of the seventeenth century.[30] Moreover, according to certain accounts, Henri IV took pleasure in having chapters of the *Théâtre* read to him nightly for a half hour after dinner.[31] Such an endorsement, whether true or a cultural myth, helps explain why Olivier de Serres became known as the "father of French agriculture," a status reinforced by the number of technical schools, high schools, and other organizations that bear his name in France today.[32]

The concept of terroir is central to the *Théâtre*. Nowhere before had human interaction with the earth been accentuated to such a degree as in de Serres's manual, where theories of how people should identify with the land play out in the material organization of the perfect country estate, of the sort represented in the background of de Serres's authorial portrait. The

OLIVIER DE SERRES

FIGURE 3. Portrait of Olivier de Serres, from *Théâtre d'agriculture*. The "father of French agriculture" is here depicted in front of his home, the Domaine du Pradel, in the Vivarais region; the estate remains open to visitors today. Courtesy of Association Vivante Ardèche / Château de Vogüé.

depiction, which dates from one of the first editions at the beginning of the seventeenth century, portrays de Serres positioned in the foreground of the scene, bearing an air of distinguished confidence. His image occupies the majority of the pictorial space: it is only in the background that one makes out rolling hills with neatly partitioned fields and uniform rows of crops. This man, as his self-assured aura conveys, rules with sovereignty over a methodically organized estate, heeding only reason and the call of the (Protestant) Church.[33]

More important, the word *terroir* appears eighty-seven times in the *Théâtre d'agriculture,* and de Serres makes clear that the foremost matter at hand is the question of its determining force, which shapes food and drink—and wine in particular: "The climate and the terroir provide wine with its taste and force in accordance with their properties, so that it is completely impossible to account for the diversity of wine by the species of grapes. Accordingly, the same vine put in different places will produce different kinds of wine as diverse as the soils where it is planted."[34] As did Estienne and Liébault in their *Maison rustique,* de Serres separates macro- and microclimatic differences, crediting terroir and not the grape for giving wine different tastes and qualities. Nevertheless, although such passages sound modern, they constitute something of an aberration in Olivier de Serres's overall portrayal of terroir. Mostly, de Serres *does not* emphasize the outward characteristics of products by recourse to telluric causes, but rather values an understanding of terroir insofar as it can help readers make planting decisions and shape their lives into harmony with the natural surroundings.[35] Instead of looking from the outside *inward* toward terroir in order to account for sensorial judgments, de Serres looks from the earth *outward,* starting with the terroir as a guide for dictating planting choices. This outward vision is a part of the *Théâtre*'s emphasis on using each estate's various animal and vegetable "actors" to create a specific agricultural outcome for the owner. As such, it is worth elaborating on just who this "owner" or head of the estate was.

De Serres's premise, and that of Henri IV, was that France's nobility could be incited to watch over food production in a more economic and intelligent fashion than it had heretofore. To elevate the stature of a book on farming, a vocation that was largely derided by the upper classes, de Serres peppers his manual with quotes and references from an erudite corpus of wisdom literature spanning from Hesiod in the seventh and sixth century BCE to Virgil and Columella in the first century CE.[36] He mentions dozens of prestigious names, assuming his sophisticated readers will recognize them. Through such quotations and allusions, together with techniques ranging from extended metaphors and personification to colorful accumulations describing bountiful harvests, he makes his manual literary, turning farming and agricultural prose into an object as appealing in its style as edifying in its substance. This edification also comes in part from the work's Christian overtones and the supposed moral rectitude possessed by the head of the estate who has provided for his family, producing the crops he needs as a function of the different sorts of land available to him. In this way, de Serres succeeds in empowering the estate owner while lifting agriculture and terroir to a prestigious plane of consciousness—and transmits all this in a readable manual that would influence generations of readers, imbuing them with a love of the land.

Even the organization of the *Théâtre* reflects a terroir-oriented architecture. Instead of calling the chapters "days" as did Augostino Gallo, or "books" as did Estienne and Liébault, de Serres refers to them as "places" *(lieux).* Not surprisingly, the first "place," and the first line of the book, calls on the reader to understand the unique qualities of the terroir intended for planting: "Agriculture's foundation is in the understanding of the nature of the terroir that one wishes to cultivate."[37] The rational farmer, explains de Serres, should distribute his crops according to the diverse growing potentials of soils. He recommends that readers assess this potential using a method that Estienne and Liébault also borrowed from Virgil and Columella, in which the prospective farmer steeps dirt in water, then tastes the water. In de Serres, farming must be the result of a precise assessment and intimate understanding of one's soil, together with a pragmatic aim to maximize the quality and quantity of its harvest.

In spite of this pragmatic, technical approach to gauging the terroir, the reader also quickly perceives the close bond that links humans and the land they work. De Serres emphasizes not the one-sided mastery of the rational subject over the immaterial object, but an intimate reciprocal relationship profoundly implicating both humans and the earth: "As the earth is humanity's common mother and wet nurse and each man desires to live there suitably, by the same token, it seems that nature instilled in us an inclination to honor and think highly of agriculture."[38] This passage and others like it make the case for humankind's dependence upon and bond with nature and the earth, raising the latter in the estimation of the farmer to a figure meriting humanity's utmost respect. He elevates working the land to correspond both with the romanticized images and ethical standards of agriculture associated with ancient Hesiodic poetry (de Serres mentions Hesiod several times, at one point directly quoting six lines of verse) and with more modern romanticized images of mother nature, such as those appearing in Montaigne.[39] He joins to this an ethical construct: readers are called upon to honor the land by working it as well as understanding its different qualities.[40] Most importantly, de Serres reduces the distance between human beings and terroir that appeared in Bodin. The latter unromantically stated the effects climate and terroir have on humans, constructing them as influences that sully and adulterate the integrity of their speech and actions. For de Serres, who positions humans and the earth on the same hierarchal plane, it is quite the opposite.

This last observation bears out not only in the title but also in the spirit of de Serres's work, since the *Théâtre d'agriculture* is indeed a "theater," where plants and animals play roles and the human laborer is both the director sitting above the stage-set of plantings and an actor taking part in the estate. Just as the book's organization into *lieux* brings geographical considerations to the forefront, the language effectively brings the land to life, a detail that has been recognized by modern commentators: "The anthropomorphizing contributes to the charm of the text: the sheep *rejoice* in the alfalfa, which seems *exquisite* to the cows; there is *great friendliness between livestock with wool* and *those with hair,* or *if the earth relishes more carrying hay or wheat, it principally chooses hay.*"[41] By employing this sort of personification, de Serres acculturates nature, not only conferring human status to the earth but also, once again, appealing to the educated reader's literary sensibilities and removing the paradigm of terroir from a purely technical context.[42] In other words, even as agricultural notions are presented as a rational science, their literary aspect remains prominent. Nevertheless, though one finds in the *Théâtre* qualities of the georgic and bucolic literature popular at the time, one of the differences between de Serres and the poets of the Pléiade is that the bacchic mythology is missing.[43] In fact, de Serres pointedly excludes myth from his volume in order to encourage a scientific understanding of the earth.

Notwithstanding this difference, de Serres *did* share with the poets of the Pléiade a proclivity for creating identity through regional language. The *Théâtre d'agriculture* is set in Provence and de Serres addresses his reading audience with a vocabulary that is chock-full of diverse regional terms. He offers provincial dictums and clarifies a number of lexical variances, including different translations, such as those for alfalfa (*luzerne* versus *sainfoin*) or those describing mixes of white and red carnations (*de rozete* or *piquassats*)—

and often he adopts the Provençal versions over the Parisian.[44] At the beginning of the seventeenth century, de Serres's work thus constituted a walk through a lexical garden that accentuated the real and metaphorical "flowers" of his estate in the Vivarais. These variations in language put an emphasis on the regional richness and diversity of France. Just as Grandgousier imbibes all of France by eating diversely named specialties from far-reaching regions, de Serres entices his readers with a lexical smorgasbord that demonstrates France's regional variety while making the case for the book's underlying thesis supporting the importance of terroir.

By way of concluding our examination of terroir in the Renaissance, one could say that de Serres—like Montaigne, Bodin, Rabelais, and the poets of the Pléiade—painted a picture that was both modern and distinctly early modern. It was modern because the French recognized that physiographic aspects of the land had an effect on flavors, and because there were the beginnings of a nationalistic and nostalgic relationship between people and specific places as illustrated through agricultural production. It was early modern in the sense that, as far as food was concerned, terroir was more often used in the technical context of deciding where to grow particular crops than in the context of culinary appreciation. In fact, when terroir was used in the context of explaining outward effects, it focused more on human beings than flavors. People, rather than food, were appreciated as "terroir driven." Most of all, the above authors reinforced terroir as a polysemic notion in French, created and developed from various sources in order to explain the determining power of the earth and the physical world around them.

THREE

_____

Courtside Purity and the Académie Française's Attack on the Earth

WHEN THE *THÉÂTRE D'AGRICULTURE* APPEARED in 1600, climate and terroir had already been used to create expectations for the behavior of people and the taste of produce in a wide range of contexts, from poetry and political philosophy to farming and medical science. At that point, terroir had mostly positive or neutral connotations rather than negative ones. The first third of the seventeenth century did little to change that, but as Louis XIV's power as an absolute monarch was continuously reaffirmed, the centralized power of Paris and the court started to consume France's attention, and the provinces—together with terroir—took on sharply negative associations.[1] Ironically, it was this very derision for what Parisian society considered lowly backwater rurality that led to terroir becoming all the more firmly embedded in French culture and cuisine.

One can also correlate the gravitation toward Paris with the standardization of the French language, which began in earnest with the creation of the Académie française in 1635. Just as terroir and regional identity owed part of their early construction to the Pléiade and its reflections on language, their fall from popularity was accelerated by changing linguistic standards, as varying regional "flavors" in accents and dialects were spurned in favor of homogeneity in expression. The desire for a "pure," cosmopolitan tongue spread from speech to taste, affecting trends in cuisine as segments of the population attempted to lose whatever regional patina they themselves might have—or might be perceived by others as having—by pointedly seeking "pure" and "neutral" foods. This chapter details those transformations and demonstrates through evolving dictionary definitions how the word *terroir* itself expanded to become a greater measure for human comportment.

The metric laid out by anthropologist Mary Douglas in *Purity and Danger* (1966) provides one map for how trends in language, identity, and terroir might have interrelated in seventeenth-century France. Douglas analyzes the historical obsession with purity and cleanliness in many societies, correlating with it the fear of dirt, disorder, and contagion. Dirt, as Douglas points out in the preface of a new edition, is an elusive concept that defies simple explanation.[2] "Dirtiness" pertains not only to hygiene or concerns about contagion, but often also to disorder: a disruption in an established pattern or order, an anomaly, a speck, and so on may be considered dirty. It is within the context of this last series of descriptors—breaks in pattern and anomalies— that one might explain how terroir became "unclean" in relation to speech in seventeenth-century France. Intolerance for any sort of disorder in a highly structured absolutist reign motivated an evolution in the aesthetic, linguistic, and culinary codes of the century. Douglas's theories, as will become clear over the course of this chapter, are revelatory in all three of these realms.

LINGUISTIC PERFECTION IN COURT SOCIETY AND THE VERBAL BLEMISHES OF THE PROVINCES

At the beginning of the seventeenth century, despite the various extended and metaphorical uses of terroir in Montaigne and the poets of the Pléiade, dictionary definitions of the concept remained primarily agricultural. In 1606, for example, Nicot's *Thrésor de la langue française* listed terroir as denoting any specific municipal plot, soil, or land appropriate for one agricultural crop or another.[3] This first sense did not vanish as the century wore on: it appeared in an even more complete definition in Furetière's *Dictionnaire universel* in 1690, which defines terroir as "land considered according to its nature and qualities, and with respect to agriculture. Plants, trees, only grow well in the proper terroir. Willows, alders, poplars require a humid and swampy terroir; vines need a dry and stony terroir of rock. Wheat needs rich and fertile terroir."[4] The word's primary sense remained just as Olivier de Serres had employed it, as a term appropriate to agricultural discussions about making proper choices in planting and crop selection.

Yet, the dictionaries also document terroir's transformation. Rather than existing merely as an association between crops and the cultivating process, terroir appears in these dictionaries as part of the aesthetics of perception. As the Furetière definition continues, it focuses on the tasting of flavors instead of the question of where to plant crops. It also turns decidedly negative: "One says that the wine has a taste of terroir when it has some disagreeable quality that comes to it from the nature of the terroir where the vine is planted." In some ways, the definition is much closer to terroir's modern aesthetic meaning, since it focuses on the outward expression of qualities instead of the innate suitability of the soil or the particular municipal associations of the piece of land in question. In this definition, one perceives terroir not merely by running one's hands through the soil or by tasting water in which it has been steeped, but also by noting the qualities it instills in its produce. But there are important differences from the modern connotations of terroir. Instead of purity of flavor or a faithful representation of the origin, terroir was often used in this period to indicate adulteration and disorder—a break in the "pattern" of flavor expectations, as Douglas would put it—as well as rusticity. Other renderings could be more extreme: Charles Pajot's French-Latin dictionary of 1694 translates *"le goût de terroir"* simply as *"virus terrenum,"* meaning "poison or stench of the earth."

Such negative usages spread and the word became employed in a derogative sense altogether outside the context of agriculture. Beginning in its 1701 edition, Furetière's dictionary formalized tendencies that had appeared with increasing frequency throughout the second half of the seventeenth century in its description of how the term *terroir* applies to people: "It [terroir] is also used figuratively for a bad habit acquired in one's place of birth. The people from the provinces cannot rid themselves of a particular vice from the terroir strongly opposed to politeness [. . .]. One says that a man smells of the terroir in order to say that he has the defects that one ordinarily attributes to people of his land."[5] Terroir thus appeared in association with unrefined flavors, unpleasant smells, and, in the case of people, the poor behavior they displayed.[6]

There is a lot more to be said about these nuances, but the point to be made at the outset is that these new definitions did not appear until later in the seventeenth century, *after* the advent of the Académie française and a series of iterations in which the concept of terroir was transformed by applications in the context of language. It was from this point, after the linguistic transformation, that identities—in food as well as in people—qualified by the notion of terroir took on increasingly pejorative associations, further entrenching and exasperating the supposed dichotomy between the purity of Paris and the unkempt filth of the provinces.

In fact, even before the creation of the Académie française, sentiments toward speech began to shift in a way that would have implications for France's evolving linguistic identity and for terroir. For one, anything seen as too ponderous in speech was derided. This change was reflected in evolving fashions in oratory. As the historian Marc Fumaroli (himself currently a member of the Académie) explains it, in the sixteenth century, the classical standard of eloquence was that of the fourth-century BCE Greek orator Demosthenes, whose speeches were predicated on conveying the intellectual core and weight of the message. In the seventeenth century, however, the lighter and more elegant turns of phrase of Ciceronian aesthetics became the new model, and by the 1620s and 1630s "style was more important than substance."[7]

This Ciceronian tradition of speech was further reinforced by the vogue in France for the writings of Castiglione, a Renaissance Italian author and diplomat who aspired toward eloquence through loftiness and measured civility (douceur) rather than through the "force" of argument or the sources of its "invention" and inspiration.[8] Castiglione would in turn inspire Nicolas Faret, who published in 1630 a broadly influential survival guide for the seventeenth-century gentleman called "The Honest Man or the Art of Succeeding in the Court" (L'Honnête Homme ou l'art de plaire à la cour). Among its many recommendations, it prescribes that the honnête homme (best translated as the "gentleman") should be worldly and able to speak knowledgeably about many subjects rather than focused too deeply on any one thing.[9] This aesthetic, which also implied an effervescent, witty eloquence, set the stage for the negative connotations that would soon taint the term terroir, a word whose etymological roots seemed "heavy" and ponderous.

Another indication of the evolving linguistic context occurs in a 1634 letter to the Cardinal de Richelieu from Messieurs de Bautru, du Chastellet, and de Boisrobert, all three of whom would be inaugural members of the Académie française. In it, they urge Richelieu to consider the need to set a high standard for French and to "clean from the language the rubbish (ordures) that it had contracted, either in the mouth of the commoners, in the palace crowds, in the impurities of chicanery, or in the incorrect usages of courts."[10] This project of cleansing the language would quickly be nuanced in regards to the perceived sources of contagion. By the middle of the century, authorities on fine speech such as Claude Favre de Vaugelas began to refer to the French court not as dirtying the language, as de Bautru, du Chastellet, and de Boisrobert had only a decade before, but rather as establishing the standard for high language and culture. The provinces, on the other hand, became increasingly known as the source of impurities and of the rubbish infecting the French language.

The unruly, heavy, and dirty connotations surrounding the provinces were, in fact, targeted by the Académie from the outset of its efforts to regulate the French language by creating rules on accepted pronunciation and spellings that marked clear changes from the preceding decades. According to the twenty-fourth article of the Académie's statutes, it would seek to clean and refine the French language: "The principal function of the Académie will be to work with all the care and diligence possible to give certain rules to our language, to make it pure and eloquent and able to treat the arts and sciences."[11] This effort to standardize, harmonize, and cull the language according to a centralized set of rules cast the provincial variety of dialects and usages as tainted anomalies, thereby marginalizing those whose French did not meet Parisian standards.[12]

The extent to which the seventeenth-century Académie française contradicted the values of the sixteenth century becomes clear when its precepts are juxtaposed against those of Henri Estienne, writing six decades earlier. For Estienne, purity emanates precisely from the provinces of France, which are uncorrupted by the pernicious influences that lurk in the court. In his 1579 "Superiority of the French Language" (Précellence du langage français), Estienne states that the "heart" of France, its deepest reaches, unsullied by outside influences, is the source of the best language: "as for language, I could call the heart of France the places where its naivety and purity is best preserved."[13] Estienne puts forth a system of values for language that shares characteristics with those exemplified by Montaigne and his cannibals: purity is equated with innocence and naivety. There is, in his telling, an Edenic quality to the language of those who live deep within nature, uncorrupted by society and civilization.

The belief that the undertraveled provinces were bastions of purity was reversed in the seventeenth century, and it is in this context that the word *terroir* was frequently employed to qualify language.[14] In a monument of the movement toward this new conception of linguistic perfection, his 1647 *Remarques sur la langue française,* Claude Favre de Vaugelas praises the translator Jacques Amyot, exclaiming that Amyot's expression is "naturally French, without any of the mixes common in the provincial way of speaking, which always corrupts the purity of the authentic French language."[15] In a formulation that would later be reflected in the sentiments of court writers and thinkers, Vaugelas frames the French nation and its language according to a linguistic purity that eradicates the influence of the countryside. He warns that sophisticated readers must be exceedingly careful not to contract the insidious vocabulary, accent, and verbal mannerisms of the provinces, referring to them as if they were plague-affected zones: "One must not unwittingly let oneself be corrupted by the scourge of the provinces by staying there for too long."[16] More charitably, Vaugelas also allows that people from the countryside, at the very least, often realize that their language is corrupted. Using the word *terroir* to indicate the unrefined, negative aspects of provinciality, Vaugelas concedes that certain people have fought against rusticity and by "continually resisting the vices of their terroir [...] latched onto excellent masters whom they decided to imitate."[17] Vaugelas democratically counsels that by leaving the terroir of the provinces with great haste and seeking out well-versed and untainted Parisian models, individuals outside the court may master good language and overcome their unpalatable linguistic blemishes.

The notion of terroir as the scourge of the uncivilized bumpkin was repeatedly reaffirmed during the second half of the seventeenth century. Jean Baptiste Morvan Bellegarde, in a 1697 passage that the 1701 Furetière dictionary would borrow heavily from, vividly details the insidious influence of the earth, warning that people too entrenched in terroir will never be able to purify themselves, regardless of the measures they take: "People from the provinces, no matter what they do, cannot rid themselves of a sort of vice of the terroir that is opposed to politeness; they please people at first by their niceties, but as the interaction goes on, one invariably quickly finds in their manners and actions that little something that enormously repels elegant people who have a true understanding of politeness."[18] Provincial terroir in this iteration does not simply influence one's comportment, but rather permanently corrodes one's taste and capacity for reflection. Furthermore, the effect is so strong that Bellegarde denies the possibility that it can be resolved through self-analysis or time spent in polite company.

Between these extremes, terroir appeared in a number of more mitigated forms to connote rusticity and any number of imperfections in language and behavior. The most common of these included phrases such as "to smell of the terroir" *("sentir le terroir")* and "to have the taste of terroir" *("avoir le goût de terroir").*[19] Each of these formulations indicated that the person in question was far from the polite, educated, urbane ideal of the aristocrat, or even from the polished *honnête homme,* who, though perhaps of lower birth status, had culled his social acumen to its highest potential. The concept of politeness—and attendant concern with whatever might imperil it—became so central in French society, in fact, that the figurative use of terroir in terms of language and comportment grew more common than its use with respect to food. Drawing on an anecdote from antiquity, one particularly popular turn of phrase called attention to the lack of polish in the language of rural speakers by equating the Latin *patavinitas* (derived from "Paduanism," that is, a trait of somebody from Padua) with *goût de terroir:* "Who could find today in Livy that Paduanism *(patavinité),* or that *goût de terroir* that Asinius Pollio reproached him for? Those who are brought up in the elegance of the court can certainly perceive that little something in speech that smells of the provinces, even in the most polite authors."[20] This equation of *patavinité* with *goût de terroir* ultimately became well enough established to appear as a permanent part of the early modern French cultural record, as an entry in Diderot's and d'Alembert's *Encyclopédie.*

One can thus define ideal speech in the second half of the seventeenth century as speech devoid of provincialisms, free of any sort of heavy or strong accent, and expressing with clarity, correctness, decorum, and measure the speaker's thought. Additionally, by operating as a neutral vehicle, an ideal language would communicate meaning without adulteration or alteration. The best speech, explained Dominique Bouhours, is that whose flavor is as unmodified and neutral in taste as water: "Beautiful language resembles a pure and clean water that has no taste; it is self-evident, flowing from its source; it goes where its natural inclination takes it."[21] The image functions through the metaphorical transference of water's visual clarity into the realm of speech: superior language is not turbid, but limpid and pure. Bouhours's remark invites class comparisons as well, since a similar metaphor, *"un sang aussi pur que l'eau,"* was frequently used to characterize the purity of aristocratic blood.[22] Blood and speech as clear as water were conflated as signs of nobility, while the connotations of terroir were just the opposite.

From language, the paradigm widened to include knowledge, which also was better if it was devoid of terroir. This is precisely how Béat Louis de Muralt phrases it in the next century, in his *Lettres fanatiques,* in which terroir is represented as an impurity corrupting the transmission of ideas, bringing turbidity to what would otherwise be the bright light of science: "It should be the same, it seems, with the sciences as with rivers that grow from streams produced by the countries where they pass, but this is not the case. They [sciences] are more like rivers that meander across flat countries, and only receive back from the places they pass the water they initially brought, and even that water comes back to them cloudier than when it started, and brings them only the mire or the *goût du terroir* from where they have passed."[23] Muralt makes clear that one must not count on individuals to add to and enrich the body of knowledge. The effect is rather the contrary, especially in the "flat countryside" and backwater boonies where not much goes on. In these places, turbidity takes hold, with terroir adversely flavoring knowledge and leading to cumbersome impurities. In knowledge, exactly as in language, the *goût de terroir* is what sullies and infects otherwise pure ideas; it acts as a sludge *(la fange)* that corrupts reason and speech.

The association of such impurity with terroir found a parallel in the over-turning of another important value from the sixteenth century. The Renaissance topos of truth lying under the soil—as in Rabelais's *Dive bouteille* or in de Serres's conception of the earth as the determiner of agricultural verities—was reversed. To speak in a very broad sense, hidden significance was no longer to be found below the earth but rather was to be revealed when the earth was washed away, uncovering underlying reality. For the Académie and the court, provincial France's way of speaking did not hold a refreshing genuineness that had been hidden by the trappings of Parisian cosmopolitanism, but was a polluting force that called for cleansing. In short, rather than the essence, the earth constituted an excrescence.

This aberrative aspect of earthiness appears, with an interesting twist that links terroir and ethical values to food, in Claude and Pierre Perrault's "Diverse Works of Physics and Mecanics" *(Oeuvres diverses de physique et de mécanique),* first published in 1663. The Perrault brothers, in a long passage on the physical senses, use an enlightening example to represent aberrations in tastes as due to defects in the soul. When we are robbed, they explain, we hand over the money to save our lives. Losing the money is bad, but we know that losing our lives would be far worse. Thus, a phenomenon that is normally bad becomes relatively good. There is, they propose, a similar relationship between certain individuals and food and drink that has been "corrupted" by terroir. Many of us find the smell of terroir unpleasant, they explain, but certain people, for whom terroir imparts some unknown good flavors to foods, will not only choose to eat such foods, but will even find bad smells to be good. As the Perrault brothers claim, "It happens that the usefulness that the soul finds [in such foods], whose qualities are made known by taste, keeps the bad odor from having its ordinary effect, meaning that it is not disagreeable."[24] Some people continue to enjoy foods considered universally good (bread, wine, milk, fruits, and cooked meat) but also relish peculiar, imperfect tastes that are not generally accepted, such as those imparted by the terroir: "the other source of pleasure is in the taste and smell of foods that are not as generally pleasurable and that displease some people, like wines that have *un goût de terroir*, soured or spoiled milk as in old cheese, fruits and vegetables in which the juice that plants take up through the earth is imperfectly cooked [...]. [O]ne supposes that those who like the taste and odor of those things have a unique disposition."[25] Food here is not merely a question of arbitrary personal preference, but joins the same moral register as knowledge, manners, and speech. There is something anomalous about terroir, reflected in the imperfect food some people eat, the murky knowledge they profess, and the jargon they speak. Although the Perrault brothers admit that at least a small minority of people like the smell of terroir in their foods and wines, the passage is clear in suggesting that these are deviant cases. It goes on to explain that such abnormalities have their origins in childhood, when "confused thoughts" about what the soul perceives as its needs shaped the individual's inclinations and tastes in an unusual way.

This and other delineations of sensorial "normality" by opposition allowed food to become a construct wherein tastes were objectified and used to draw larger conclusions about those who possessed them. Those with good taste were the most readily able to sense or "taste" rusticity elsewhere. In other words, the person who was "neutral" and "unblemished" in language, comportment, and taste was able to perceive aberration in others specifically because he or she had not been corrupted, either in soul or in palate, by terroir. Not coincidentally, the more the smell of terroir became a sign of rusticity, the more being able to detect it was a sign of sophistication. It was as if noticing dirt, contamination, or a deviation from normality elsewhere, and being generally intolerant of aberrations in food and language, were a sign of one's own purity and breeding.[26]

THE RETURN OF THE EARTH: TERROIR'S SEVENTEENTH-CENTURY PROPONENTS

In spite of the general stigma that had been attached to people and produce who were associated with terroir, a countermovement occurred at the height of Louis XIV's power in the last third of the seventeenth century. This opposing trend underscored ambivalence concerning the system of terroir-related values while reaffirming persistent French beliefs in the earth's systemic hold on the qualities of plants and the dispositions of human beings. In matters of language, knowledge, and food, terroir was not, it asserted, exclusively negative. Moreover, in many of the counterexamples offered in this period, terroir was not a figurative expression of rusticity, as the Furetière dictionary had qualified it at the turn of the seventeenth century, but an actual force physiologically determining people in the same way that it determined plants.

Arguments that mitigate the negative interpretation of terroir occur in several varieties. One of these is exemplified in the *Examination of Common Prejudices* of Claude Buffier, a now forgotten seventeenth-century text that sought to disabuse readers of vulgar prejudices. In it, Buffier reaffirms that one's terroir marks one's speech and acknowledges that this circumstance denigrates the provinces in the eyes of Paris and the court. He also judges that while there are legitimate differences between accents, one cannot make a qualitative judgment concerning which accent is better. In other words, Buffier, who had an enormous influence on Montesquieu (more on this in chapter 6), shifted the paradigm of terroir away from a pejorative pure/impure dichotomy toward a vision of terroir as one of the acceptable, normative factors that influence speech.

Buffier lays out what is at stake in a dialogue that opposes Timagène, a snobby Parisian, to Téandre, a character possessing a more mitigated view of different speaking styles. Both characters share a vision in which climate has a decisive influence on language, but interpret it in different ways. Timagène speaks first, blaming terroir for differences in regional dialects: "Each language seems to be influenced by the nature of the terroir where those who speak live: such that the Gascon and the Provençal have a lively and amusing *jargon,* whereas the Normand and the Picard possess something of a rude drawl."[27] Timagène's derision of the regional dialects is evident. Even if he does concede that Provençal is "lively" and "amusing," he still qualifies it as "*jargon,*" which translated as "corrupted language" at the time.[28] In fact, it becomes clear that anything other than the Parisian terroir-free accent could be subject to mockery. Téandre attempts to talk some sense into Timagène, pointing out the latter's bias: "The example is plausible [...] but to discern whether you are right to find the Gascon language more agreeable than the Normand, you have to judge without prejudice or interest."[29] Timagène at first denies having any bias at all, since he is not from any of the provincial regions. To which Téandre rejoins that as a native of Paris, he is prejudiced without realizing it: "You are from Paris: you were raised among people instructed that

FIGURE 4. This contemporary map depicts the languages and dialects that shaped identities and traditions in pre-Revolutionary France. The rubric *"français de l'Île-de-France,"* or what Timagène represented as "pure" French, represents just a small portion of France's historical linguistic diversity. Courtesy of Bordas Publishers.

Normand *jargon* is ruder than Gascon, and that Picard is more stupid than Provençal. This is a natural prejudice for you that you don't perceive."[30] This relativism asserts that although the Parisian has adopted the role of a neutral judge, he is in fact biased without knowing it. What is at stake here is not whether climate determines language (as both conclude clearly that it does, and terroir is much less a metaphor in this example than a real, tangible cause of variety), but whether different value judgments may be applied to different trends within speech, and whether there is an objectively *better* way of speaking.

As compelling as this example is, with its direct reference to terroir, it is not as important as that given by the Chevalier de Méré, an advocate for refined conversation, style, and comportment (that of the gentleman or *honnête homme*), widely considered by his contemporaries to be an authority in defining good taste and polite behavior during the latter half of the seventeenth century.[31] As an arbiter of style, Méré admits that language is not only a reflection of character and intellectual acumen, but also an expression of physical origins: "It is true that we possess that little something from the places where we are born, especially if we pass our lives there, and differences of mind and temperament are reflected in language."[32] Méré lends credence to the influence of natal origin (an idea that Bodin sought to discredit, as we saw in chapter 2), but also admits that the effect of place takes increasing hold and intensifies as we grow. For Méré, regional differences not only affect our way of expressing ourselves but also reflect more important differences in our minds and personalities.

Yet Méré also stipulates that the cultivated person should not succumb too entirely to terroir. A gentleman should be natural in reflecting his terroir, but not too natural *("trop naturel")* or unrefined: he should not go to seed in his province. Rather, he should speak an unmarked, universally acceptable currency: "Pronunciation, as I mentioned, to be good and perfect should be worldly, and polish itself through contact with other languages. I add to this that it should not reveal which place or country is the home of the one speaking."[33] Although Méré goes on to say that he finds pleasure in certain accents, adopting the attitude that appeared in Buffier, he is clear in advising those who aspire to polite society to be pure (untainted by terroir or origin) and cosmopolitan. Méré thus does not call for language to reflect regional dialects and the native terroir as Montaigne or the Pléiade poets might have; instead he advises that speakers walk the line between being natural and authentic in order to remain cultivated and refined.[34]

Along with Méré, several other significant examples demonstrate the ambivalence that surrounded the practice of using terroir as a mark of human identity in the seventeenth century. The above paragraphs suggested that pure reason, in line with eloquence, should not be encumbered with the bodily weight of terroir, nor indeed with any corporeal blemish. This view corresponded with the predominating Cartesian doctrine that formed the rational ethos of the seventeenth century, separating mind from body and creating an ideal of unhindered objective thought. While by and large the judicious thinker in the seventeenth century considered that knowledge could only be muddied by the backwaters of the provinces and that the physical influence of the body should be prevented from affecting the pure thought of the rational mind, at the same time a countercurrent conceded that geographic origins could in fact have a natural and normative role in determining the kind of reason and knowledge each person might possess.

Taking a stance that expresses the dominant Cartesian position, Adrien Baillet, a seventeenth-century priest and Descartes's first biographer, opposed the notion that material influences could determine thought and speech. Writing of a brand of literary criticism in which authors were judged according to their climate and terroir, Baillet laments that so much importance should be accorded to the determining influence of origin. Yet, notwithstanding his connection to Descartes and a religious background that would endorse Christian values and convictions instead of climatic determinism to decide agency, Baillet nevertheless concedes that the climate is not without some bearing on an individual's comportment: "Although we have said above that the qualities of a man's mind are personal, and there is a sort of injustice to attribute to a climate, a territory, or a province the vices and virtues that we observe in authors, nevertheless, rather than breaking with most critics, one must agree with them that authors, being composed of corporal matter as well as spiritual substance, are affected in this at least by the quality of the air they breathe and the terrain that nourishes them."[35] Baillet does not suggest that human beings are composed of a material soul and he is unremitting in his judgment that climate will not change the quality of an author's work. Even so, he provides valuable testimony that the seventeenth-century practice of using climate theory to understand authors was as widespread as the use of concepts like terroir to judge language production.

The passage is worthy of consideration for two other reasons. First, Baillet perceives an epistemological tension between human behavior and climatic determinism, which suggests that the ambivalence we have seen in the Perrault brothers regarding terroir in the culinary and larger nonculinary applications was widespread. Second, Baillet personally concedes that the air and the ground must have some influence on human beings without casting that fact in a pejorative light.[36] There is then good reason to believe that *some* segments of the population in seventeenth-century France considered human beings to be naturally linked to the earth, without attaching forcibly negative connotations to that relationship.

Baillet's description appeared three years before a more important work that contributed to defining France as a country with respect to its European and North African neighbors. In his 1688 *Digression sur les Anciens et les Modernes,* the well-known author Bernard le Bovier de Fontenelle makes the case that the "ancients" held no intrinsic advantage over the "moderns," as the former were shaped from the "same clay that we are made of." He does, however, accord a major role to terroir and the effect of the environment. In discerning between the French and the Italians, Fontenelle's model allowed for difference not only in tastes, but also in reason and rational thought. Individual opinions and ideas are shaped according to climate and terroir, in his reasoning, and not all are of equal value. He offers that

> if the trees of all of the centuries are equally large, the trees of all the countries are not. It is the same thing for the differences between minds. Different ideas are like plants or flowers, which do not all grow as well in every sort of climate. Perhaps our terroir in France is not right for the reasoning that the Egyptians do, no more than for their palm trees, and without going so far, maybe the orange trees that do not grow as well here as in Italy demonstrate that there is in Italy a certain bent of the mind that is not completely similar to that in France.[37]

Fontenelle demonstrates how tightly identified the world of plants and the agricultural register remained with the world of humans and their modes of reasoning. He equates thoughts to flowers and fruit, with their sensitivity to climate, thereby marking a retreat from an ideal of language or reason "as pure as water." According to Fontenelle, reason "tastes" different with respect to the terroirs that produce it. By contrast, readers with twenty-first-century assumptions are likely to believe that the litmus test for good, "objective" thinking is that it can be executed in terms of a logical chain of unerring, demonstrable conclusions. Reason, in these terms, should not vary according to climate or have a particular "taste." Yet for Fontenelle, reason is just as variegated as are the national and regional characters of countries and places.

The fact that this type of metaphor, linking products of the soil and products of the mind, was so widely used is also telling when it comes to the complicated, even obsessive, relationship that France had with plants, agriculture, and the earth. The metaphor concerning the effects of terroir had ceased to be used only figuratively: it was no longer simply a synonym for rusticity, but rather an indication that the earth really did shape the intellectual properties of its human "produce." Despite opposing currents of thought on the subject, terroir, by the end of the seventeenth century, had come to mean with ever-increasing seriousness what Montaigne and Bodin had suggested in the previous century, that the material influence of the earth shapes the qualities of mind and soul. As Fontenelle puts it, "It is unremittingly sure that by the chaining and reciprocal dependence that occurs between all parts of the material world, the climate differences that are felt on the planets must extend to the brain, and have some sort of effect there."[38] By specifically comparing ideas to plants and flowers, Fontenelle proposes that thought exists in types as diverse as the types of weather and soil. He also partially defuses the battle between "the Ancients" and "the Moderns," since he does not accentuate what is different between them but what, by the effect of the climate, is the same.[39] Finally, Fontenelle puts a firm essentialist accent on terroir as a nationalistic concept, using it to frame France's identity in comparison to that of other countries. The fauna and flora of France represent normality, while the Egyptians with their palm trees and Italians with their orange trees are necessarily imbued with a more exotic type of reason, undoubtedly less measured and moderate than that of France.

To be fair, Fontenelle goes on to nuance his theories by allowing that even if soil and climate do have an effect on thought, art and culture have more enduring influences. He also makes clear that since the human brain is less material than a plant, it is easier to transplant human beings to Paris from Rome than, say, to grow oranges successfully on the banks of the Seine. Fontenelle's example would have relieved Bodin of his concerns about autochthony and human relations insofar as he makes plausible the idea that humans are able to adapt easily to new climes and become part of environmentally determined communities. Nevertheless, rather than allowing for the relativism that Buffier ascribed to language, where no one manner of speaking was better than another, Fontenelle ascribes a system of values to rational thought that allows some "trees" to be taller than others. His comparisons aim to differentiate countries according to their greatness *(grandeur)* and achievements, rather than merely focusing on diversity and accepting that all things are equally good. What began as a seemingly innocuous observation, that climate influences character, opens the door to both an essentialist vision of human beings and a system for defining French national identity.

Finally, although Fontenelle admits that terroir affected reason, the implications of the remark for his French readers were relatively charitable, because it was widely held that the climate in France was perfectly temperate. Thus while the French might need to concede that they did not look at the world as Cartesian exemplars, with their minds objectively separate from their bodies, there was solace to be had in the fact that because France's climate was mild, it would consequently not significantly divert reason from truth. This strategy of characterizing the nation based on its moderate climate was redeployed a number of times in many different contexts over the following one hundred years, leading up to the Revolution. France was the best country in comparison to others because its climate did not appreciably taint speech, comportment, and thought. Paris, according to similar reasoning, and because it was also frequented by the highest percentage of cosmopolitan people, was even more perfect: it was the best milieu for language because it lay at the geographical middle of a moderate country, its centrality equated with objectivity and opposed to the physical and intellectual marginality of the provinces.

SEASONING POLITE LANGUAGE AND CLEAN CUISINE

The work of the Académie and evolving social politics became increasingly reflected in the material culture of cuisine in seventeenth-century France. There was, for example, a contemporaneous discourse that suggested that food preferences in the most refined and cosmopolitan people shared many of the qualities extolled above in terms of eloquent language, of purity and neutrality. Noteworthy examples occur in an avuncular letter from the well-known seventeenth-century epicurean Saint-Évremond, as well as in a speech made by the Chevalier de Méré.

Saint-Évremond was an expert in matters of fine dining, and in certain respects played a role in the realm of cuisine similar to that played by the Chevalier de Méré in speech and polite behavior. Chapter 5 will take up the former's colorful personality in greater detail, but one letter, on the importance of purity in foods, written circa 1675 is especially pertinent here.[40] In it, Saint-Évremond attempts to cheer up the Comte d'Olonne, a friend exiled to the provinces in the latter half of the seventeenth century. He begins with the consoling thought that even if there are no *"honnêtes gens"* so far from Paris, the Count can always find solace in good books and good foods. Conflating the two subjects in the pages of his letter, Saint-Évremond prefaces his remarks by stipulating that people of quality know "goodness by the exactitude of their taste and gravitate toward it automatically."[41] That said, he offers certain practical tips to the Count, expounding on the joys of simple but excellent books (Lucien, Petronius, and Cervantes) and the solace that comes from honest living, careful selection of foods, and sobriety in one's culinary exploits.

Putting a premium on the same values of purity, refinement, and natural elegance that appeared in the inaugural writings of the Académie française, Saint-Évremond explains that, with respect to matters of seasoning, one must be inordinately demanding at the table. To this end, he warns the Count to avoid adulterating mixes and ragouts: "all of these culinary mixes and compositions, called ragouts and hors d'oeuvres, must be understood by you to be sorts of poisons. If you only eat a little of them, they will only harm you a little: if you eat a lot of them, it is not possible that their pepper, vinegar, and onions will fail to ruin your taste and compromise your health in the end."[42] Complex, impure flavors corrupt taste and ruin health. Simple sauces, preferably those one makes oneself, are the most wholesome. Although salt and oranges are, according to Saint-Évremond, the two most "natural" seasonings, herbs are more exquisite than spices though still not suited equally well to all things. One must above all, Saint-Évremond concludes, use extreme discernment and discretion in dispensing seasonings. Just as the refined speaker eschewed all but the purest of language, the informed eater is encouraged to avoid the mishmash of "mixes" or "compositions" and to shy away from strong flavors, not only for pretensions of good taste, but also for well-being. Saint-Évremond makes clear that it is precisely in observing this practice that the persons of quality reveal themselves as such, gravitating toward foods that most mirror the natural purity of their physical composition and noble blood, which, like their words, should be "as pure as water."[43]

Elsewhere in the letter other parallels between the linguistic and culinary registers emerge. Saint-Évremond explains, for example, that seasonings, much like words according to Vaugelas and Bouhours, must bring out the natural flavors of foods without revealing their own flavors: "One must employ them [the seasonings] with discernment to the foods for which they are the best accommodated, and dispense them with as much discretion, so that they bring out the flavor of the food while hardly letting their own be perceived."[44] Seasoning, an addition that at first seems superfluous in natural cooking, can in fact extract the "essence" of the food, paradoxically perfecting its natural qualities through organic artifice. The passage recalls the "nudity" Montaigne strove for in his own writing, and the Scythians' use of the natural artifice of the local terroir to generate pure, natural smells and personal beauty. In Saint-Évremond's characterization, refined individuals are meant to strive through the use of seasonings to achieve the culinary perfection that nature would have in its optimal iteration. Whereas Montaigne encourages a return to perfect nature through the beautifying process, Saint-Évremond suggests that nature by itself is not sufficient and needs perfection through the judicious use of artifice. However, the rhetoric of both cuisine and words, in order to be most effective, must not be perceived: it must sound and taste natural and intrinsic.

Examining the practice of seasoning through the optic of language demonstrates that the latter entered into a direct dialogue with food, and shows how closely related the two ways of thinking were in the seventeenth century. Evoking the "seasoning" of speech in his *Discours de la conversation* in 1677, the Chevalier de Méré discusses ideal language by employing the metaphor of condiments (Méré uses the Italian word *condimento*). Méré's foray into the culinary lexicon aims to help his readers to understand the perfect tone of expression in conversation. In it, he allows that adding "condiments" to the discourse to give it some flavor is perfectly acceptable as long as the language as a whole remains "pure": "One must use as much as possible an easy and flowing expression; but it is only appreciated when it seems apt, and within the purity of language [. . .]. I find moreover that one needs what the Italians call the *condimento,* or seasoning. For blandness easily brings disgust. So one must take care not to be insipid and without flavor."[45] For Méré, this measured use of *condimento* is one of the adjustments that serve to bring the conversational dish to perfection, making it flavorful while keeping it natural. The speaker must make this adjustment, Méré hastens to add, while doing nothing to corrupt the speech's natural attributes, or causing it to appear too "studied." The speaker must furthermore "give more care to the naïveté than the perfection of things," without "too much embellishing."[46] In other words, just as simple sauces were preferred to mixed compositions in the culinary register, so in the register of speech: naive, simple, not overly embellished speech was considered the most eloquent. Here again, "seasoning" does not imply that one should change the natural qualities of the cuisine or speech, but only that one can paradoxically use artifice to make either food or language *more* captivating without diminishing its inherent nature.[47]

These examples, in which authors conflate food and language, began appearing in a slightly altered form in a late seventeenth-century generation of writing on food that promoted questions of aesthetics over those of health. Such cookbook authors railed against mixed, extravagant, and ill-conceived preparations. In the *Art de bien traiter* (1672), one of the seventeenth century's well-known cookbooks, the author (whom we know only by the initials

L. S. R.) warns against overflowing plates, overabundances of ragouts *(ragoûts)* and mixed hashes *(galimafrées),* and extraordinary compilations of meats.[48] The book specifies that the new reign of politeness in France renders obsolete all of the extravagant, disordered presentations of food in favor of, among other things, the "exquisite choice of foods, the finesse of their seasoning, the politeness and cleanliness of their service."[49] Although L. S. R goes on to explain that different people have different predominate humors, and that it is preferable to meet their individual physical needs (recalling the Perrault brothers' acknowledgment that some readers with altered souls prefer foods that taste of terroir), the aesthetic values he upholds in the world of cuisine are the same as those recommended by purveyors of fine language earlier in the century.

From all of this one could conclude that both the parallelism and the ambivalence that connected language, food, and terroir in France had as much to do with the state of politics and changing social hierarchies as with seventeenth-century culinary advancements. Mostly, the valorization of linguistic and culinary purity derived from the centralization of power and the rise to prestige of the court of Versailles. The parameters provided by Mary Douglas, with her attention to how a break in a pattern or an interruption of an order could qualify as a dirty or impure aberration, are clearly relevant to the discussion. Certainly terroir-flavored language was considered "sullied" insofar as it broke with the new national linguistic standards of the Académie française. Geographically specific accents and lexicons constituted an anomaly, out of place with the universal model enforced by centralized royal power. Ironically, insofar as terroir represented the individuality of a geographical place or region outside Paris, it was left weirdly without an accepted *social* place in the order of Versailles and the absolutist regime. In other words, smelling, sounding, or tasting of a physical place in language, food, or taste was equivalent to being socially out of place in seventeenth-century court society. As will become clear in the next chapter, qualifying terroir in this way becomes all the more meaningful when one considers another symbol of French absolutist culture: the garden of Versailles. The ordered symmetry of its rows of trees, and patterns of flowers neatly arranged and geographically orchestrated, represented values greatly at odds with those of terroir-infected language and produce.

FOUR

France's Green Evolution

TERROIR'S EXPULSION FROM VERSAILLES

AS LOUIS XIV'S POWER APPROACHED its apogee in the second half of the seventeenth century and members of the court affected a maximum of urbane sophistication, Versailles began to represent the archetype of cosmopolitanism. It was the utopic "no-place" in a context in which being marked by the provinces, or by any sort of terroir, was akin to being afflicted by a cultural blight. The material culture of the garden reflected aesthetic values concerning refined language and comportment. It also expressed another important change: between the early and late seventeenth century elite members of French society, with some exceptions, increasingly refused to entertain the sort of symbiotic relationship with the land that had been advocated by Olivier de Serres. Instead, in a class-driven society with a locus of power centered squarely on Paris and the court, idyllic representations no longer featured humans working harmoniously from within nature, but working authoritatively *over* and above it.

As we saw in chapter 2, the Académie française had already begun to attempt to codify and purify language of its irregularities, create universal rules, and distill from language the essence that it might have had were it not for the aberrations that circumstances of history and the climes of the provinces inadvertently produced. Roughly the same attitude appeared with respect to nature, agricultural pursuits, and gardens. Rather than being subordinated to the influence of the climate and its vagaries, individuals sought to overturn its effects, using the garden as a representation of human autonomy and power over nature. This translated into the creation of symbolic landscapes governed by geometry, method, order, and artificially instilled diversity.[1] Ironically, in the pursuit of gardening, a practice specifically devoted to earth and dirt, terroir once again appeared in the pejorative

context of deviation and insalubrity. One needed to rule over the soil, separating the landscape from one's own identity instead of assimilating the two.

This evolution sits in diametrical opposition to the depictions of farming
made in sixteenth- and early seventeenth-century literature. Prior to the construction of Versailles and the release of a spate of books on gardening that
replaced the Renaissance vogue for literature on estate management, one of the
most iconic representations of nature was the idealized notion that appeared
in Olivier de Serres's *Théâtre d'agriculture*. To fully understand the transitions
that took place in France, it is necessary first to outline several key images
promoted by de Serres, and then identify the shift away from them. One of the
most prominent characterizations in the *Théâtre d'agriculture* is that of
the estate owner himself. The *père de famille,* as de Serres calls him, works with
the earth to understand its potential and becomes an integral part of the land
he cultivates. In return, nature springs to life around him. For de Serres, estate
management entails "living" agriculture as part of a system where the *père de
famille* is both the *Théâtre*'s main actor and its director.

For the *Théâtre*'s first readers in the seventeenth century, the significance
of the holistic system did not end there. The *père de famille* not only depicted
Olivier de Serres, the "Seigneur du Pradel," watching over his estate but also,
considering the image in larger moral and practical terms, brought to mind
France's king, Henri IV.[2] For de Serres and his readers the symbolism could
not be more clear: the father's overarching role, whether he be the father of
the family, the seigneur of a fiefdom, or the head of the country, was to use
reason and experience to facilitate agriculture and interact personally with
each aspect of rural life, understanding the various terroirs (regions) of his
estate (kingdom) while ensuring the planting of fields, the management of
people and livestock, and the production of a bountiful harvest.[3]

At the *Théâtre*'s center is a microcosmic focus on the soil of the estate—
and an overriding ethos that would be radically transformed throughout the
century. From the first sentence of the first page, le *père de famille* is called on
to understand the earth: "The foundation of agriculture is the knowledge of
the nature of the terroirs that we want to cultivate."[4] The *père de famille*
interacts with the terroir, examines it, smells it, and even tastes it to determine its qualities and know its limits. That taste and the local geography,
along with the soil's color and smell, dictate the farmer's rational response to
his land and the interventions he should undertake for agricultural success.

But success in terms of economic productivity was not the only reason to
consider the soil. Through the humors in Hippocratic and Galenic medicine,

the medical science that remained central until the latter part of the seventeenth century considered the nature of the soil to be of critical importance when it came to health. Olivier de Serres speaks specifically of various maladies that may be caused by humors and the natural remedies that one can concoct in one's own garden to cure them, evoking an array of examples ranging from the juice of endive and fennel to an expectorant syrup of squillactic oxymel (a mix of honey and diluted vinegar with the dried bulb of the sea squill). The strong correlation between one's soil and one's physical constitution explained de Serres's deeper connection with the land. The earth, in the *Théâtre*, contains "hidden" properties, and by assessing it with the tools of reason and observation, readers will be able to make the correct choices, coexist harmoniously with it, and benefit in terms of health and wealth.

In no way, however, does de Serres suggest that human beings should exist on a higher moral plane than the earth they nurture. Rather, we live within its medium and should strive to understand it. We can and should cultivate it, de Serres emphasizes, and even overcome it when there are challenges, but we must coincide with it. That is why, along with assessment through the senses and the use of reason and experience, de Serres invites his readers to respect nature's limits, observing borders and boundaries in plants. One cannot, for example, grow anything anywhere: such attempts are "vain efforts, to think that one can grow wild trees elsewhere and otherwise than their natural tendency takes them."[5] Certain soils allow only for certain crops, and de Serres reminds his readers that they cannot turn mountains into plains and plains into mountains.[6] In its discourse on recognizing terroirs, limits, and borders, in terms of both places and seasons, the *Théâtre* owes heavily to the *Georgics* (de Serres mentions Virgil eleven times and paraphrases *Georgics* 2, 109, while discussing terroir). Once again, along with several other ancient agricultural authors—especially Columella, Cato, and Varro—Virgil remained central to the interactions Renaissance writers entertained with the land.[7]

Most of all, de Serres conveys the constant feeling that the *père de famille* is wholly invested and implicated with nature in a hands-on way. Although from the first page de Serres uses reason to seek the proper proportion of clay and fine sand in soil, he also remains personally attached to the earth, which he animates and personifies through metaphors: "Because just as salt seasons foods, clay and fine sand, being distributed in terroirs in perfect proportion, by nature or human intervention, make them easier to work, to keep in or cast off humidity appropriately; and by these means, tamed, trained, fattened, they happily bring us all sorts of fruits."[8] By interacting with the terroir through a variety of techniques, the *père de famille* succeeds in bringing the earth to productive life, "taming" and "fattening" it to adjust its seemingly human disposition. Cultivated, happy and fat soils gaily produce a variety of fruits, pleasing the *père's* eye as he wanders among them, and provide sustenance for those he cares about. The animated theater is of course directed by the *père,* but he also acts *within* it and, above all, does nothing to risk denaturing it.

THE FALL OF THE *THÉÂTRE* AND TERROIR FROM THE GARDENER'S GRACE

Despite its prestige early in the century, the *Théâtre* fell progressively from favor in France during the seventeenth century. In part, this was because de Serres was Protestant and the already shaky tolerance for Protestantism dissipated after the death of Henri IV in 1610. But the vision of the French entertaining an intimate relationship with their fields fell from favor for other more important reasons. Some of them have to do with the diminished prestige of the nobles and their seigneurial estates after the Fronde, the civil wars from 1648 to 1653 in which the Cardinal Mazarin defeated the insurrection posed by the provincial aristocracy and paved the way for the absolutist power of Louis XIV. With power henceforth concentrated centrally, the provincial jewels lost their splendor when compared to the glory of the absolutist Parisian crown. The change was also connected to terroir's concomitant lexical fall from grace. Still other rationales for the shift may be found in a new practice of gardening, in which the conviction of technical mastery and moral superiority over nature would in many circles replace de Serres's holistic vision.

To this last point, as esteem for the provinces fell off and was subsumed by a growing fascination with the ascendant supremacy of Paris, talk of fields and agronomy went out of vogue, replaced by a developing interest in gardens. Instead of practical issues of estate management and sustenance, readers sought an aesthetic vision of nature artfully crafted, beautified, and controlled by humans. Jacques Boyceau de la Barauderie's 1638 *Traité du jardinage*—a work that undoubtedly influenced Le Nôtre, the principal architect of Versailles, and La Quintinie, the creator of Louis XIV's *potager* or vegetable garden—exemplifies this evolution.

Both de Serres and Boyceau were Protestant. Both privileged the ethics of working the land, bemoaning that such an important task had fallen to the hands of ignorant laborers when it had once been a royal and godly endeavor. Both also suggested that a keen understanding of nature, diverse climatic conditions, air, and water was necessary for success. Nevertheless, Boyceau's treatise replaced that of de Serres by speaking more palatably to the public of his time. He could in no way be construed as targeting the *père de famille* or the estate owner situated in one of the many regions scattered through the provinces of France who had been served by parishes possessing copies of de Serre's *Théâtre*. Instead, Boyceau wrote for the gardener, seeking to follow the "rules and maxims" necessary to obtain the beauty found in the royal houses of Paris, Fontainebleau, and Saint-Germain.

Whereas de Serres opens the *Théâtre*'s first edition with an image of gardens surrounded by France's mountains and fields, placing an emphasis on the country's national agricultural production, Boyceau's title imagery and text highlight lawns, groves, and garden beds *(pelouses, bosqueuts, parterres)* and state as his objective the consideration of "ornaments serving to beautify *(embellir)* the garden." The textual focus also changed radically in Boyceau. As Thierry Mariage remarks, whereas only 13.5 percent of de Serres's *Théâtre* leaves utility behind to consider pleasure gardens, only 12.5 percent of Boyceau's treatise is dedicated to utility instead of beauty.[9] The priorities of the two works are almost symmetrically flipped, and this change is reflected by the use of the word *terroir* itself. It appears eighty-seven times in de Serres, but only in ten instances in Boyceau. In fact, the word's growing negative associations helped to eradicate it almost completely from the vocabulary of beautification in garden aesthetics, and it appeared with radically fewer instances in other gardening manuals in the following years.[10]

In its depiction of garden culture, Boyceau's work helped to solidify a negative association with terroir and agriculture, since it distinguishes between urban areas and the countryside, relegating the production of provincial fields to the lowly laborer: "Leaving to the laborer *(paysan)* the crops of the countryside and the care of wheat [...] our principal efforts are thus employed in the gardens."[11] Instead of accentuating sustenance and production, Boyceau is preoccupied by the same aesthetic concerns of order, symmetry, and purity that we have already observed at work with respect to language and literature, and that would capture the attention of cookbook writers in the decades to come.[12] He goes, in fact, even further, urging his readers to seek to perfect nature in a way that had not been realized in the real world, adding adornments and ornaments in order to "embellish."[13]

Boyceau's accent on beauty and shift from valorizing the countryside constituted in 1638 the midpoint of an evolution away from the symbiosis with nature described by de Serres in 1600 and toward the diametrical transformation that would occur in the gardens of Versailles in the 1660s. By the end of this process, we can observe the complete disjunction between the idealized harmony that came from cooperating with nature in the georgic setting depicted by de Serres and the urbane cosmopolitanism of the new court aesthetic. Rather than communing with the countryside, Versailles radiated outward as a sovereign, artificial icon of glory, constituting a multifaceted representation of the absolutist regime of Louis XIV at the height of France's historical power and prestige. Modern critics such as Mukerji, Garrigues, Baridon, and Goldstein have followed Norbert Elias's lead in emphasizing the extent to which the gardens of Versailles constituted a display of the king's mastery over both the human and natural world, and an attempt to bring perfection to the latter.[14]

VERSAILLES: THE MASTERY OF THE TERRESTRIAL WORLD

The dominance of the natural world was a metaphor with broad significance. Versailles represented, in garden form, France's military power, scientific mastery, and, as Chandra Mukerji puts it in chapter 5 of her book, the king's astute social choreography. At Versailles, the world of the garden became an image for the entire kingdom, as plants and trees underwent extreme measures of grooming to depict the subordination of nature to the king. Elias explains how trees were shown as metaphorically obedient as the king's subjects in the court: "It suits the king's taste to group the trees and plants in his garden in clear forms that are easily overlooked, as the courtiers are grouped by ceremonial. The trees and bushes must be trimmed in such a way that no trace of disorderly, uncontrolled growth is visible. The paths and flowerbeds must be so arranged that the structure of the garden show the same clarity and elegance as that of the royal buildings."[15] As with the Académie's rules for language, anything unkempt or lacking uniformity was excised in an attempt to subordinate imperfect nature and attain excellence. Even at the time, Versailles was such a well-known icon for its domination over nature that near contemporaries, such as Saint-Simon, were overtly critical after the king's death, reporting that he did violence to nature: "There it gave the king pleasure to tyrannize Nature and to tame her by expending art and money [...]. One feels repelled by the constraint that is everywhere imposed on Nature."[16]

Much has been written about this mastery of nature in Versailles as a whole, but the king's vegetable garden in particular effectively tells the story of the broader shift in values and the reversal of the French relationship with terroir. The nine-hectare space known as the *potager du roi* provides an excellent example of how nature was mastered and transformed into a *terroirless* place. From its very inception, the king's vegetable garden stood in opposition to the notion of terroir as practiced by Olivier de Serres and his generation. De Serres had recommended the assessment of terroir as the starting point in any gardening or farming endeavor. By first understanding the land's natural qualities, one could then properly employ the techniques of agriculture to produce a rich harvest. Louis XIV, however, shocked his chief gardener, La Quintinie, by ordering his garden to be planted on the site commonly referred to as the *étang puant,* or "stinking pond."[17] Instead of respecting the natural potential of the earth and choosing a planting site accordingly, he chose to *remake* the natural setting to order. Between 1676 and 1683, La Quintinie oversaw at great expense an artificial transformation of the land in order to plant on just the sort of area that de Serres exhorted his readers to avoid.[18] The result was that the swamp was drained and immense quantities of clean dirt were brought in from a neighboring area, fertilized, and further supplemented from the mammoth excavation of what would become the artificial lake called *la pièce d'eau des suisses.*[19]

This artificial construction of a terroir that did not previously exist is emblematic of the mentality Versailles was built upon: reason and science could master nature. Madame de Scudéry, well known in the court and salon culture of the time, testified to the king's dominance over nature in her 1669 novella *La Promenade de Versailles,* in which a "beautiful foreigner" visits Versailles for the first time and is astonished by its magnificence. The emphasis is not on Louis XIV's understanding and assimilation of humankind and the natural world, but on his talent in using artifice to control nature:

"From what I see," said the beautiful foreigner to me, "your prince enjoys making art overcome and beautify nature everywhere."

"To confirm your sentiment," I said to her, "I only have to say to you that it is no hardship for him to change the place of ponds, and one of these days, he'll change around two or three of them."[20]

The king "overcomes" and "beautifies" nature. He is able to move natural features of the land, such as swamps, in order to create the representation he desires.

It is therefore not surprising to learn through historical accounts that intricate machines and conveyor systems were used to move the earth and elaborate systems of irrigation and drainage were constructed to confirm the king's dominance over natural conditions.[21] In constructing the garden, La Quintinie's defiance of the natural constraints of place, as ordered by Louis XIV, was coupled with a defiance of space and time.[22] His tools included a trellis system and the espalier style of pruning trees to a wall, channeling them to look not dissimilar to human subjects standing at attention, branches forced out horizontally like arms.[23] Heat from the stone walls and a pruning method that forced branches to grow along strict lines maximized solar radiation and were further examples of nature mastered by human science and reason. As a result of such techniques, fruits ripened early, challenging the limits of the natural cycle and altering parameters of natural time as well as space. Although several agricultural techniques to speed nature along had already been used in the past, including in the work of de Serres (e.g., hot beds with manure, greenhouses, grafting, etc.), Versailles represented a complete change in the ambitions of gardening through the pointed extremes it employed to control and contradict nature. Rather than marshaling forces to understand nature, as de Serres had advocated, the *potager du roi* set out to transform it.

Perhaps the most telling sign of this transformation occurred in the organization of the space itself. Outside the *potager,* the parks of Versailles were formed of groves, hedges, fountains, beds of flowers, and statuary with mythological representations. In this setting, the visitor walked at the same physical level as such pagan gods as Apollo. In the vegetable garden, however, passageways were constructed on the top of tall walls from which the viewer could look down and survey the fruits and vegetables from above. The space represented a dramatic shift from de Serres's *Théâtre,* in which the *père de famille* was both a director and an actor interacting on the same plane as animals and plants. Instead, it constituted a theater where the spectator surveyed nature from above.[24] Finally, although we know through the testimony of La Quintinie and others that the king enjoyed bringing visitors into the gardens to pick fruit, and often ventured personally into the garden to interact with nature, his activities were limited to harvesting here and there or displaying his scientific mastery and control of nature through new pruning techniques.[25]

FIGURE 5. The physical organization of the *potager du roi* at Versailles has changed since the seventeenth century, but the raised wall on the left gives an idea of how the king and his visitors would have seen the gardens from above, in dominance over the natural scene. Photo by Gianni Dagli Orti, courtesy of the Art Archive at Art Resource, NY.

Perhaps most strikingly, the glory and nobility of Versailles was due to the fact that, through the acculturation of nature, it possessed no terroir at all. Not only was the king's garden placed on an artificial terroirless site, but also the produce cultivated by La Quintinie offers an incontrovertible example of the changes in attitude toward farming and gardening. Rather than seeking the most well-known terroir for any one product and growing fruits or vegetables that would produce the best correlation between flavors and soil types, the king was happiest when he could produce at Versailles fruits that could be mistaken for those from other parts of the world, including his orange trees from Portugal, white figs, and peas often grown out of season.[26] His domination over nature was conveyed by fruits as pure as the visitors to Versailles were cosmopolitan: both aspired to perfection, unmarked and uncorrupted by terroir.

This is finally the most resonant point in the juxtaposition between the depiction of nature early in the seventeenth century and that of nature during Louis XIV's reign in the second half of the century. For Olivier de Serres, terroir needed to smell good in order to promise a succulent harvest, but La Quintinie wrote that the best earth was completely neutral and had no smell at all. In the beginning of his treatise on gardening, La Quintinie employs the stock example of wines to prove that fruits and vegetables take on the taste of terroir. The best terroir, however, he explains, was "no terroir." The soil should have no flavor at all, in order to allow for the purest expression of the fruit in question:

> Moreover, it seems to me that what makes a parcel of land truly good is that it has absolutely no odor and no taste [. . .]. The example of wines that take on the taste of the terroir serves as a convincing proof of this truth, as it is always the case that the sap, which is prepared by the roots, is simply made of water which, being in the land where the roots are to work, is necessarily imbibed with the flavor and qualities of this earth and retains them [. . .]. The land in order to be good must be wholly like water which is good, meaning neither acrid nor insipid, nor sweet: it should not smell of anything whatsoever, neither good nor bad.[27]

Rather than allowing for diversity in soil, La Quintinie sought out terroir that was perfectly neutral, resembling what he qualified to be good water. Thus, forty years after the first attempts to purify the French language of terroir in Vaugelas, and in the years following Dominique Bouhours's assessment that the best language should be as neutral and pure as water, the same aesthetic appeared in the perfected French garden. In each of these iterations, the bodily influence of the earth was seen as a corruption that blemished the immaculacy, essence, and expression of nature's best fruits and vegetables.[28]

PHILOSOPHICAL RUPTURES BETWEEN MIND AND BODY AND NEW VISIONS OF THE LAND

Versailles depicted Louis XIV's motivation to display political influence by demonstrating power over nature, but there was a philosophical impetus at work as well, one that helped reshape French identity with respect to nature and the material representation of land, gardens, and agriculture. This influence, which privileged the mind and derided the body, was motivated by a philosophical division between the dualist theories of Descartes and the monist explanations of human agency proposed by seventeenth-century

Epicureans. The scope of the debate helped lay the groundwork for a further evolution that would transform not only the French relationship to the land, but also the burgeoning literature on cuisine that arose after 1650.

Descartes's emphasis on pure reason and rational method was widely known at the time (his *Discours de la méthode* was published in 1637), but to what extent garden aesthetics in Versailles were a reflection of Cartesian influence is complicated and the subject of significant debate.[29] Key notions at Versailles—such as perspective, geometry, and rationalism—certainly fit well with Cartesian thought, but the importance of many of these themes predated Descartes, as they occur in de Serres and elsewhere. On the other hand, the humbling of the physical body in favor of an emphasis on the sovereignty of the mind was clearly reinforced by Cartesian thinking, and is of direct relevance to the evolution of terroir and the hierarchal positioning of humans as standing above earthly influences in seventeenth-century garden imagery.

Writing his *Discours de la méthode* in French instead of Latin in order to reach a wider audience, Descartes seeks to establish that we owe our dignity and superiority to the power of reason. Human beings, he explains, are composed of two separate orders: the higher order of the mind, and the lower order of the body, which includes the mechanical corporal functions and the passions that we share with animals. Descartes claims that the two are joined by the pineal gland, the point at which bodily sensations are articulated and deciphered by the rational mind. The mind, in this context, is meant to judge the sensations of the body with detachment, considering them as if they belonged to a separate object of analysis. One might envision the mind as much like the viewer at Versailles observing the *potager* from atop the wall, contemplating the earthly body with detachment while dictating rational decisions to enact upon it.

Descartes's formulation entirely separates the prestige of being human from human physicality; it also proposes that human existence can be confirmed independently of the bodily senses through mere rational deduction, encapsulated in Descartes's phrase "I think, therefore I am" (*Je pense donc je suis*). Indeed, all that we can know for certain in the world, according to Descartes, is detected by the intellectual power of the mind. Sensorial data—indeed all impressions from the body—are subject to error and must therefore be methodically examined and interpreted by reason. Thus, according to the logic of Descartes, neither the human body nor any other corporal entity should alter the conclusions arrived upon by reason.

The visual effects created by playing with perspective in the gardens at Versailles were a case in point: trickery to the senses whose truth reason alone could decipher. For Descartes and all Cartesians, pure thought, language, and comportment should operate independent of the influence of sensory data, bodily forces, and climatic determinism—including, say, the effect of terroir.[30]

Many aspects of the Cartesian model were transcribed in the new vision of the French garden as presented at Versailles, in its calculated technical mastery of nature and reasoned configuration. As Mukerji puts it, "There is something about the formality, materialism, and impersonality of Cartesian thought and French formal gardens that makes them seem part of a contiguous, if not the same, cultural system."[31] Yet seventeenth- and eighteenth-century French intellectuals continued to offer counterexamples to the Cartesian ideals of mind-body separation and comportment based on unhindered reason. One notable example above is that of de Muralt, with his image of pure knowledge that can be affected by the body, like water that becomes turbid as it flows through the hinterlands and is polluted by terroir; or Fontenelle's comparison of humans to trees, growing different types of reason depending on the terroir of their countries. Such examples challenged the symbolism of the garden as a place where humans could demonstrate intellectual control over the landscape.

The philosophies most systemically in conflict with Descartes's postulation of a mind that possesses detached mastery of the body qua nature, however, were Epicureanism and the persistence of Hippocratic and Galenic medical theories. Together, the two wrested from French intellectual opinion the notion that a sense of human identity could be as detached and autonomous with respect to the landscape as the rationalized landscapes of Versailles seemed to suggest.

Pierre Gassendi (1592–1655), while less well known than Descartes today, commonly receives the honor for reviving the Epicurean philosophical school in seventeenth-century France. He authored a modern interpretation of the work of Epicurus, and was followed by disciples such as Jean-François Sarasin (1611–54) and François Bernier (1625–88).[32] The group ushered Epicurean materialist ideas into the realm of serious conversation. More importantly, Gassendi attacked Cartesian thought and attempted to legitimize Epicureanism by proving that it was neither the philosophy of excess, nor fundamentally incongruous with Christianity, nor representative of a strict atomistic determinism that would curtail the freedom of human agency.[33]

This last issue, dating back to the writings of Democritus in the fifth century BCE, constituted one of the fundamental difficulties of atomism, since as a monist, materialist philosophy it depicted the soul as corporeal rather than spiritual. This resulted in a sticking point: the materiality of the soul implied that it was subject to the laws of physics. There was therefore little room for Epicurean proponents to claim complete autonomy over their own actions, since in a purely physical world all thought and agency falls within an unbreakable chain of cause and effect, standing thus in contrast to Descartes's dualist system of body and mind, which assured the agent complete autonomy over the body. Though Gassendi proposed a soul that was only *partially* material, trying to carve out room for the autonomy of human agency, the Epicurean conception still proved overly deterministic for the tastes of many potential proselytes.[34]

One iteration of Epicurean theory in the realm of physiological taste and flavor is highly telling insofar as it premised normality not on the function of reason independent of the body, but on the constitution of the taster. François Bernier explained that taste sensation was physical. He took up a stock example of sweetness and bitterness that dated to Epicurus and Lucretius, and wrote that the flavor of substances hitting the tongue was determined both by the particles of the matter and by the pores in our tongues. Sweet tastes come from round atoms that fit with ease through the corresponding pores of the tongue. Bitter tastes come from angular atoms that abrade, flay, or enter the tongue with difficulty.[35]

In Bernier's explanation, it is clear that flavor should occur according to a normative paradigm in which humans perceive tastes in mostly the same ways, as most individuals possess tongues that have similar pore shapes. The exception is when people age or are sick, at which point their tasting mechanism becomes enfeebled. In other words, in a corollary to the malformed soul that the Perrault brothers offered as an explication for the propensity to search out terroir-driven food, it is not that the intellectual perception of flavors has gone awry, but that an aberrant physical constitution has twisted reality. In this way, flavor can be said to dwell both in the food we are eating (the shape of its atoms) and in the senses of the taster (the constitution of the pores). Bernier does not, however, conclude that only illness and age can explain differences in taste. There can be, he suggests, other reasons for variations in preferences, but, like Lucretius, he focuses exclusively on variety as a deviation from the norm.[36] Epicureans like Bernier held that sensation generally represents something that is *true* in a more direct sense, insofar as it reveals valuable data about the taster's physical composition and the world he or she lives in. This materialist, Epicurean view held strong in the latter part of the century as taste in foods and wine became a central issue. It set the stage for physicality to play a primary role in culinary refinement, restoring to the body a primary role in making aesthetic judgments about the truth of the world.

The Epicurean materialist vision reconnected human identity to the physicality of climate and landscape in a way that forced a reconsideration of detached vision and rational mastery in formal garden aesthetics. In an article, "The New Division of the Earth by the Different Species or Races of Men that Inhabit it," published in 1684 in a popular scholarly journal, François Bernier explains that empirical evidence gathered on voyages around the world had taught him about differences in populations, and that geographical origins were correlated with different "species" or "races."[37] He speaks first in broad terms, commenting mostly on how the exterior appearance of humans is influenced by climate and soil: "Because although men in the exterior form of their bodies, and principally the face are almost all different from each other, according to the diverse cantons of earth they inhabit [. . .] I nevertheless noticed that there are four or five species or races of men for whom the difference is so observable that it can serve as warranted grounding for a new division of the earth."[38] Bernier propounds the same Epicurean discourse on diversity and limits that we saw in Virgil's *Georgics,* in which the inhabitants of the earth are as corporally diverse as the physical districts from which they originate. Although Bernier groups these differences into four or five larger, general categories, he also notes that variety is observable between small territorial districts. Most importantly, his discourse opens the door to essentialist distinctions about the intrinsic value of one population over another. It also suggests that inherent capacities of the body and mind (as far as the soul is considered material by Epicureans) may be influenced by geographic origin.

In fact, as if he were worried that his intended readers (most of them French men) would take umbrage at being cast as determined by their climate, Bernier's examples are devoted to women and foreigners from distant places, leaving white European men comfortably out of the equation. His discussion about terrestrial diversity takes the form of aesthetic judgments, absurd to twenty-first-century readers, about the physical traits of ethnic groups, and in particular, the beauty of women, qualifying the effects of climate and terroir in terms of alterity. He also acknowledges the power of "seed" *(semence)* alongside the effects of climate, allowing readers to conclude that personal characteristics are biological as well as environmental. Invoking terroir directly, he explains that any given woman's "beauty does not only come from water, food, the terroir, and the air, but also from the seed, which is unique to certain races or species."[39] This explanation couples class, gender, and race alongside origin in its explication of physical traits. Yet Bernier stops short of stating that the thoughts or intellectual prowess of people are the result of exterior factors.

Nevertheless, the proverbial well was poisoned by such observations: the façade of the European white man's mind rising above the influence of body and earth to represent an imaginary paragon of reason and purity was increasingly beginning to show cracks as the seventeenth century drew toward a close. This change was motivated by the philosophical debate outlined above, but became increasingly relevant in the context of social and political conditions. Within an extremely hierarchal society and a locus of power centered on Versailles and Louis XIV, individuals sought ways both to assimilate with certain class groups and to distinguish themselves from others. This dynamic resulted in new depictions of human relationships, reflected both in representations of landscapes and in culinary culture.

COOKING FOR CLASS: HIGH REASON AND THE RETURN OF THE BODY

When it came to displaying purified, discerning tastes, there were many reasons to avoid terroir and its negative connotations, and several ways to vilify the *other* as entrenched and determined by provincial rusticity. As a result of class dynamics, direct and indirect references to Cartesian and Epicurean modes of thought appeared, partially reshaped, in commentaries on taste and the burgeoning culture of cuisine in the second half of the seventeenth century. The proliferation of new cookbooks, in particular, played a primary role in reflecting this evolution.

In one important change related to transforming social hierarchies, cookbooks shifted from focusing on the health of the eater to discussing questions of culinary aesthetics, cachet, and social status. As Jean-Louis Flandrin has pointed out, earlier in the century, in sources like *Le Trésor de santé* (1607), eaters were encouraged to indulge in foods that would complete natural deficiencies in their characters. In the second half of the seventeenth century, however, with an increasingly large bourgeois class, a greater number of individuals had access to luxury items that would advertise their knowledge of elite social conventions and suggest they possessed superior taste. Prestige and sophistication were packaged for sale, offered in the form of purchased noble titles *(charges);* in the material culture of castles, landscapes modeled after Versailles, and lavish clothes; and in high-class choices in cuisine.[40]

It was in this context that, along with new trends in eating, transformations in cooking took place, and many of the Cartesian standards for adherence to reason and method that had been applied to creating successful gardens were applied to the rational mastery of cooking. Most prominent was the idea, inspired at least partially by Descartes, that a formulaic and studied method could lead to excellence in cooking. To achieve perfection, one needed merely to follow a recipe that indicated exact measure, technique, and proportion, and to take care in choosing proper ingredients.[41] This approach represented a change from the past, when choices about food had overwhelmingly been based on one's intrinsic physical constitution and humors. Now individuals could follow simple, methodical procedures to eat their way up the social ladder.

In this respect, at the height of absolute power in France, one could say that the tools of prestige, at least in the realm of cuisine, were democratized. Method and reason were rootless, objective, and mostly immune to discourses on class, blood, or humors, allowing the bourgeois person to cook (or perhaps be cooked for) and eat like a member of the elite. In other words, by using the same technical mastery that was imposed on nature in the perfect French garden, combined with correct measure and proper ingredients, one could achieve on the microcosmic level of the plate the perfection of Versailles. One did not have to have the financial resources to move mountains or drain swamps in order to show that one was noble in spirit if not in birth. The body, with its baggage of heredity and bloodlines, was shifted to the margins in this picture.

Members of the bourgeois population, such as Nicolas de Bonnefons, the author of the successful cookbook *Délices de la campagne* (1651), thus increasingly sought out the proper tools to succeed in the kitchen.[42] Bonnefons makes clear in his preface that the success of the professional chef or home cook (Bonnefons dedicates the book to the *"femme ménagère"*) has something to do with the household's financial resources, but also allows that his work addresses a readership of varied income levels. He is fastidious in technique and pays great attention to the origin of ingredients, the equipment called for, and procedures for producing the best possible finished product. In this respect, Bonnefons provides a rational method for meeting the challenges and limits of nature, though he in no way suggests that it is possible to transform nature as entirely as was accomplished at Versailles.

François Massialot, who published *Le Cuisinier royal et bourgeois* in 1691, provides another excellent example, clearly conflating classes even in the title of his book. Elaborating on the book's ambitions, Massialot explains that his reader, by shining the "beam of spirit and reason" on the subject, and combining that effort with good taste, could accede to the highest social order, at least in the realm of cuisine.[43] The effect was even more pronounced in the cookbooks that would follow in the next century. The *Cuisinière bourgeoise* (1742), published by a writer known simply as Menon, explains in the pages of its preface that the book's author would adjust his precepts to the fortune of his readers "and to the nature of the foods they are obligated to limit themselves to. It is not for nobles that he writes, it is for the bourgeois: but one could say that he ennobles common food through the seasonings with which he enhances them [. . .] the cooks that he instructs will find in his lessons an easy method for [. . .] giving to the most common [foods] a flavor that is not common."[44] In this conception, seasonings are not limited to bringing out the natural qualities of the food, as advocated by Saint-Évremond, but instead should be employed to transform a "common" primary matter into an "ennobled" end product. Menon does not suggest that one can entirely overcome nature, as had been achieved at Versailles, but he fervently instills the notion that readers can climb in class and eat like nobles through the use of the proper methods, precepts, and techniques.[45]

Despite the democratizing influence of reason, and partially *because* of it, there was a significant reaction from those intent on reaffirming the hierarchical lines between the classes. Instead of targeting the question from the angle of food production, it was easier to attack taste and appreciation. Taste was not something that could be rationally decided: good taste had more to do with who a person was than with what a person thought. Ironically, it was often the bourgeois themselves who were the most vociferous in upholding the standards of good taste in this context, presumably because their own pretension to social prestige was premised on distinguishing that which made them merit a higher social stature in comparison to others. Consequently, as Jean-Louis Flandrin puts it, cookbooks of the time strongly advocated a definition of good taste that was not formulaic in the same way that recipes themselves were. One could evidently use reason and method to cook well, but not to be a gifted taster. As Flandrin explains, "from the mid-seventeenth century, then, cookbook authors discuss their art; and they do it with respect to 'good taste,' which seems outside time and space. This good taste, in fact, was willingly opposed by them to the gastronomic roving of individuals and whole groups of people."[46] This "gastronomic roving," as it turns out, was most commonly attributed by cookbook writers to non-Europeans. To take up Massialot once again, he declares that it is only in Europe (and principally, in France) that "cleanliness, good taste, and finesse in the seasoning of plates and the ingredients in them" prevail.[47]

In other words, instead of insisting that eating and appreciating flavors depended on the same skills of reason and method that were called on to produce the plates, most cookbooks reconnected good taste and polite comportment with a set of qualities one could not obtain through the use of reason alone. As a result, the brand of theorizing that appeared in the Epicurean François Bernier made its way to the table. To begin with, cookbook authors began to foreground France itself as a propitious place to cook, because the French had superior tastes. Cookbooks papered over class difference, not only by giving rational method a place in cooking, but also by displacing good taste from the qualities of the individual to those of the nation. Many cookbook titles were indicative of the trend. Works such as *Le Cuisinier français* by La Varenne and *Le Jardinier français* by Bonnefons (both published in 1651) made food a French affair, while the authors explained in their prefaces that the French excelled as a people in cooking. Through following the precepts of these books, readers could both reaffirm their Frenchness and rise in the social order by eating like royalty.

The rhetorical technique used in this genre of texts is worth commenting on. Instead of casting climatic determinism in terms of a dichotomy separating Paris and the provinces, the cookbooks advocated for a national identity for all of France, based on the country's central location in Europe. To put it simply, bourgeois cookbook writers turned to the same environmental determinism that had been used to set Paris above the provinces, in which the latter were weighted down by the sludge of terroir. That is, writers began to correlate the general excellence of French taste in foods with the French environment. The French, they claimed, were able to appreciate good food because they came from a moderate climate where neither the people nor their foods were "overspiced" or "oversunned." Climatic determinism was no longer exclusively an insult, but rather became a measure by which one could, at least on a broad level, reaffirm the good tastes of those lucky enough to be shaped by the right climate.

In this vein, speaking of La Varenne's recipes, the competing cookbook author L.S.R. disparagingly explains that the former's tastes *(goûts)* embraced "miseries that one would endure more willingly among Arabs and other marginal people than in a purified climate like our own, where salubriousness, refinement, and good tastes are the object and matter of our most sustained attentiveness."[48] Delicate flavors, cleanliness, and good taste—the same sorts of factors that appear in reference to wines that did not smell of terroir—were naturally sought by people whose palates had not been marred by living in the extremes of foreign climates. Environmental determinism appeared in a positive light, not because L.S.R. thought he and his readers were *above* the corporal influence of terroir, but because the French people as a whole come from a "purified climate." Perhaps their judgment was not as "objective" as in the Cartesian model, which detached reason from bodily influence, but it was just as irreproachable because the (French) body in question was geographically perfect.

The most resounding example of this new dynamic occurs in 1670 in François-Savinien d'Alquier's *Les Délices de la France, avec une description des provinces et des villes du royaume.* Alquier praises France's perfection in comparison to other European and non-European countries. He does this not by negating the effect of the climate, but by extolling its perfect moderation:

> Because, in reasoning according to all maxims and all the principles of science, one must admit that our State must be very perfect, and very abundant in all the things we need. The reason for this that I have arrived at is that, being in the sky's most tempered climate, and situated between the two Tropics, it is necessarily moderate, and as a consequence, abundant, the middle between two extremes being the source of natural goodness, as well as virtue […]. Experience proves to us clearly that the effects are that much more noble and more perfect in that they are a part of the nature of their causes.[49]

Alquier uses exact moderation as the model of excellence, applying an ethical tone to his observation with words like "noble" and "virtue," in a luxurious vision of agricultural wealth and abundance that explains France's overall perfection through its climate. The human and plant registers are once again conflated here as a perfect representation of "unplaced" geographical merit: they owe their ideal qualities to a utopian perfection of space that is excellent because it is moderate and neutral. Most importantly, in Alquier's formulation it is place—not race—that "ennobles" the French.

This last remark notwithstanding, it should be noted that terroir creeps back into the national vision, in a depiction of France as the "perfect garden." French produce (both people and plants), like the best dirt in La Quintinie's garden, was as neutral and unblemished as the purest spring water. In a culinary context that also sheds light on beliefs about human beings, ambivalence toward terroir remained prominent. Though France was conceived as a perfect place, terroir's role remained marginalized, ambivalent, and for that, all the more solidly entrenched in the culinary and literary connoisseurship that developed alongside the culture of language and gardens in the seventeenth century.

FIVE

Saint-Évremond and the Invention of Geographical Connoisseurship

AS WE HAVE SEEN, in the sixteenth century and much of the seventeenth century, terroir was both viewed as a real determining force on produce and human beings and derided for its provincial or unclean connotations in language and in gardens. Indeed, terroir became a crass and unruly manifestation of nature in humans and plants, one that culture was meant to refine, if not altogether expunge. In terms of food and terroir, perhaps the most telling testimony is that of the epicurean Saint-Évremond, who appeared briefly in chapter 3 in the context of seasoning. Saint-Évremond was France's early prototype of a wine and food snob and widely known in the seventeenth century as the era's most finicky eater. More importantly, he was the self-proclaimed founder of place-based eating, and even referred to himself as the quasi-inventor of "geographical connoisseurship" *("La Gourmande Géographie / Dont je suis comme l'inventeur").*[1] His story reveals how certain values relevant to language and garden aesthetics made their way into the culture of the table. From there, with the help of a persistent vein of Galenic and Hippocratic medical science, theories on terroir continued to frame French identity as well as to reinforce aesthetic values, both at and away from the table, in a nascent brand of literary criticism.

FOOD SNOBBERY IN THE SEVENTEENTH CENTURY

Saint-Évremond's relevance to the history of terroir is prominent in a satire of his prandial fussiness written by a certain M. Boisrobert between 1657 and 1659.[2] In it, Saint-Évremond, along with the Marquis de Bois-Dauphin (Mme de Sablé's son) and the Comte d'Olonne (the one later exiled to the

93

provinces) refuses to drink all wine except that issuing from three particular slopes *(côteaux)* in Champagne: Ay, Hautvilliers, and Avenay. Champagne, although a still wine at that time, was already imbued with prestige, having long been the choice of royalty and other elite personalities. Boisrobert reports that the trio of men quickly became known, for their finickiness, as the "Côteaux."[3] This playful bit of banter gained momentum in 1665 when a second author, Jean Donneau de Visé, satirized them in a play called *The Côteaux, or the Gourmets Marquis.*[4] There is evidence that the three men fully embraced the nickname, employing it in reference to themselves in public, thus fanning the mixture of fame and notoriety that grew in regard to their particularity about dining and wine.[5]

The Côteaux's reputation for exaggerated fastidiousness was in fact essential to the French genesis of what we know today as eating based on the aesthetics of terroir and origin. Although the self-proclaimed inventor of *"la gourmande géographie"* and his cronies were not the first to talk about such matters, they certainly popularized that conversation.[6] Culinary heroism, like that of the Côteaux, became high profile in the mid- to late seventeenth century. At the height of court society, it was essential to draw distinctions between oneself and the less discriminating individual in order to ascend in the social hierarchy. Being a good taster, someone sensitive to delicate flavors, implied that one was a refined character, pure in mind and body, and not tainted by terroir nor marked by the provinciality and crassness associated with the earth's influence.

Accordingly, there was more than a bit of admiration mixed in with the satire as the reputation of the Côteaux grew. In tasting a food, their astute palates could detect its origin, and that rare skill correlated with their elite class:

> *Oronte:* Marquis, who then are the members of this Côteaux?
>
> *Valère:* They are discerning fellows, who like the good bits,
> And who, knowing them, have through experience attained
> The most infallible and best taste in all of France.
> Of today's aficionados, they are the most elite and distinguished.
> Presented with game, they can say by the smell
> Its place of provenance.[7]

The satirical description of the eaters depicts them as finicky to a fault, but a glorifying tone weakens the bite of the criticism. The passage insists on the status of the Côteaux (they are marquises), correlating it with good taste by calling them the "elite" of gourmets. They are also highly discerning *(délicat)*, distinguished, and generally infallible in terms of food connoisseurship.

In addition to discerning the best foods, the Côteaux further differentiated themselves by requesting only pure, unadulterated products. Turning back to the letter from Saint-Évremond to the Comte d'Olonne considered in chapter 3, it is clear that Saint-Évremond's concept of good cooking is grounded in the unerring authenticity of the food's taste and its consequent healthfulness: "A very natural healthful soup, neither too diluted nor over-concentrated, must be preferred ordinarily to all others as much for the precision of its taste as for the usefulness of its consumption [...]. The fat quail caught in the country, a pheasant, a partridge, a rabbit, each tasting as they should taste, are the true meats that can in different seasons be the delight of your meal."[8] Both soup and game, Saint-Évremond specifies, should be perfectly cooked and unadulterated. Flavors should be natural and conform to the expectations that one would have for the dish in question. To a degree bordering on fanaticism, Saint-Évremond and the Côteaux insisted on a minimum of sauces and a maximum of "natural" flavors.

In this schema, the connoisseur did not "eat for the place," but rather, treasured provenances that *did not* leave a mark on the food. That is, the Côteaux did not seek variety from specific terroirs for the unique tastes they left on produce, nor the *goût de terroir* in itself, but ate geographically to determine which foods were the best representations of their kind. Having made that judgment, they would accept nothing else. As the Bishop of Lemans related in a chiding tone, they took their inclinations to an extreme: "These men [...] can only eat river veal [*veau de rivière,* veal specially fattened in fields bordering the Seine, near the city of Rouen]: they must have partridges from the Auvergne; their rabbits must be from the Roche-Guyon or Versine; and as for wine, they can only drink that from the three slopes, Ay, Hautvilliers, and Avenay."[9]

Place-based eating for these connoisseurs was just the *opposite* of how we currently think of the notion. It was not framed in terms of the complexity that terroir would add, such as the mineral fragrance that today's connoisseur might expect to smell in a wine from Chablis, but in terms of which place of origin possessed the most pure, healthful, and delicate produce. We can extrapolate that the foods of top pedigree, those chosen by the Côteaux, were considered flawless translations of nature, containing perfect flavors in accordance with the ideal the taster had for each food type. This seventeenth-century concern with the "natural" has been examined by critics as an aesthetic construction. As Jean-Pierre Dens puts it in terms of art, "the seventeenth-century *("classique")* natural is always a conventional naturalness predicated on conformity between a work and its ideal model [. . .]. It does not issue from what is real, but from aesthetic consonance that is itself the product of a social relationship."[10] Here, the relationship is between elite, high-class connoisseurs and the unadulterated food they seek as the equivalent to their "pure-blooded" constitutions. Thus, the very natural, healthful soup *("bien naturelle")* mentioned above by Saint-Évremond is a soup whose ingredients attain an archetypal purity, the very reflection of Saint-Évremond's own constitution and merit.

This being the case, the best terroir was a terroir that left no earthy flavor whatsoever, allowing the unmitigated essence of the food to show through. Nowhere is this clearer than in the example of the Champagne d'Ay, the wine most coveted by the Côteaux. Saint-Évremond boasted that Ay was natural—not in the sense used by Méré, in which *"trop naturel"* meant unrefined—but insofar as it issued unblemished from its terroir. As such, it was ideally suited to promoting the health and enjoyment of elite connoisseurs. Saint-Évremond writes: "If you ask which of these wines I prefer, without allowing me to stray into the taste trends inspired by false connoisseurs, I would say to you that the good wine of Ay is the most natural of all wines, the healthiest, and the most purified of any odor of terroir—and of the most exquisite pleasurability in its flavor of peaches, which is unique to it, and the best in my opinion of all flavors."[11] Here the ambivalence regarding terroir in the seventeenth century is on full display. The most sophisticated of tasters demanded not only that a wine or food be characteristic of its terroir *(naturel),* but also that it not smell strongly of the place, that is, that it be free of the *goût de terroir* that the Perrault brothers referred to as an aberration appreciated solely by those with altered souls. Or, as Peter Shoemaker recently qualified Saint-Évremond's fabled preference for the wine of Ay: "Ironically, then, it is not the presence of a *goût de terroir,* but rather its absence that marks these wines as coming from a specific place."[12] The absence of impurities allowed for the defining essence—at least as Saint-Évremond perceived it—of delicate peach flavors to appear.

This conundrum—that a wine had to be knowable according to its place (so that the connoisseur could demonstrate prowess in identifying it), but could in no way smell directly of the terrestrial individuality of that place—makes sense when one puts it in the context of the social jockeying taking place in seventeenth-century court society. If a connoisseur were to admit a

FIGURE 6. The slopes of Ay depicted on an early twentieth-century postcard. Ay was the origin of France's best wine, according to Saint-Évremond and the three Côteaux.

fondness for the product of a terroir, he or she would risk being negatively identified as someone who liked unwholesome foods or did not possess a sufficiently acute palate to detect them. This concern led to increasing snobbism in food choices, since it was easier to show that one had supremely good taste by deriding a large variety of foods and accusing them of having bad flavors (that those with less·acute perceptions and refined constitutions were unable to detect) than by making a positive pronouncement about good taste and risking being labeled as unrefined by others. This sort of culinary discrimination was reinforced in no small measure by the medical wisdom of the seventeenth century.

MEDICAL TAKES ON A GLASS OF WINE

Advances in medicine in the second half of the seventeenth century were leaving behind Renaissance theories on the humors and turning increasingly to discussions on the chemical composition of the blood.[13] Nevertheless, equating the intrinsic qualities of foods and the effects they would have on particular groups of people remained popular. This is not altogether surprising: in a world where one could purchase royal offices in order to become noble, those belonging to the inherited aristocracy attempted to defend their status. Thus the refined, "pure-blooded" population—and those wishing to appear as such—insisted that their high-class physiological constitutions naturally led them to seek out elegant foods, premising their assertions on a tradition of medical science that remained useful for its function in reaffirming social class. In other words, the "return of the body" as a relevant factor in taste, discussed in the last chapter, was upheld not only by Epicurean theory, but by materialist medical conceptions that remained prevalent in certain circles.

Prominent ideas on these matters were stoked by several versions of a discourse lingering from the previous century, including that of Nicolas Abraham de la Framboisière, the royal physician of Henri IV and Louis XIII. La Framboisière, writing in the early part of the seventeenth century, both influenced later thinkers and echoed remarks made in the sixteenth century on the virtues and drawbacks of different wines by qualifying them according to both their origins and colors: "Wines possess different natures and virtues according to the country's diversity of climates and terroirs. French wines grown near Paris and the surrounding area are mostly white and rosé. There are few red wines, and even fewer black wines."[14] By invoking both wine color and terroir in the medical lexicon, La Framboisière helped define the parameters used to categorize wines throughout the seventeenth century along the lines of color and origin.[15] Paris was mostly equated with lighter wines, white or rosé in color, which were considered devoid of excessive marks of terroir and thought to be the most delicate. Red wines, on the other hand, which got progressively darker—from light red *(vin rouges)* to dark red *(vins noirs)*—as one went toward Burgundy and Bordeaux, were understood to contain more terrestrial components.

La Framboisière goes on to explain that white wines are more limpid than red wines but contain fewer nutrients. On the other hand, they can be counted on to provoke frequent urination and cleanse the veins of heavy, melancholic particles: "Wines of a fine and light substance, like water, provide little nourishment to the body, but they are quickly digested, and provoke copious urination. They are appropriate for refined people and agree with those who have amassed in their veins an accumulation of large, melancholic humors."[16] White wines are perfect for those who live preciously *(mignardement),* with affected deportment. La Framboisière adds that such wines are also appropriate for the effete drinker, students, residents of cities, and all those who lead sedentary lives. The whites do not further weigh down the melancholy-producing qualities of the blood, and produce a salutary effect by not providing more nutriments than a delicate system can assimilate.

Red wines have a more rude and terrestrial constitution *("sont de substance plus grosse et terrestre")*. They contain more iodine, more nutrients in general, and increase the production of blood. They also possess coarse particles that obstruct the pores. This is why red wines, explains La Framboisière, are better for those who live hard *(durement)*, like "laborers, vintners, and other people who work a lot, and those who have loosely constituted bodies with more space than matter."[17] The latter have open pores and "sweat very easily" *("sont sujet à suer à tous propos")*. They are thus able to sweat out obstructions. In turn, they are also able to benefit from the extra nourishment that these wines contain.

All of this explains why the *goût de terroir* was used in the seventeenth century most often in reference to red wines, which contained visible sediment and smelled more strongly of their origins. The reds, it would appear, had more character in the mouth and left a stronger olfactory impression than the whites. They were also usually considered more rustic, which is exactly how their detractors qualified them, associating them with rustic individuals, profusely sweating laborers, and the working class in general. One important illustration that such medical theories remained in vogue in the late seventeenth century, and that they dovetailed with the Epicurean ideas of an individual like Saint-Évremond, is provided by an article written by Pierre Bayle in the 1680s, relating the theories of Benjamin Broekhuisen.

Broekhuisen constructs an argument based on Galenic and Hippocratic doctrines, like that of La Framboisière, but packages it in a materialist, Epicurean vision. His work not only confirms many of the stereotypes that appeared above, but also provides important nuances. Bayle introduces Broekhuisen's work, which was first published in Dutch and later translated into French as "Economy of the Body of the Animal" *(l'Oeconomie du corps de l'animal)* in his widely read *Journal des Savans*.[18] For Broekhuisen, all that characterizes a human's or animal's movements comes from the food it eats and the air it breathes. Broekhuisen provides theories about air issuing from the earth and the sea and gives specifics on a number of geographical climates in particular. In certain places, he explains, humans need to take countermeasures to combat the climate. He makes it clear that in the face of such climates, homeostasis can only be maintained through the proactive stance of an individual. In Holland, for example, one needs to burn incense, such as that of benzoin or cloves, before getting out of bed each morning in order to change the pernicious qualities of the air, which would otherwise adversely affect the movement and constitution of the lungs and the rest of the body.[19] Although Broekhuisen concludes that there are no hard and fast rules about what an individual ought to eat, he encourages readers to take into account their environments, since constitutions change in incalculable ways according to the cycle of seasons and divergent lifestyles.

That said, in spite of a clear attribution of physiological diversity to external factors, Broekhuisen also correlates social classes, diet, and wine color. People say, writes Broekhuisen, that peasants and lowly people are "stupid" and "animal-like." This is because they eat foods that are "very rude and terrestrial, which can only make for a very rude chyle and blood."[20] People "of quality," on the other hand, have "almost always higher intelligence, and are capable of greater vocations and the most sublime of sciences, because they choose the best foods, whose juices, being more purified by subtle matter, create a more subtle blood as well, and their intellect is consequently more open and penetrating."[21] Broekhuisen reports that peasants, with their thick, squalid blood, are stronger but slower, while the higher classes are more subtle and spirited, possessing an intelligence unencumbered by terrestrial components. This dichotomy corresponds perfectly to the class prejudices noted above regarding red and white wine and the weighty unpleasantness associated with terroir. Interestingly, the text does not cast the lower classes as intrinsically inferior. Though Broekhuisen does not say so explicitly, peasants, it would appear by reading between the lines, could actually improve their intelligence and deportment if they were to eat better foods. Broekhuisen's analysis, correlating a lack of intelligence with heavy terrestrial foods, was not just an isolated opinion, but became a part of the definition of "food" *(aliment)* in the Furetière dictionary, proving how widespread and commonplace the bias became.[22]

Finally, Broekhuisen's account not only employs Hippocratic and Galenic themes but is remarkably atomist in its explanation of the suitability of different beverages for different individuals. The point is important because it demonstrates just how easy it was to conflate medicine at the time with the kind of Epicurean thought that François Bernier employed, with his theories on the pores of the tongue and his explanation of climate-based determining factors. Indeed, notwithstanding concurrent Cartesian trends separating mind and body, medicine and Epicurean philosophy constituted in many ways a united front demonstrating the power of the physical world on human beings. When it came to providing a technical explanation for the medical phenomena he described, Broekhuisen offers that red wine is composed of little hooks that slow the blood. The description derives from Epicureanism and from key passages in Lucretius's *On the Nature of Things,* in which the author associates hooked atoms with large, oily matters.[23] Thus in Broekhuisen, readers met with a doubly-reinforced medical and philosophical discourse, correlating encumbered blood and coarse food with slow thinking and low social status, and proving that red wine was only appropriate for people possessing physically rustic and "porous" compositions big enough to allow the hooks to pass. White wine, though less nutritious—less "terrestrial"—contained molecules that were rounder and circulated more easily in the veins.[24]

The last point, that white wines offered less nutrition than reds and were appropriate for high-class individuals, provides a glimpse into how the theories on social distinction that Pierre Bourdieu applied to French society are relevant to—and perhaps owe a part of their genesis to—seventeenth-century trends. Bourdieu explains that individuals wishing to present themselves as elite gravitate toward food that has less nutritive value to suggest that their tastes are more refined and do not correspond directly to an economic and bodily physical need to maximize the energy content in the choices they make. Using the term *dénégation de la fonction,* Bourdieu points out that individuals looking to distinguish themselves in categories ranging from food to language to clothing deride anything that is construed along the lines of pure functionality rather than aesthetic value. This leads to his juxtaposition of the *goût de luxe* to the *goût de nécessité.* Those possessing the "taste of necessity," at least in the context of twentieth-century French society, would gravitate toward an alimentary consumption of "heavy, fatty, strong foods."[25] Those possessing the "taste of luxury," in contrast, would prefer fresh fruits and vegetables, as well as foods that do not cause weight gain. In the first case, the pragmatism of nutritional content is the primary driving force, while in the second an association of eating for sustenance's sake alone is disparaged.

One can see how in the seventeenth century, too, an early version of this social distinction is likely to have applied, and would have reinforced the medical undergirding that disdained red wine as the heavy, more nutritious wine suitable for physical laborers. As Peter Shoemaker puts it, referring to the seventeenth century, "despite all of the talk of nature and simplicity, it is difficult to escape the suspicion that a new form of elitism was at play. The new trendy vegetables—artichokes, peas, asparagus, lettuce, chicory, etc.—were all fairly low in caloric content and relatively expensive to obtain."[26] The culinary elitism described by Bourdieu is pertinent in explaining eating practices popular in French court society as early as the seventeenth century, and provides additional insight into the stigma attached to terroir at the time.

Thus, philosophical, medical, and social considerations articulated in terms of class clearly conspired to reinforce a development in taste that relegated flavors associated with earth away from the realm of acceptability. Yet, notwithstanding the general trend toward devaluing terroir, other cultural testimony from the time reveals that there is more to the story. Environmental determinism, reinforced as much through literary as through culinary trends, helped weave terroir-based notions all the more deeply into French society.

TERROIR, SATIRE, AND LITERARY CRITICISM

Although the above passages suggest that connoisseurs chose their foods carefully to avoid being dragged down or incapacitated by terroir, when it came to literary characters, seventeenth-century readers expected *all* classes of people to act in accordance with their geographical terroir. In different genres, ranging from theater and novels to satire, the correlation between food, people, and their origin was both a formula used to create verisimilar characters and a satirical tool wielded against those who aspired to a higher social class by feigning sophistication at the table. Literary representations of culinary etiquette—or the lack thereof—provided an especially effective tool for revealing the pretensions of the ever-increasing number of individuals who attempted to define their class by means of their culinary refinement. This strategy, while apparently widespread, most often failed. For an author like Saint-Évremond, "the way to make yourself ridiculous where food and drink are concerned is to try to display a discrimination you do not possess."[27] Accordingly, seventeenth-century authors scrutinized taste in food—and, by extension, aesthetic judgments in general—with the goal of warning off those who would seek to use pretentions of good taste to climb the social ladder.[28]

The best example of the genre appears in Nicolas Boileau's third satire, the burlesque *Repas ridicule* (1665).[29] The satire's protagonist, a poet of some pretension himself, is lured to a dinner by the promise of drinking fine wine and eating good food in the company of the esteemed Molière. Unfortunately, he is disappointed on all counts and must stomach a frightful speech on contemporary writers as his pompous host *(un fat)* serves up horrific fare, lowly Parisian rabbits that reek of their unglamorous diet:

> Upon a hare flanked by six scrawny chickens,
> There were three rabbits, domestic animals
> Who, raised from their tender years in Paris,
> Still smelled of the cabbage they had been fed.[30]

Here, the unpolished guests are described by the same term *(étiques,* "scrawny") used for the chickens and come across as veritable animals themselves, with rustic behavior that precisely mirrors the table's unsophisticated fare. All the while, the host offers revolting food served in an indiscriminate mishmash (again, a practice that contemporary cookbooks cautioned against), which is wolfed down by the guests.[31] As the passage progresses, the text mirrors more and more closely the medical discourse of Broekhuisen and his colleagues, unmistakably assimilating the eaters and the eaten, fulfilling its satirical function in carefully disparaging the first by focusing on the lowly origins of the second.[32]

Whether it be the host's excessive use of garish spices—"Do you like nutmeg? We put it everywhere"—or the appraising words of the other guests, who try to hide their humble origins behind a façade of connoisseurship, the bluff fails miserably.[33] The satirical tone of the passage is accentuated by one bumpkin in particular. Boisterously advertising his undiscerning palate while pretending that he possesses the refinement of the Côteaux, he indiscriminately conflates the qualities of lowly domesticated rabbits and pigeons with the merits of their more prestigious wild counterparts:

> Especially a certain braggart, whose famished beak
> Had followed the smoke of this feast,
> And who claimed himself proficient in the ways of the Côteaux,
> Praised amply the victuals as he ate.
> I laughed to see him, with his scrawny face,
> His old grayed collar flap, and his ancient wig,
> Promote our caged varmints to wild rabbits,
> And turn our Cauchois pigeons into superb ringdoves.[34]

The braggart *(hableur),* with his animal-like "famished beak," pretends to be of high culinary rank, but could not be more ridiculous in his appreciation of the low-quality foods he elevates to gourmet fare. Through his eating, he makes a statement about both his class and origin. We know from his rustic mores that he is from the country (a *campagnard,* the text advises), and not a sophisticated Parisian, and that he has followed smoke to the dinner as would a starving animal. As for his low class, among the several indications the text provides is the fact that he mistakes domesticated game for (superior) wild game. This fits the logic of the text, since the right to hunt *(le droit de chasse)* was traditionally a privilege reserved only for nobles, presumably making the correct appreciation of wild game an indication of class and refinement.

Once the bad taste of the host and guests is established in the context of the feast, the satire draws a parallel to bad taste in a wider context, as the hayseeds turn from discussing food to a conversation on literature, where they champion various subpar authors. By having these characters show incomprehension for the real masters, like Racine, and advocate for literary hacks (their list includes washed-up or passé authors as well as individual enemies of Boileau), the satire correlates bad physiological taste with bad aesthetic taste, and generally inferior intellect. It is at this moment that the narrator takes flight, his own tastes as cerebrally embattled as his stomach, vowing never to be trapped again at such a disagreeable meal.

The satire's message is clear: as the crude occupants of Boileau's table gravitate toward cheap knock-offs, produce of inferior origins, overseasoning, and second-rate literature, they unerringly conform to their own low-class origins. The corrective lesson of the satire could not be more obvious in its warning to the seventeenth-century reader to eat within one's rank and class, or risk the ridicule of being called out as an imposter. What's more, the equivalence that Boileau makes between bad taste at the table and bad taste in art and literature became increasingly commonplace. As Voltaire would later opine: "Just as bad taste in the physical sense consists in being pleased only by excessively biting and extravagant seasonings, bad taste in the arts exists in only finding pleasure in overly studied ornaments, and not perceiving nature's beautiful essence."[35]

READERS' TASTE AND FICTIONAL FRENCH IDENTITIES IN TERROIR

When it comes to understanding the expectations of French readers in the seventeenth century, the above scene is important for another reason. By creating representations in which characters' tastes mirror their social origins, Boileau conforms to the directives he propounded in his *Art poétique,* where he added earth and climate to class as guidelines determining the actions of literary characters. With respect, for example, to Madame de Scudéry's historical roman à clef, *Clélie,* which portrays individuals from the author's seventeenth-century social milieu in the course of depicting the exploits of the Roman heroine Clelia, Boileau warns:

> Reserve for each their own character.
> Of centuries, countries, study the customs.
> Climates often create diverse humors.
> Make sure then not to give, as in *Clélie,*
> Neither the appearance, nor the French spirit to ancient Italy.[36]

Clélie falls short of reader expectations, says Boileau, because it does away with geographical determiners, proposing that a character from ancient Rome could possess a modernized, French style of comportment. Boileau both propounds a brand of literary criticism based on climatic determinism and alludes directly to Hippocratic medicine, suggesting that medical considerations about behavior based on humors would have remained commonplace enough to appear as self-evident truths to readers.

One of the most telling examples of creating character identity through climate comes from Saint-Évremond himself. Although Saint-Évremond believed that the best food, like individuals of high standards, ought to escape the imprint of the terroir, in his writings on literature he directed that for the sake of verisimilitude authors must take into account the impact of the climate on their characters. In books, that is, unlike in life, determinism by the environment was accepted as occurring independently of the characters' social class, education, and the mitigating force of correct dietary habits that Broekhuisen advocated for above. Even for a member of the aristocracy to escape the definition of terroir in literature was to break the laws of verisimilitude. This is the criticism that Saint-Évremond leveled in 1668 at Racine's *Alexandre,* whose protagonist, Porus, had been too "Frenchified" to appear credible in Saint-Évremond's judgment: "I imagined a greatness of soul in Porus that would seem more foreign to us, that the hero from India should have a different personality than ours. Another sky, so to speak, another sun, and another soil produced other animals and fruits in that place; men there seemed dissimilar in their faces, and even more so, if I dare say, because of a different type of reasoning, moral values, and wisdom, specific to the region that seemed to predominate there and drive different minds in a different world."[37] Saint-Évremond accentuates the familiar human-animal-plant metaphor, and attributes a determining force to the climate, not only with respect to physical appearance, but also in terms of ethical qualities and even modes of reasoning. Moreover, if Saint-Évremond replaces *"terroir"* here with *"terre,"* associating it with the sky and sun, he likely does so to avoid the negative connotations the former word had accumulated. He is not making a judgment on whether it is laudable or incriminating for a literary character to be marked by his or her origin, but like Boileau, merely stating that for a literary text to be plausible, the author must account for the provenance of the characters in depicting their behavior.

Saint-Évremond's consideration of the power of the climate as a determining factor continued to develop as he reconciled his culinary and literary discourses with theories about how the physical conditions of place shape the comportment of human beings in real life. In an essay, *"Sur nos comedies"* (1677), published nine years after his thoughts about Racine's *Alexandre,* Saint-Évremond modified his literary theory not only to include a discussion of fictional characters, but also to discuss how climate influences the expectations of readers as well. In the first pages of the latter essay, he bemoans the fact that, although the ancients created comedy to mimic ordinary human life via characters whose personality reflected nature's diverse humors, the current tendency is to populate literary works with identical personalities in an overabundance of gallant tales. Taking up a specific example, Saint-Évremond reproaches a minor seventeenth-century author, La Calprenède, for his work *Cleopatra,* in which the author depicts the book's lovers as resolving to talk instead of take action in the throes of passionate and emotionally charged scenes.

Saint-Évremond does not limit his vision to the literary characters in question: rather, he expands his reflection to include the reader as well. He offers the example of a well-born Spanish woman (the Princess of Insenghien) who was incredulous that, in the heat of an encounter, the two adoring lovers would resort to mere talk instead of consummating their affair. Saint-Évremond admits that the princess is justified in her criticism, and that "La Calprenède, although French, should have remembered that for lovers born under a sun much hotter than that of Spain, words were pretty useless in these circumstances."[38] Saint-Évremond, however, amends his criticism, adding that the woman's remark would be better founded in Spain, where "as all of the gallantry of the Spanish came from the Moors, there remains in them

I am not sure what other African flavor, foreign to other nations."[39] This, he explains, combined with the lore of the gallant stories traditionally recounted in Spanish culture to create a people with different expectations from their French counterparts. As a result, Saint-Évremond's final judgment of La Calprenède is nuanced. The author of *Cleopatra* makes an error because he does not take into account the origin of the characters and the "hot-blood-edness" that would have led them to consummate their passion, but he is correct in that he *does* take into account French readers and their expectations (more cultural than climatic) that lovers in such situations are more inclined to talk than get down to business.[40]

As we can see, as soon as he considers the effects of climate on real-life situations, outside the context of food and literary characters, Saint-Évremond's discourse is not as straightforward as it would first appear. Specifically, he admits that climate and terroir are not alone in affecting human comportment: reason, education, and culture all also have parts to play.[41] Given this admission, it is fascinating to reflect that literature was held to the litmus test of climate long before wines and foods were critically and systematically judged in the same way. In some circles, literary characters were neither verisimilar nor credible if they did not reflect the terroir, while foods, at least for Saint-Évremond, were not palatable if they did.

QUESTIONS OF CLASS AND THE QUARREL BETWEEN BURGUNDY AND CHAMPAGNE

Turning back to the wines of Ay, it is now easier to define the aesthetic expectations Saint-Évremond helped to build around them: the wine phenomenon conveys in a microcosmic form the negative status of terroir in the seventeenth century. Yet, even on the culinary front, there was some ambivalence to account for. The question can be traced to a behind-the-scenes debate on wines that began in the middle of the seventeenth century. Around the same time that Saint-Évremond began praising the qualities of the wine of Ay, the first of several skirmishes broke out in the medical world pitting the wines of Champagne against those of Burgundy. The upshot of the debate ultimately inspired France to modify its drinking practices, reshape the status of red wines, and take the first step toward a new, eighteenth-century view of terroir. Here again, Saint-Évremond and the legend of his culinary prowess figured at center stage.

When it came to competition between regional wines, Burgundy's main strategies in the quarrel with Champagne about who made better wine were precisely the ones that Champagne had used against Burgundy: medical merit and favoritism from the aristocratic elite. Although several medical theses written as early as the 1650s touted the advantages of Burgundy over Champagne, the real blow, and arguably the blow that pushed Champagne toward accepting an identity as an effervescent wine, did not come until 1694.[42] In that year, Louis XIV's doctor, Guy-Crescent Fagon, declared that the wines of Champagne were too acidic for the king's stomach, and that the king would henceforth drink only Burgundy wines.[43] Given the regional patriotism that had fueled such disputes in the past, it is unsurprising that Fagon was Burgundian himself. But other reasons motivated his pronouncement.

For most of the latter half of the seventeenth century, the wines of Champagne were favored by medical texts because they supposedly contained a large proportion of water and provoked healthful, frequent urination (a belief that remained part of the *doxa* for some time: it was repeated in Diderot and d'Alembert's *Encyclopédie* entry for *"Vin"* fifty years later). Fagon, however, deflated Champagne's boast on this subject by explaining that the more frequent urination they provoked was caused by their excessive amount of tartrates, which were slightly prickly and flattering on the tongue but dangerous because they did not properly mix with food and aid in digestion, as Burgundy did. Instead, the tartrates, as Fagon explains it, go unmixed into the body, where they aggravate the nerves because of their sharp points and "sour the blood." Thus, though they pass through the system more quickly, the wines of Champagne cause greater health risks, most notably that of gout. Burgundy, on the other hand, as Fagon explains it, contains more "spirits" *(esprits)* that mollify the tartrates and caress the tongue. The wines thus reduce the risk of debilitating illnesses. After the king changed to a Burgundy regime, Fagon concludes, his step was much lighter, and he could sometimes walk for truly remarkable distances.[44]

In the years following this pronouncement, there was an intensified succession of verbal attacks and counterattacks from denizens of Champagne against inhabitants of Burgundy, with members of both the medical and literary worlds aiding the wine-producing region they most favored. One member of the medical faculty of Reims, Gilles Culoteau, engaged in a heated exchange of letters with M. de Salins of Dijon, and submitted that the wines of Burgundy conveyed a frightful odor. He complains that the wines exhibit a smell that is "a burnt exhalation that injures the organ and which smells of the reddish, mineral dirt of the land."[45] Culoteau then goes on to endorse the wines of Champagne, by praising their superior brand of terroir in terms that were contrary to the heavy and dirty connotations that the word had picked up during the previous century. The best wine, he writes, is that of Reims, whose components are "subtle and volatile, because it grows in a sweet and light earth, exuding such an agreeable fragrance that one smells the perfume even before one tastes it."[46] These "subtle, volatile" particles constituted a stereotype that purveyors of good taste used ever-increasingly in the eighteenth century, with respect to both the effervescent and noneffervescent versions of Champagne wines, to correlate consumption with high class and superior intelligence.

Although Culoteau attributes the subtlety of the wines of Champagne to their soil of origin, choosing adjectives that recalled those used by specialists in their medical and mechanical observations about wines suitable for the upper classes, as he developed his article further, soil was mostly left out of the picture. In fact, Culoteau finishes his diatribe against Burgundy by deliberately casting aside all scientific evidence and subscribing to the higher authority of people with taste and discernment *(délicatesse)*. He quotes Saint-Évremond's observations on Champagne wines verbatim and then adduces a variety of accounts of how the region's wines have traditionally appealed to prestigious individuals ranging from kings, emperors, and popes to France's best authors (Racine and La Fontaine) as proof of Champagne's superiority.

The elegant character of Champagne and its rhetorical consanguinity with individuals of class, good taste, and intelligence became increasingly important in asserting the wine's disconnection from all that was base and close to the ground. In the years immediately following, several regional poets from both sides of the quarrel offered works dedicated to their respective wines, including their associations with nobility and inspirational aspects of the libations.[47] Still, despite a valiant defense by Champagne's proponents, red wines started to make a comeback in the first decades of the seventeenth century. This was, perhaps not coincidentally, a time when the wines of Champagne resorted in greater and greater numbers toward effervescence. *Paillet* and *clairet,* Champagne's nomenclature for the light red, still wines produced in the region, steadily lost popularity in the Parisian markets during the first part of the eighteenth century.[48]

One hypothesis to explain this change and the rising popularity of Champagne as an effervescent beverage is that the Champenois chose to stand pat and continue to advance the rhetoric of bubbly lightness rather than try to compete with the Burgundians on their own playing field. Indeed, it was immediately after Fagon's denigration of what were predominantly the still wines of Champagne that the image of Champagne as a producer of primarily sparkling wines began to take shape. Given what we know, it seems plausible to conclude that after Fagon's pronouncement, some individuals reconciled themselves to drinking wines associated with terroir (this was verifiably the case by the 1720s, when accounts such as those of Claude Arnoux sung the praise of Burgundy *because* of its terroir), while others continued to denigrate the ground and search for wines that would "elevate" their spirits and be disassociated from terroir.[49]

This hypothesis appears all the more credible if one considers the analysis offered by Benoît Musset in his recent volume on the early modern history of Champagne. Musset calls attention to the first painted depiction of effervescent Champagne, called *Déjeuner d'huîtres,* a work Louis XV commissioned from the painter Jean-François de Troÿ, which seems to offer visual confirmation of the values laid out above. The work was intended for display in an inner chamber at Versailles, to be seen only by the select members of the court who would have accompanied the king after a day of hunting.[50] It depicts Champagne being served at a festive occasion, marked by the sort of prestigious associations that the wine possesses today. It also reinforces the dichotomy between ponderous, vulgar earth-bound fare on the one hand and the delicate, light, and pure wine and cuisine preferred by the high-class elite on the other. The difference is vividly displayed in the visual representation: one of the richly dressed, stately participants lets fly a cork while the rest of the guests converse, gesticulate, drink, and look toward the ceiling with animated amusement. At their feet, lowly domestics collect the spent oyster shells and bottles that aristocratic guests have cast to the ground. Champagne, the effervescent kind, had thus found a point of entry into noble circles despite having been expelled from Louis XIV's diet because of its acidity.[51]

Through representations similar to that of de Troÿ, Champagne codified its prestige in the French mind and became an icon for class and style. Voltaire, for example, chose the Champagne d'Ay in his famous poem "Le Mondain," an ode to luxury written in 1736, the year after de Troÿ's painting appeared. There, instead of reinforcing the beverage's exclusiveness, Voltaire democratizes Champagne's royal, elite image, redrawing it to belong to the French in general. He appropriates images similar to those depicted by de Troÿ, but applies them not only to the Champagne d'Ay, but also as a national symbol for French vivacity of spirit:

FIGURE 7. *The Oyster Lunch,* commissioned by Louis XV from Jean-François de Troÿ in 1735. Courtesy of RMN Grand Palais / The Art Archive at Art Resource, NY.

> From a wine of Ay whose foam is hurried
> From the bottle with force propelled,
> Like a lightning bolt blasts the cork,
> It shoots, we laugh, it hits the ceiling.
> The effervescent froth of this cool wine
> Is of our French people the shining image.[52]

Champagne, in this conception, lifts ordinary French drinkers to the lofty realms of aristocracy and allows them to metaphorically rub shoulders with the prestigious cosmopolitan elite in the courts of France, England, and

Russia—who were increasingly drinking the wine.[53] Champagne became a national beverage that broadcast sophistication and cosmopolitanism insofar as it was a product whose taste was not associated with provinciality or cumbersome images of terroir and rustic, heavy wines.

WINES AND WORDS AT THE END OF THE
SEVENTEENTH CENTURY

It is worth acknowledging in conclusion the different aspects of terroir and climatic determinism that this chapter has touched upon. Through Saint-Évremond, it becomes clear how interconnected conversations on language, wine, literature, and food were at the time, and how a new breed of place-based connoisseurship in food was linked to questions of health, social climbing, and class. On the one hand, advocates of fine cuisine sought to distinguish themselves by eating food according to its origin but, in doing so, were generally seeking products that did not smell of any sort of terrestrial quality and did not have a *goût de terroir,* whereas on the other, authorities in literary analysis had recourse to terroir and climatic determinism, with the conviction that a literary work's characters *ought* to express the influence of their place of origin. The wines of Champagne, in particular, incarnated the "no-terroir" aesthetic that dominated at the time, and their ongoing conflict with those of Burgundy, given the heavier associations of the latter, attests to the ongoing ambivalence that had been a signature in terroir's evolution since the Renaissance.

A final example of this ambivalence in material culture demonstrates how deeply representative culinary practices were of the broader questions preoccupying French society during the final years of Louis XIV's reign. Owing to the successive skirmishes in letters between supporters of Champagne and Burgundy, the two regions became strong icons, different but each equally rooted in the French imagination—one generally more light, buoyant, and stylish, the other darker, more solid, and terrestrial. This distinction become a benchmark, well enough established in the collective cultural imagination that it could be used figuratively in discussions of other matters. The best example is that of François de Maucroix, a close friend of the fabulist La Fontaine, also from the Champagne region, who contrasted the two wines as he characterized different types of eloquence. On the one hand, he recalled Demosthenes, whose rhetorical style accentuated the force and substance of an argument, the type of oratory, as noted in chapter 3, that had been popular in Renaissance France. In the seventeenth century, Cicero's model replaced Demosthenes with a style of speech that favored smoothness and agreeability, attempting to win over the listener through pleasure instead of succeeding by the sheer solidity of the argument, as the stereotype went.

Taking up these ideals for eloquent speech in 1706, de Maucroix explains that there is now, in the eighteenth century, ambivalence in France about both styles, and concludes that both could be equally convincing. To make his point, he summons the examples of Burgundy and Champagne.

> And so, guess what I compare Demosthenes and Cicero to? The first, to your good wines of Burgundy, and the second to our wines of Champagne. In Burgundy wine, there is more force, more vigor, and it does not cosset to such a degree its man, it knocks him down more brusquely: that is Demosthenes. The wine of Champagne is more fine, more delicate, it entertains more and for a longer time, but in the end it has no less of an effect: that is Cicero.[54]

Allowing that some tables prefer the wines of Burgundy, and others prefer that of Champagne, Maucroix signals that aesthetic preferences in both wine and speech are evolving. Just as in the seventeenth century decorum and high style outweighed the substantive humanism and erudition of the sixteenth century, lighter Champagne wines were more popular than earthy, fuller-bodied Burgundies. By the beginning of the eighteenth century, though the dichotomy between the two speech and wine styles was still intact, there was more uncertainty concerning which was better and more acceptable. This indecision in wine and words reflected the beginning of terroir's changing fortune in French society.

SIX

————

Terroir and Nation Building

BOULAINVILLIERS, DU BOS, AND
THE CASE OF CLASS

AT THE END OF LOUIS XIV'S RULE, in the first years of the eighteenth century, a political and ideological debate encouraged the French to look at the ground in a new way. Terroir's sullied seventeenth-century image evolved according to a new vision that influenced how people understood the state, its citizens, and their relationship with the land. To put it another way, when theories regarding social class and what constituted Frenchness not only challenged the king's absolute power and authority but became a threat to France's collective identity, consanguinity, and image of itself as a unified country, terroir made its return. Its conveyance was a discourse on aesthetics, an unlikely source that helped inspire a nationalistic trend and ultimately led the country to reconsider how it defined itself with respect to French soil. Moreover, this eighteenth-century ideology may have had lingering effects, since the French *droit du sol* or *jus soli,* the granting of citizenship at the age of majority to anyone born on French soil of foreign parents, would not be considered in the same way today had this pre-Revolutionary conversation not changed the French outlook on terroir and climatic determinism.[1]

At the center of this debate was the Count Boulainvilliers. Boulainvilliers was a military officer, historian, political theorist, and astrologist born in 1658.[2] Although today he is most often considered as a historical figure of secondary importance, his efforts to bring recognition and entitlement to the landed gentry (the *noblesse terrienne*) were the subject of passionate debate at the beginning of the eighteenth century. In fact, one could argue that the backlash raised against Boulainvilliers's extremism—and the biological determinism implied by his outlook—helps explain the acceptance of a renewed vein of environmental determinism in France in the eighteenth century, one that put the emphasis on climate instead of blood. The most prominent examples of this environmental determinism are the political writings of Montesquieu in *De l'esprit des lois* and the burgeoning theories of Buffon's *Histoire naturelle,* which circulated soon after.[3] Yet these two authorities merely reinforced and further popularized ideas developed by other authors, writing in different disciplines with different motivations. The theories on art and literature of the Abbé Du Bos, and to a lesser degree the travel accounts of Jean Chardin, embraced environmental determinism three decades before the major works of Montesquieu and Buffon. In fact, when it comes to explaining how climate theory contributed to constructing ideas of the French nation, it is hard to overstate Du Bos's influence. Not only was he widely known for his writings, he was endorsed by Voltaire, who praised his magnum opus, *Réflexions critiques sur la poésie et sur la peinture* (1719), referring to Du Bos as the grand master of all matters aesthetic.[4]

Du Bos's background as an early aesthetic theorist is precisely what makes him important: he conflated national identity, environmental determinism, and terroir not in a historical consideration couched in political theory, as Montesquieu did, nor in the context of natural history, as Buffon did, but in the course of formulating a new vision of painting and poetry. In doing so, he brought theories of climate and terroir to the surface of French consciousness by employing them with respect to the sorts of aesthetic judgments people would make on a daily basis. His accounts also confirm the usefulness of terroir as a broader indicator of social values, since there is ample evidence that Du Bos was directly motivated by Boulainvilliers to connect theories on climate-determined appreciation of literature and art to larger questions concerning France's identity. What follows demonstrates how Du Bos's rules for art and literature helped reverse the seventeenth century's take on terroir, shape its vision of nation, and inspire new thoughts on food and wine.

THE COUNT BOULAINVILLIERS

André Devyver's *Pure Blood* (*Le Sang épuré,* 1973) and, more recently, Marcel Detienne's *How to Be Autochthonous: From the Pure Athenian to the Rooted French* (*Comment être autochtone: Pur athénien au français enraciné,* 2004) are among many recent texts to have argued that Henri de Boulainvilliers perpetuated and exasperated a debate concerning the origins of France's citizens, sovereignty, the proper form of government, and even the implied inherent superiority of some classes over others, a debate that began in earnest in the early years of the eighteenth century. In simple terms, the controversy was between the *thèse royaliste,* a theory that upheld absolute rule by the king, and the *thèse nobiliaire,* which advocated in its most extreme iterations for the supremacy of and rule by France's noble population.

These contrasting opinions led to a prolonged reflection on identity and a heightened national consciousness.[5] Before unpacking the details, it is important to indicate from the onset that there has been a great deal of disagreement concerning Boulainvilliers's message, his "real" motivations, and what one ought to read into his writings. Hannah Arendt and Michel Foucault are two authoritative twentieth-century voices to have depicted Boulainvilliers as one of the precursors of modern biological racism, but Claude Nicolet and Harold Ellis are among contemporary apologists for Boulainvilliers, warning that historians have perennially misinterpreted his work.[6] There is no question that what Boulainvilliers intended in his writings is worthy of a more subtle interpretation than he often receives, but what is much more pertinent in this context is not the message Boulainvilliers ultimately meant to convey, but rather how he was construed by the influential thinkers of his century (e.g., Du Bos, Voltaire, and the framers of post-Revolutionary France, such as Emmanuel Joseph Sieyès) and how reactions to him shaped the notion of terroir and identity. This chapter will focus on the latter aspect of his influence, while suggesting along the way that even if the twentieth century was extreme in its condemnation of Boulainvilliers, those interpretations were not entirely unfounded.

Let us return to the eighteenth century. Boulainvilliers and his fellow proponents of the noble point of view questioned the legitimacy of the absolutist regime, the law of royal succession, and the sovereignty of French kings from Clovis to Louis XIV (in fact, Boulainvilliers claimed that historically the French kings were only elected magistrates and not absolute authorities).[7] More importantly, Boulainvilliers spoke for members of the landed gentry who had been increasingly disenfranchised by the Fronde and the loss of power they had experienced in the previous century. These individuals traced their lineage to ancestors responsible for what they viewed as the conquest of Gaul. The prestige of French blood, as the theory went, came from the Franks, who invaded Gaul beginning in the fifth century, after the fall of the Roman Empire, conquering its inhabitants by means of courage and the might of the sword.

Boulainvilliers, who documented his own family's noble lineage to the fifteenth century, claimed that this prowess of the sword in the Frankish conquest of Gaul created in essence a "master-slave relationship," establishing the inherent superiority of Franks over Gauls, who were weaker and thus rightfully subjugated.[8] According to this logic, there were thus three different classes of people in France: those descended from pure-blooded Franks, who were entitled to rule; commoners or peasants, who were mostly descended from the Gauls who had been conquered and subjugated (with some admixture of the original Roman conquerors in the fifth and sixth century); and finally, those who had usurped the noble ascendancy of the feudal system by using the transplanted system of Roman aristocracy to take over and begin administering the state from the time of Clovis on. This last category explained the absolutist regime as it evolved to exist under Louis XIV.[9]

Boulainvilliers, in his posthumously published *Essai sur la noblesse* (1732), which was widely known in various versions before its publication, brought to light what the author considered to be the illegitimate power of the king, who unfairly disrupted the natural order, ruling through tyranny and impinging on the liberty of the rightful, noble heirs of France.[10] Boulainvilliers was further scandalized by the profusion of "nobles of the robe" *(gens de robe)* during the reign of Louis XIV, the result of opening a bevy of administrative and judicial positions to the bourgeois by selling royal charges (titles). Boulainvilliers lamented that money corrupted the governing system and displaced noble virtue, allowing aristocracy to be watered down by those who had no true military measure of noble valor.[11] Most importantly, Boulainvilliers put racial characteristics at the center of his argument (hence his classification by Arendt, Foucault, and others as one of the modern fathers of racism), claiming that the original, pure-blooded French—and thus the rightful heirs of power—were blond-haired Franks all of roughly the same height, a token of the purity of their race and its freedom from mixture with that of the Gallo-Romans.[12] Still, Boulainvilliers concluded, there had been a decline: over time, "the necessity of money drove the nobility to such a loss of pride that they are no longer ashamed of mixing their blood with the most vile of commoners."[13]

Boulainvilliers was not extreme enough to call for these "original rulers" to retake leadership, but his writing on class in his *Essai sur la noblesse* did create a divisive debate on the identity of France's inhabitants, particularly his claim that the Franks, as the victorious party, should not have condoned the mixing of their blood with that of their inferiors.[14] Boulainvilliers construed eighteenth-century France as degraded from a former feudal society where the nobles protected the land and the vassals farmed it.[15] Terroir and agriculture had already been disdained in the seventeenth century, as the provincial antipodes of Louis XIV and the cosmopolitan Versailles, but Boulainvilliers added to the conventional derision of peasants and agricultural work by contrasting it with the noble pursuits of warriors.[16]

Boulainvilliers was not alone in his theories about the origin of France. What is surprising, however, is how much support his ideas received on various levels from some of the French Enlightenment's central thinkers. Montesquieu, for example, who was himself from the provinces and of noble origins, subscribed to many of the general tenets of Boulainvilliers's claims for the superiority of the noble class in book 11 of his *De l'esprit des lois*. Although he upheld that monarchy was the best form of government, he remained sympathetic to the idea of an empowered noble class with a legitimate voice in the ruling of French affairs, a step that would constitute a movement toward separation and balancing of powers within the state. Later, in book 30, Montesquieu explicitly states that his position lies squarely between those of Boulainvilliers and the Abbé Du Bos.[17] It is the latter, the Abbé Du Bos, however, who is most important in the context of the evolution of terroir. Although he would later be acknowledged by Montesquieu as the principal adversary of Boulainvilliers, stridently upholding an opposing theory, much of what Boulainvilliers thought about ancient French origins and the invasion of the Franks from Germanic territories was at first supported by Du Bos.

Du Bos was an absolutist, but even as late as 1719, in his *Réflexions critiques sur la poésie et sur la peinture,* Du Bos opined that "the Romans were chased from their homes" and "enslaved" by "brutal conquerors from beneath the northern snows."[18] He however contested that their history of military victory would make them individually superior or qualify them as the rightful heirs and rulers of France. Moreover, Du Bos later changed course and posited that perhaps the Gauls had welcomed the Franks, and that there had been no military conflicts of the sort that Boulainvilliers and other proponents of the *thèse nobiliaire* spoke about.[19] Without a conquest, there could be no *droit de conquête,* and no hierarchical difference between the Franks and the Gallo-Romans.

In fact, Du Bos and Boulainvilliers parted ways, it would seem, precisely at the point where a theory about historical origins turned into a divisive racist theory that threatened France's unity and identity. This hypothesis appears all the more plausible when we take into account the purported testimony of Du Bos during a session of the States General (États généraux) regarding the necessity that France avoid unrest for the sake of a happy, peaceful society: "The happiness of the people, which is the only goal we ought to aspire to, is more jeopardized by seditions against established laws than by all the laws that the supreme power can establish. All of the passions of King Louis XI caused France to suffer less than the first time the reformers took up arms."[20] Applying that principle to the debate at hand in the session, Du Bos upheld that the general welfare of the French people was better maintained by adhering to the king's absolute power than by challenging it. In other words, even if Du Bos had agreed to an extent with Boulainvillier's interpretation of history along racial lines, he would have been eager to adopt a moderate position to preserve peace in France at all costs. In fact, it is the strength of this desire for social harmony that helped shape how he articulated his theories on truth and beauty.

IMPLICATIONS OF DU BOS'S IDEAS ON BEAUTY

Although Du Bos explicitly advanced his theories on the amicable relationships between the Franks and Gauls in 1734 to resolve the debate between royalists and nobles, his more effective argument for the promotion of social accord was diffused obliquely over a decade earlier, in his work defining a climate-based conception of identity. There, he specifically invoked the effect of terroir on identity three decades before Montesquieu propounded his own wide-reaching theories on climatic determinism. It was at least partially the popularity of Du Bos's theories—and the escape they allowed from what was perceived as Boulainvilliers's biological elitist ideas—that began to reverse the aversion for the earth that occurred in the seventeenth century. The irony is that these theories promoted a different sort of racism, suggesting hierarchical differences based on geographic locales.[21] This is the way that it would appear later in Buffon's *Natural History,* where Buffon, supporting a theory of monogenesis, opined that although black people and white people came from the same race, the inferiority of the warmer climate in Africa had led to degradation of the species in blacks.[22]

In his *Réflexions critiques sur la poésie et sur la peinture,* Du Bos set out to explain the origins of aesthetic values. Since seventeenth-century thinkers had insisted that taste and class were strongly correlated, it is striking that Du Bos constructs his paradigm based on taste and *nation,* omitting class as a priority. He also raises the status of terroir, changing it from a negative descriptor for food and people into an identifying characteristic of the climate and a key to determining the aesthetic tastes of a population.

In reinforcing connection with the earth in terms of aesthetics—the very connection that had been cast into opprobrium in the seventeenth century—Du Bos also undermines the claims of biological superiority that were made by proponents of a pure-blooded, Frankish race. Although Du Bos does not specifically point to terroir and climate as a source of nation building, his reasoning gave like-minded readers the ammunition they would need to defeat Boulainvilliers. In this regard, it is not insignificant to note that Du Bos was familiar with Bodin and Broekhuisen as well as with Fontenelle and Jean Chardin, and their writings on environmental determinism.[23] In fact, his initial approach to the subject seems to simply reiterate standard climate theory, echoing the thoughts of previous authors. Du Bos characterizes the climates of other lands as deviating from perfection and provides a long list of countries that are inferior because of environmental conditions, juxtaposing them with France, which is perfectly situated in a moderate climate. Here again, his paradigm resembled the vision of terroir proposed in the previous century: France had the best climate, since it was perfectly neutral and balanced. France was ideal not for the qualities that the terroir instilled, but for the qualities that it *did not* instill.

Du Bos illustrates his point with examples of the extremes found in countries with less benevolent climates, such as that of horses from Saint-Domingue, that is, the present-day Haiti (too small), or men from China (too cowardly). Again, in the tradition of French writers such as Bodin, Bernier, and Chardin, many of Du Bos's pejorative examples have to do with physical or personal traits. But after a few ethnic slurs couched in the language of pseudoscience, Du Bos begins to talk about the climate in more moderate terms. He explains that people of foreign descent eventually acquire the characteristics of the adopted country where they are born: "Foreigners who have become acclimated to whatever country in question have always become like the original inhabitants of the country where they have moved after a certain number of generations. The principal European nations have today the particular character of ancient peoples who lived on the land they live on today, even though these nations are not descendants of these ancient peoples. I will explain with some examples."[24] Du Bos uses the example of the Catalans, a people descended in part from the Goths who invaded northern Spain and southern France. This invading people abolished the original language of the Catalans and imposed their own brand of diverse idioms, which went against the natural grain of the remaining Catalan people. Yet the Goths ultimately succumbed to the effect of the climate and, owing to the influence of "nature" (in this example, the quality of the air), became once again like the autochthonous population of the region: "But nature brought back to life in today's Catalans the mores and inclinations of the Catalans from the time of the Scipios."[25]

Du Bos goes on to admit that Gaul had been conquered by Germanic peoples (an opinion he would rescind by 1734), but explains that the fact is irrelevant since the character of the nation depends primarily on the effects of the climate, which in this case transformed the Germanic people into Gauls: "Although the French descend more from the Germans and other barbarians established in Gaul than the Gauls, they have the same inclinations and character of mind as the ancient Gauls."[26] That is, Du Bos relegates race to a secondary role, explaining that because of the climate the Germanic Franks took on the characteristics of the country they settled in. He draws on testimony from Livy, noteworthy in itself since Livy is also the source that Boulainvilliers used to support his own conclusions, before adding the crushing blow: "It has always been clear that climate is more powerful than blood or origins."[27] Any sort of biological racism supported in Boulainvillier's line of thinking is critically denied here: the country's climate determines people in a way that their blood cannot override.

What is perhaps even more fascinating is that, in order to support his theories hinting at nationhood, Du Bos has recourse to the biological characteristics of plants, creating an identity for France's people based on its agriculture. He takes up key aspects of Fontenelle's reflection on the "Ancients" and the "Moderns" and, like Fontenelle, makes judgments on the relative merit of countries: some "trees" are bigger and more beautiful than others. He uses a number of examples to evaluate the effect of terroir: Flax thrives in certain terroirs, in others it languishes. Melons only grow well in some terroirs, and a vine from Champagne planted in Brie will soon no longer produce palatable wine.[28]

In each case, the lynchpin for Du Bos is terroir. He explains that the quality of the air, which influences people, itself is determined by the quality of the earth and its different minerals. He stipulates that humans do not choose their aesthetic propensities and aversions according to the tenets of good taste dictated by the purity of their blood. Nor are reason and education wholly responsible. Rather, according to Du Bos, people are programmed by their provenances: "Just as two seeds from the same plant produce fruits whose qualities are different when these seeds are sown in different terroirs or when they are sown in the same terroir in different years, similarly, two children who are born with brains composed in precisely the same manner will become two different adults as far as intellect and inclinations if one of these children is raised in Sweden and the other in Andalucia. They will even be different, although raised in the same country, if they are raised during years with different temperatures."[29] The passage concerns itself not only with the general characteristics (e.g., laziness, courage) that occupied the other authors who had written on climatic determinism up to that point, but also with *how* the terroir alters the blood and soul.

In other words, Du Bos explains that body and soul are united and that the quality of the blood is specifically linked to that of the air, which is in turn influenced by the terroir: "During man's life, as long as the spiritual soul remains united with the body, the character of our mind and of our inclinations greatly depends on the qualities of our blood [. . .]. Now, the qualities of the blood greatly depend on the air that we breathe [. . .]. That is why nations that live under different climates are so different as far as the mind and inclinations. But the qualities of the air themselves depend on the qualities of emanations from the earth that the air envelops."[30] Along with representing an evolution in climate theory, Du Bos's take on different national behaviors constitutes a decisive break from Cartesian dualist thought insofar as it provides for a central influence that both the body and external factors of the environment have on the mind.

It is worth observing that Du Bos, in his comparisons of people and plants, homogenizes them: both are acted upon by the soil. Both change qualities when they are transplanted: "The vine stock that is transplanted from Champagne to Brie quickly produces a wine in which one no longer recognizes the qualities that it produced in its first terroir. It is true that animals do not take after the soil of the earth like trees and plants. But as much as it is the air that gives them life, and it is the earth that nourishes them, their qualities are no less dependent on the place where they grow up than the qualities of trees and plants are dependent on the land where they grow."[31] Being *flavored* by one's terroir thus does not appear as an aberration in his argument, as it would have in most contexts in the seventeenth century, but rather as perfectly normal. Certainly, one must note that in the quotation about "transplanting" people above, Du Bos deflects any potentially unpleasant domestic implications of environmental determinism by using foreign countries (Sweden and Spain) as examples. Nevertheless, as he expounds about the parallel effects of terroir on people and on plants, he is categorical in tying his evaluation of the effects of the environment to the constitution of humans in general.

Before Du Bos, the influence of terroir was considered mostly in relation to those lacking autonomy of intellect, possessing imperfect language, or having deportment sullied by the provinces. While literary characters, women, and foreigners were understood to reflect their provenances, in the vast majority of cases the French white male was portrayed as autonomously rising above his terroir. In Du Bos, however, there is a general "democratization," and terroir appears without explicitly derisive connotations.[32] Du Bos also attempts to be precise in his explication of terroir. Developing the specifics of terroir by using a scientific lexicon and naming minerals, Du Bos presents the concept with more detail than it had ever seen before, rivaling the analytic precision of medical writings.

Finally, Du Bos politicized the concept, using terroir to define a French identity and national character. Comparing France with Italy, Du Bos explains that the soil of the latter country is replete with minerals that shape the character of the Italians and distinguish them from the French: "In many places in Italy, the earth is full of alum, sulfur, bitumen, and other minerals. Where these mineral deposits are found in France they are not of the same quality or proportion to the other deposits as they are in Italy. One finds almost everywhere in France that the tuff is of marl, a sort of fat, whitish, tender stone, containing a quantity of volatile salts."[33] Du Bos posits that a signature national soil—marl, a tender whitish stone filled with volatile salts—broadly characterizes France's terroir. The description of marl is important, since, as the last chapter showed, volatile salts were considered positive components in food, conducive to light, spirited character, and the wit and intelligence associated with aristocratic spirit. In other words, Du Bos hints at a national "nobility" based on soil instead of blood. This assertion, that the French have a character attributable to the soil, would be reconfirmed by the eighteenth century's most important Enlightenment thinkers, beginning with Montesquieu.

MONTESQUIEU AND THE LAWS OF THE LAND

Montesquieu echoed some of Du Bos's argument, but he developed his own brand of climate theory in larger strokes, with the specific intent of depicting national characters. His task was not to create aesthetic norms, but to establish legislative standards for different climates, to match the personalities of their people. In book 14 of *De l'esprit des lois* (1748), Montesquieu notes general differences between countries and regions, recommending that specific laws be created to accommodate and sometimes to counteract the effects of climate. Although Montesquieu does not speak of individual terroirs in this part of his writing, we can assume that this is at least partially because if a region were too variable on a microclimatic level, it would be impossible to suggest an appropriate set of laws for the region as a whole. In order to avoid frustrating the practical application of his theories, he speaks less of the soil and more of the general climate.

Elsewhere, however, Montesquieu does explicitly link soil quality to human comportment. He writes in particular of marl, the chalk and clay mixture that Du Bos invoked above. Marl, or *marne*, was primarily known at the time as the name of a river and as the predominating soil type in Champagne, the source of the particular flavor of its wines.[34] Like Du Bos three decades earlier, Montesquieu attributes the national character of the French to marl. He does so in terms remarkably similar to those of Voltaire's characterization of French people and Champagne in the poem "Le Mondain," which was discussed in chapter 5:

> The nature of the earth contributes much to the difference of dispositions. Most French provinces have, at the underlying level, a sort of white chalk that is called marl, which we cover soils with to fertilize them. This marl is full of volatile spirits that enter into our blood through the food [. . .] with which we nourish ourselves, and by the air that we breathe, in which it is mixed [. . .]. Now, such volatile spirits, once in the air, must produce some sort of effect. This effect is a certain lightness, a fickleness, this French vivaciousness.[35]

The French levity of spirit Montesquieu is referring to mimics the bubbly effects of Champagne, marking the latter quite consonantly as the national drink Voltaire had deemed it a decade earlier. As Montesquieu notes, French subtlety and spirituality do not come from blood but from the climate: "The air carries, like plants, particles of earth from each land. It acts upon us to the point that our temperament is determined by it."[36] In other words, the qualities of lightness, airiness, and delicacy that the previous century valued have not ceased to be laudable traits, but now are paradoxically attributed to the qualities of the ground.

Just as Voltaire democratized and glorified the French in "Le Mondain," comparing their nature to the airy lightness of Champagne, and just as Du

Bos had suggested that the French were superior to the Italians because of the presence of tuff and marl in French soil, Montesquieu went to the roots of Champagne, with its white marly soils, to qualify the national character as light and airy. Montesquieu leaves absolutely no ambiguity regarding the mark made by the earth, giving precise examples of the effects that local foods would have on people: "The things that we feed upon have, in each land, analogous qualities with the nature of the terrain. One finds iron in honey: it must be that those particles of metal slip into the plants and flowers, whence the bees take it. We find it in the blood [. . .]. That's why minds and characters are truly dependent on the difference of terroirs."[37] Such constructions of personal and national character based on terroir, similar to and no doubt inspired by Du Bos (Montesquieu knew the latter's work well even if the two were famously not always in agreement), provided a conflicting model, from one of the eighteenth century's most influential thinkers, to Descartes's seventeenth-century doctrine of pure thought and the ideal separation between mind and body.

Ironically, Montesquieu's logic also fed a racism that was as iniquitous as that of Boulainvilliers. That racism, developed extensively in three books of *De l'esprit des lois,* is much more known and roundly criticized today than that of the obscure writings of Boulainvilliers. That is because it opened the door to justifying France's colonial enterprise and the slavery it entailed. Slavery, though reprehensible in Montesquieu's opinion, is much more justifiable in countries with warm climates that "encourage laziness." If the denizens of these lands were not forced to work, he intimates, there would be no productivity at all, leading to decadence and moral dissolution.[38] Although Montesquieu does not specifically mention the Caribbean or the French slave trade, it was an easy logical leap to apply his writings on India and China to regions closer to home.[39]

It is worth noting in light of this discussion that Chardin, Du Bos, Montesquieu, and Buffon, though influential, were not alone in the sort of climatic determinism described above: authors in the eighteenth century were generally persistent in assimilating humans and plants into climatic systems. This occurred not only in metaphorical terms, but also in the more literal descriptions of human behavior made by philosophers and scientists of the period. A well-known physician and contemporary of Montesquieu, Julien Offray de La Mettrie, also a strident opponent of Cartesian thought, actually penned works titled *L'homme-machine* and *L'homme-plante.* Three decades after Du Bos's treatise on art and literature, and in the same year as

Montesquieu's *De l'esprit des lois,* La Mettrie wrote that "such is the dominance of the climate, that a man who changes climates feels this change in spite of himself. He is an ambulatory plant who transplanted himself; if the climate is no longer the same, it is proper that he should degenerate or improve."[40]

TERROIR'S EXPANSION IN THE AESTHETIC WORLD: FROM PALETTE TO PALATE

In the pages of his writing on aesthetics, Du Bos explained the earth's role in shaping art as easily perceived through the simple mechanics of sensorial evaluation, just as its role in shaping food was. Who has not, he inquires, noticed that the different countries exude different colors of light? That is because, he continues, the ground colors the air, just as it colors people and flavors wines. Du Bos then launches into a variety of agricultural and wine-related terms, such as *fermentation* and *yeasts,* to explain the "emanations" of the earth and their effect on people, which account for diversity in both humans and plants. Talented artists realize this and capture the earth's unique regional conditions in the colors of their paintings:

> In Italy, for example, the quality of the air is a bluish-green, and the clouds of the horizon are of a very dark yellow and red. In Holland the quality of the air is a pale blue and the clouds of the horizon are cast only in whitish colors. One can even note the same difference in the skies in the paintings of Titian and in the paintings of Rubens, these two painters having represented nature as it appears in Italy and in Holland where they copied it [...]. Just as the qualities of the earth determine the particular flavor of fruits in many countries [...] the earth is the cause of the different tastes of wines that are grown in two adjacent regions.[41]

Here, Du Bos begins inadvertently to formalize wine tasting by using it as a metaphor and metric for judging and appreciating the accuracy of painted representations. In other words, painting, like wine, is aesthetically defined as determined and colored by its landscape, which shapes the natural space being represented. The gifted painter reproduces nature according to its varying geographical differences.

Through such comparisons, Du Bos strengthened the climatic association between people and food in the French imagination and helped turn terroir into a normative aesthetic construct. The connoisseur of today who measures the authenticity and desirability of a food according to the correspondence of its characteristics with those thought to be intrinsic to the terroir tastes flavors according to early modern models for assessing painting and literature. Though this practice first appeared with the aesthetic formalization of the earth's influence on fictional characters in the seventeenth century, as in the criticisms directed at Racine's *Alexandre* and Scudéry's *Clélie* in chapter 5, the model became much more prevalent in the worlds both of art and of food in the eighteenth century after Du Bos.

To take a prominent example, Johann Joachim Winckelmann, often referred to as the father of archeology and art history, was of monumental importance in the evolution of European aesthetic standards in the late eighteenth century.[42] He devoted several pages of his work to climate theory, borrowing directly from Du Bos.[43] Winckelmann's theories quickly became known throughout Europe, and although he was German his influential work was translated into French in the second half of the eighteenth century. He, like Du Bos, left no ambiguity when it came to the effect of the climate; the French translations of his writing further specified that terroir was a key component to appreciating artists and their work.

According to Winckelmann, everything from the hue of skin to that of the sky is influenced by the terroir and the successful painter must account for what French translators of Winckelmann's work rendered as the *goût de terroir* in artistic productions: "As man has always been the principal object of Art, artists from every country have lent the physiognomy of their nation to the faces they paint [. . .]. It is this *goût de terroir,* as we say today, that the most talented masters preserve in some part."[44] Although Winckelmann provides a circumlocution to express the concept of terroir in the German, he allows for a categorical application of climatic determinism, explaining that talented German, French, and Dutch artists represent in their paintings images of their people that are as determined by their respective national climates as would be the Chinese, Japanese, or Tartars. In other words, Winckelmann does not single out his own nationality as free from the influence of climate, nor does he make climate an effect of class. Like fictional characters in books, skillful painted depictions are called upon in these accounts to correspond to specific terroirs, presumably so that the viewer would find the scene realistic and credible.

Although the string of metaphors presented in the works of Du Bos and the translations of Winkelmann makes it clear how tightly bound wine was with appreciation of art, similar expectations were formally taken up in the world of cuisine only *after* being propounded in these influential works on art and literature. In other words, although Du Bos used metaphors of food and wine to define aesthetic norms in literature and art, generally speaking it was only in being structured, formalized, and legitimated in these domains that, through a circular movement, the same criteria became clearly articulated in the world of cuisine.

Though Du Bos was instrumental in reversing broader prejudices against terroir in the philosophical realm, when it comes to cuisine, as chapter 5 suggested, changes in red wine's fate were also the result of other factors mitigating the perception of culinary terroir. One of these was Fagon's pronouncement that the wines of Burgundy were more suitable than those of other regions for the health of Louis XIV. Fagon's diagnosis undoubtedly encouraged the aristocratic class and the bourgeoisie to accept red wines, with their more earthy flavors. Yet the transformation was far from instantaneous.[45] Clearly from the late 1690s into the first decades of the eighteenth century there remained a good deal of uncertainty and ambivalence about whether red wines from Burgundy were generally preferable to wines from Champagne. As Benoît Musset puts it, at the time red wines in France were often construed as "almost fatal for delicate individuals."[46]

It was precisely at this moment that the dishonor of being associated with the ground, as red wines with their greater quantity of terrestrial qualities *(parties terrestres)* undoubtedly were, seems to have been diminishing. Certainly, we know that medicine underwent a transformation away from physical to chemical principles for understanding human bodies. In turn, a few well-known physicians who favored chemistry over physics, such as Nicolas Lémery, began to advocate for red wines as "drugs" based on new, if not equally outlandish, understandings of how wine affected the body. Lémery explained, for example, that red wine chased away melancholia, resisted venom, and incited women's menstrual cycles.[47]

Nevertheless, though red wine had new advocates, many signs indicate that abhorrence for the terrestrial compounds widely believed to be contained in red wine abated slowly. It is with respect to this aversion that the Abbé Du Bos appears as an especially influential model in his writing, helping to disarm readers concerned about the perceived effects of terroir by preventing it from being necessarily pejorative. Since he defined the French and their tastes according to their terroir, Du Bos was instrumental in allowing that foods could be associated with their terroir without decisively negative connotations. Yet, faced with the public's ambivalence owing to an entire century of casting terroir as a negative descriptor, it is not surprising that the transformation was not instantaneous. Another step was needed to mitigate the perceived threat of the ground, and to convert the latter from a threatening scourge to a positive attribute.

That step, as it turned out, was to be taken by new definitions of what constituted a skillful chef. The chef's role was explicitly defined in the work of a widely celebrated cookbook author, known simply as Menon, who turned out to be one of the eighteenth century's most important advocates of cooking for the bourgeois class as well as a champion of the value of terroir in cuisine. Menon instructed his readers that imbibing terroir might not turn out to be directly poisonous, and could even be greatly beneficial. But an eater could not appreciate terroir in food with the same detachment that a viewer could, per Winckelmann, observe a painting's *goût de terroir*. It was necessary to avoid the danger of infecting the eater's blood with rusticity or other maladies potentially present in adversely affected terroir. The chef thus was the specialist who used science and art to clear this hurdle and transform any dangerous raw impurities into healthful comestibles.[48] Menon's 1749 work, *La Science du maître d'hôtel cuisinier,* which took it as its explicit goal to lift the culinary arts to the level of painting and poetry, also likened cooking to a science, and proposed a methodology both to search out terroir in foods and to neutralize any pernicious effect it could have on the refined connoisseur.

The beginning of the book's preface, the "Dissertation préliminaire sur la cuisine moderne" penned by Lauréault de Foncemagne, a member of the Académie française, makes an apology for cooking, extolling its merits and bemoaning the excesses and unappetizing concoctions turned out in the past. When it came to foods being appreciated according to their terroir, Foncemagne turns for support to the world of art and literature, quoting more than an entire page from Du Bos on climate theory.[49] Providing solid evidence that the world of art mediated aesthetics on food appreciation, Foncemagne quotes Du Bos verbatim, expressing the conviction that the human constitution and disposition depend on climate and food: "Physics teaches us that the diversity of foods, at least as much as that of climates, creates variety and difference not only in bodies, but also in dispositions, inclinations, and mores of nations [. . .]. The salts and spiritual sugars of these foods put in the blood of people from the north [. . .] an ethereal oil they could not get from foods from their own country."[50] Foncemagne transplants Du Bos's theories directly into the world of food and cooking. He embraces a new use of terroir: exotic foods from outside one's terroir can be consumed to make up for deficiencies due to the climate. The *goût de terroir* was no longer just a means of providing the touch of authenticity to a painter or writer's work, it was also the remedy for certain ailments.

What great changes have been made in the people of the north, Foncemagne exclaims, since they have taken to eating the sugar, spices, wine, and other foods that grow in warmer climates.[51] They have more vigor and are much more subtle in their mannerisms, he adds, since goods produced in Spain and warmer climates fill the blood of northerners with "animal spirits." The proximity of southern countries to the sun produces food that enlivens the blood and imagination. Yet, these foods come from their origins with intrinsic dangers: to ensure their healthfulness one must turn to the fastidious work of the best chefs, who "refine" *(subtiliser)* them and strip away heavy, rude, and pernicious components from their "mixes":

> Cuisine cleanses the heavy parts of foods, stripping from the mixes that it employs the terrestrial juices they contain. It perfects them, purifies them, and spiritualizes them in a way. The foods that it prepares must therefore carry to the blood a greater abundance of purer and freer spirits. From thence, more agility and vigor are seen in bodies, more vivacity and fire in the imagination, more range and power in the intellect, more delicacy and finesse in our tastes. Is it therefore too much to deem the adornments of modern cuisine among the physical causes that rescued the reign of politeness, the talents of the intellect, and the arts and the sciences from the heart of barbarism?[52]

Foncemagne does not latch onto a movement toward the natural by stipulating that foods should reflect their regional differences. His intention is not to obtain aesthetic perfection with recourse to the terroir, but rather to elaborate how the flavors of foods from specific regions can be used to transform the personality and health of the people who eat them.

Clearly, climate-specific foods are important for Foncemagne. But what is more important is that skilled chefs extract the agility and vigor from foods of southern climates while preventing northern eaters from imbibing the impurities that would lead them to adopt the barbarous behavior of southern people.[53] When joined together, climate-specific foods and chefs pay rewards in large dividends, Foncemagne explains, quoting both Du Bos and the testimony of a doctor who maintained that the health of patients had drastically improved since the products of southern climates had made their entrance

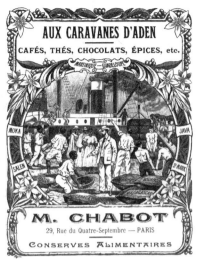

FIGURE 8. These late nineteenth- or early twentieth-century labels illustrate the status of coffee, tea, chocolate, and sugar as exotic foods, imported from the French colonies, that needed to be "purified" and refined before becoming suitable for cultivated European tastes and the French bodily constitution.

on the scene.[54] This shift marks a polar opposition to the medical theories of the previous centuries, which advised that one should not eat foods from outside of one's terroir. Thus, as terroir's status slowly changed, it helped expand and legitimize the profession of the eighteenth-century chef in new ways. Terroir created the need for a specialist who could transform the dangerous and lowly terrestrial components, using art and science to marry flavors and create a safe, enjoyable culinary experience.

On the relationship between food, art, and terroir in the eighteenth century, it is enlightening to review one of Foncemagne and Menon's principal assertions: that food, which at one time was simply a matter of the natural desire for sustenance, had become an art form.[55] Their observation appears credible. Food shared some of the same special vocabulary as art and was linked to the art world by being referenced in the eighteenth century's most authoritative works on aesthetics (Du Bos, Winckelmann) as a culinary corollary to the way that one should experience and judge literature and art. Yet when it came to appreciating either cuisine or art, there was more than the determining factor of one's terroir at stake. Culture and education were equally important.

There was, Foncemagne posited, a range of savors as vast as the spectrum of colors and sounds considered by the art world. The talented artist was the one who achieved a harmony of flavors, creating unity out of diversity. Although Foncemagne intimates that humans have a natural tendency to find harmony agreeable, he claims that the refined eater could develop a "knowledgeable palate" *(sagacité de goût)* that was lacking in others.[56] Many great artists thus do not succeed in pleasing those with "common tastes" because such eaters do not possess the wherewithal to appreciate them. Foncemagne offers as examples the Huron of North America and the "Hottentots" of Africa, claiming that such rustic people would hardly appreciate the music of even the word's best musicians. As it turned out, masterful cooks needed audiences with keen tastes to appreciate their work, and those tastes were honed as much through culture as nature. It was in fact the dialectical relationship between representations of nature and culture that would continue to lead to terroir's rehabilitation in the second half of the eighteenth century.

SEVEN

The Normalization of Terroir

PARIS AND THE PROVINCES

ALTHOUGH THE ABBÉ DU BOS, MONTESQUIEU, and Menon all played large roles in changing the overriding view of the earth in the first half of the eighteenth century, Jean-Jacques Rousseau arguably had an even more significant part in the decades leading up to the Revolution. As Adam Gopnik pointed out, Rousseau promoted the "superiority of terroir" not only to the public who voraciously read his books, but also to a broad range of well-known historical figures such as Robespierre, Chantoiseau (heralded by many as the inventor of the modern restaurant), and Marie-Antoinette, who made a pilgrimage to Rousseau's grave in Ermenonville in 1782.[1] The values in Rousseau's writing kindled a spirit of rural renewal, glamorized provincial living, and reinforced a positive role for terroir in culinary culture. Moreover, whereas in 1749 Menon advised chefs to seek from food the properties specific to its provenance only after "cooking out the impurities," fewer than twenty years later Rousseau promulgated a vision that was just the contrary.

By romanticizing the earth's hold on human beings, Rousseau inspired his readers to assimilate themselves with the natural world and seek out its qualities within themselves, redefining as pure the sorts of "impurities" that formerly would have been "cooked out."[2] As regards terroir specifically, in many ways Rousseau's writing was a logical continuation of Du Bos's aesthetics, and represented a clear change from the way that climates and terroir had been perceived by Chardin, Montesquieu, and Buffon. The latter mostly used examples of terroir and foreign climates as explications for alterity, whereas Rousseau laid the groundwork for terroir principally to incarnate French identity.[3] What followed in the years leading up to the Revolution was a nexus wherein political thought met literature and natural science, coming together to perpetuate climatic determinism as a way of creating nation and identity.

Culinary aesthetics were also a part of this evolution, as late eighteenth-century tastes in cuisine reflected values about what constituted "naturalness" in other spheres of life. New publications romanticizing farming appeared and regional agricultural societies *(sociétés d'agriculture)* sprang up. Yet, the ambivalent feelings regarding terroir were never completely eradicated. Place, terroir, and identity remained the object of major debate when the National Constituent Assembly (Assemblée nationale constituante) redrew the country's map after the Revolution in 1790 to create the departmental geographical boundaries *(départements)* France knows today.

ROUSSEAU'S COMMUNITY THROUGH
LIVING THE LAND

Rousseau is entombed across from Voltaire in the crypts of the Panthéon in Paris, and the joke goes that these two most defining voices of the French Enlightenment will discuss to eternity their differences of opinion on everything from art and social inequality to religion. In terms of their views on terroir too, the difference between the two is stark. At least in figurative language, Voltaire cast terroir as a blemish and an aberration from purity. Writing to King Frederick II of Prussia in 1772, Voltaire apologized for the dullness and awkwardness of his unpolished prose, explaining that an extended stay in the provinces, far from polite company and the conversation of Frederick the Great, had left him intellectually impoverished. Voltaire used the seventeenth-century metaphor of water for words, invoking the notion of purity in direct contraposition to the opaque befuddlement and inelegance associated with terroir, explaining that his writing style had become corrupted by his time in the country, since even "the purest waters take on the *goût du terroir* from the places they pass."[4]

To understand how Rousseau's views differed, and how he inspired a new generation of thought about terroir, place, and identity in the countryside, one has to return to 1763, to a prolonged reflection on race and identity that appeared in *Émile* (Rousseau's book on child rearing), in which the author pauses to reflect on traveling and what makes groups of people different. There, he expresses a sentiment strikingly similar to that of Boulainvilliers, lamenting that people have interbred and lost their identities: "To the extent that races are mixed and peoples confounded, one sees the gradual disappearance of those national differences."[5] Rousseau recounts that ancient peoples considered themselves autochthonous, having forgotten that their people had once migrated from somewhere else. After these ancestors had spent several generations in their new country, the climate shaped them and conferred upon them an identity, which they adopted as their intrinsic nature. According to Rousseau, that positive source of unification and community is what had been jeopardized in France. He laments that "among us, by contrast, the recent emigrations of the barbarians after the invasions of the Romans have mixed up and confounded everything. Today's French are no longer those great blond-haired and white-skinned bodies of the past."[6] Breeding between the Romans, Franks, and Gauls, had tainted France's population, a fact readily observable, Rousseau claims, in the darker complexions of the contemporary French.

The above passage's double signifiers of whiteness (the hypothetical ancestors are both *"blonds"* and *"blancs"*) as suggesting purity may have resonated in the context of the debate on slavery and the colonial enterprise that was taking place in France in the second half of the eighteenth century.[7] Yet, Rousseau's discussion in *Émile* is considerably more nuanced than the above passage would suggest, and he ultimately attributes only secondary importance to the interbreeding of "races" as a factor detracting from the integrity of France as a homogenized population. Moreover, even if at first glance Rousseau's position resembles a throwback to the sixteenth-century view, in which people were considered "pure" if they were untouched by foreign contact, in many ways he was revolutionary in terms of climatic determinism, since he aestheticized terroir in a positive way.

As his logic went, racial purity and French identity were not destroyed merely because people contaminated their blood, physical features, and temperaments by interbreeding (although that is part of the problem for Rousseau), but because they destroyed the very landscapes, climes, and terroirs that should have left an iconic mark on them: "This is why the ancient distinctions of races and the qualities of air and terroir distinguished the temperaments, looks, morals, and characters of different peoples more strongly than can be distinguished in our day. For today, European inconstancy does not leave any natural cause enough time to make its impressions, and with the forests leveled, the marshes dried up, and the land more uniformly—although worse—cultivated, there are no longer even the same physical differences from land to land and from country to country."[8] Rousseau maintains some sentiments that appeared in Du Bos, upholding that the status quo of a people is to reflect their landscape. Yet he clearly goes further, defining the conformity that humans should have with the terroir as a moral imperative discarded in contemporary society's corruption. He also adopts a tone strikingly in contrast with the aesthetic practice of Versailles, lamenting the disappearance of forests and the drying up of swamps, precisely the sort of masterful manipulation of nature that Versailles was premised upon. Whereas the scientists, architects, and engineers of Versailles created purity by importing "clean" dirt to the former swamp and transforming nature to meet their ends, Rousseau opted to define purity as nature's mark *before* it was defiled by human actions. In terms of humans themselves, although race and identity could be adulterated by either biological mixing or the altering of the environment, it is the environment that initially created a given population's character before other negative influences intervened.[9] In short, nature created the standard by which communities were formed and toward which they ought ideally to gravitate.

Rousseau's embracing of terroir as a positive quality in *Émile* takes on a new dimension when the subject of wine is evoked in his epistolary novel *La Nouvelle Héloise,* published a year before *Émile* in 1761. The example is important because it demonstrates how readily descriptions of wine and food were used to reflect the broader context of human relations. In a scene in a vineyard in *La Nouvelle Héloise,* the ambiance at the table and the taste of wine are used to describe a quasi-utopian society. But the passage also provides a telling account of how deterministic beliefs with respect to climate and nature played into the realm of fiction in the "biggest bestseller" of eighteenth-century France (as the historian Robert Darton has pointed out, the book was popular enough that people used to rent it out to read by the hour).[10]

The utopian aspect of the scene in question has been unpacked by literary critics, who have focused on the bucolic, georgic aesthetic of its representation of the grape harvest.[11] Saint-Preux, the narrator, begins a letter by launching into the pleasure of being in the countryside of Clarens, Switzerland. He exclaims that city people don't know how to appreciate the countryside's exquisite charm. They claim to treasure the rural landscape, yet paradoxically bring their city habits, paraphernalia, and even foods with them from home. Rousseau generally depicts urbanites as etiolated and close-minded, setting them in stark contrast to the simplicity and warmth of his idyllic representation of the country.

Through Saint-Preux, Rousseau paints a sepia-toned tableau of yesteryear, before women were "corrupt" and when men lived more simply. To wit, he describes harvest time at Clarens as falling under the warm, watchful, maternal eye of the owner and overseer, Madame de Warens. Here, rural life is a tableau of fertility, with rolling vines and colorful leaves openly exposing the grapes, which hang in luxurious, palpable bunches. The agricultural richness translates into human happiness, as diverse classes participate in an activity that occupies them as an ensemble. The social hierarchy both remains intact and gracefully falls away as each individual adopts his or her role, seamlessly working for the benefit of the whole: "The tasks attributed in such a manner, the common occupation, that of the grape picker, is to fill the empty vessels. Everyone is up early: we assemble together to go to the vines."[12]

Once again, the real magic comes from Mme de Warens, who skillfully assembles the workers. Saint-Preux describes wines produced by Warens that clearly double for the collective spirit the hostess creates from a group of diverse social classes working together. She makes wines with several different exotic natures from different terrains, all issuing from one harvest and one *"climat"*: "All these different wines have their particular preparation; all these concoctions are healthy and natural: and so it is that thrifty ingenuity makes up for diversity of soils, and concentrates twenty terroirs *("climats")* into a single one. You could scarcely imagine the zeal, the gaiety with which all this is performed. We sing, we laugh all day long, and the work goes only better for it. Everyone lives in the greatest familiarity; everyone is equal and no one forgets himself."[13] Rousseau substitutes the word *climat* for *terroir,* but the concept is exactly the same. In this countryside terroir, the hierarchy of class is forgotten *("tout le monde est égal")*. Instead of being on the outside, considering culture, food, and class as objects of appraisal, the narrator takes part in the scene, becoming one of the actors.

The power of Mme de Warens's concoctions, both the drink and the group of willing laborers, is that they draw the "drinker" in and allow the person both to retain an identity and become a part of the whole; the narrator comments both on the individuality of the wines in the mix and on their capacity to blend together in an unmistakably unified utopic context. Nevertheless, an important point of Rousseau's depiction is that it derives not only from the identity, but also from the alterity incarnated in the different populations. The *"climats"* are mixed, and while it is true that individuals never lose their identity, neither is the social hierarchy ever forgotten *("personne ne s'oublie")*. Even as Rousseau aims to bring about a blend in people and wine, he pointedly refers to the individual defining characteristics *("apprêts")* that remain tangibly intact in the blend. Mme de Warens's wines are the result of a melting pot in which hierarchy and class difference are simultaneously reaffirmed and forgotten.

EIGHTEENTH-CENTURY INFLUENCES
OF THE BOOK ON THE VINE

There is no question that Rousseau's writing had enormous influence on the pre-Revolutionary French population. It is, of course, an entirely different matter to ascertain with any certainty how the strength of that influence might have been reflected in the material culture of wine and terroir. Yet, an unmistakable transformation in culinary mores with respect to terroir took place in the eighteenth century, and some of that change undoubtedly owes to Rousseau's influence. The pages above have already touched upon the evolution in red wine culture during the first half of the eighteenth century: sources indicate that Paris, for instance, was consuming much more red wine from the Loire than white by the 1760s.[14] Wine consumption had also been popularized, spreading significantly to the lower classes in a way that had been almost completely absent in preceding centuries.[15] Even more clearly, however, in the years following Rousseau's writings on nature and terroir a proliferation of tangible signs indicated that terroir was becoming a new modality of perception, with people attempting to apprehend the essences of the earth through the smells and tastes it transmitted to wines.

In 1765, three years after Rousseau's publication of *Émile*, and four years after *La Nouvelle Héloise*, Louis de Jaucourt penned the entry *"Vin"* in the seventeenth volume of Diderot and d'Alembert's *Encyclopédie*. He writes: "A good Mosel wine ought to have the taste of slate, because the vines that produce these wines are enriched with slate that was left exposed to the air until being reduced to a sort of clay or rich soil. The vineyards of Hochheim near Mainz contain coal fossils that must be the reason that wines from this terroir resemble yellow amber in their taste and fragrance."[16] The *Encyclopédie* set a benchmark for the way the surrounding world was to be understood. According to Jaucourt, wines characteristically smell a certain way due to their origin or terroir—in fact, they even "ought" to reflect their terroir. Thus, a "good" Mosel wine possesses the taste of the slate used to fortify the soils of the vines. This description of how wine should be defined and experienced represented an important change. As the preceding chapters have shown, seventeenth-century connoisseurs generally sought products from a specific

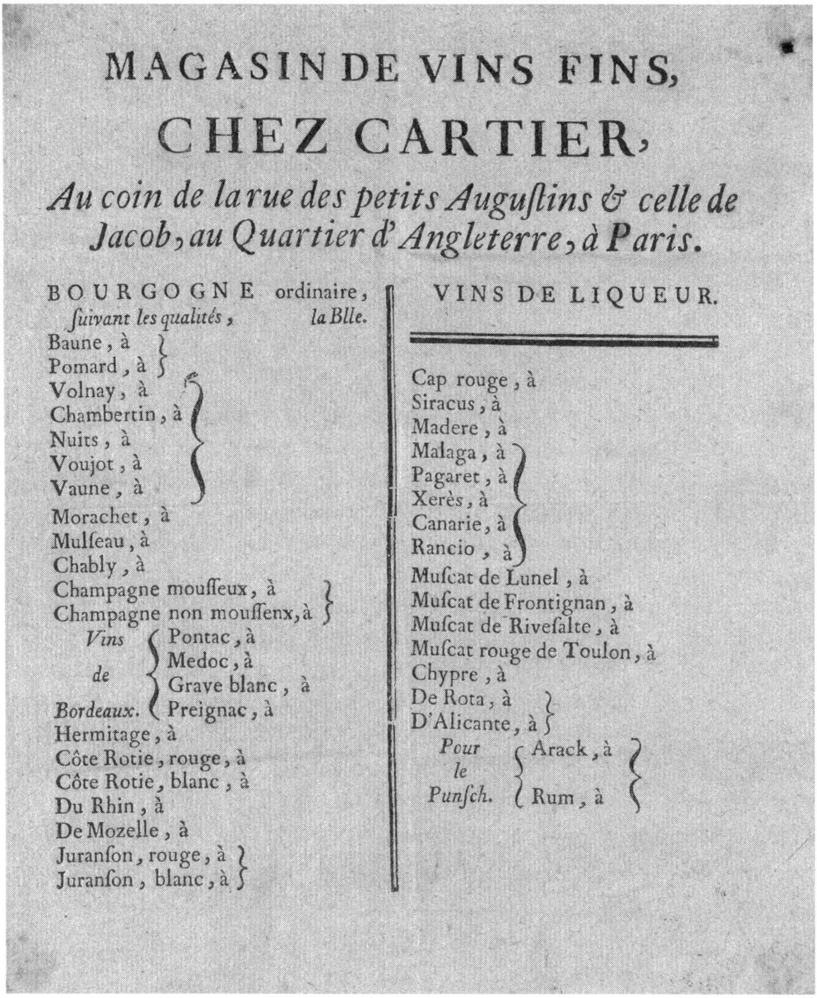

MAGASIN DE VINS FINS,

CHEZ CARTIER,

Au coin de la rue des petits Auguſtins & celle de Jacob, au Quartier d'Angleterre, à Paris.

BOURGOGNE ordinaire, *ſuivant les qualités,* la Blle.

Baune, à ⎱
Pomard, à ⎰
Volnay, à
Chambertin, à
Nuits, à
Voujot, à
Vaune, à
Morachet, à
Mulſeau, à
Chably, à
Champagne mouſſeux, à ⎱
Champagne non mouſſenx, à ⎰
Vins de Bordeaux. ⎰ Pontac, à
⎰ Medoc, à
⎰ Grave blanc, à
⎰ Preignac, à
Hermitage, à
Côte Rotie, rouge, à
Côte Rotie, blanc, à
Du Rhin, à
De Mozelle, à
Juranſon, rouge, à ⎱
Juranſon, blanc, à ⎰

VINS DE LIQUEUR.

Cap rouge, à
Siracus, à
Madere, à
Malaga, à
Pagaret, à
Xerès, à
Canarie, à
Rancio, à
Muſcat de Lunel, à
Muſcat de Frontignan, à
Muſcat de Rivefalte, à
Muſcat rouge de Toulon, à
Chypre, à
De Rota, à ⎱
D'Alicante, à ⎰
Pour le Punſch. ⎰ Arack, à ⎱
⎰ Rum, à ⎰

FIGURE 9. Wine offerings in Paris in the 1760s. This image shows how different terroirs, red and white, had come into vogue; note that Champagne is first listed as effervescent and *then* noneffervescent—an evolution from the previous century. Courtesy of Yale's Beineke Collection.

place of origin in order to ensure purity, perfection, and "non-placeness"; by contrast, Jaucourt and the eighteenth century began to seek individual qualities in a terroir. Moreover, one can surmise that a part of the pleasure of this new culinary experience came through the mixed sensory and rational process by which the taster correlated produce with provenance. One could say that Jaucourt followed Rousseau's lead: just as the latter stipulated that humans *ought* to reflect their terroir, Jaucourt went beyond the previous century's aesthetics. He spoke of specific flavor characteristics that wines from any given place *needed* to have. It was not merely a question of which area yielded the best wine, the most healthful, or the most pure, but which produced individualized flavors that were true to their place of origin.

Such writings were influential to the extent that by the end of the eighteenth century the discourse on terroir had begun to evolve substantially. For instance, one text by canonical agricultural writers explained that there were two kinds of terroir flavors. There was a natural *goût de terroir,* a welcomed flavor in wines, and an artificial *goût de terroir* that constituted a defect.

> One should distinguish between, I think, two sorts of *goût de terroir [goût naturel* and *goût artificiel de terroir]:* The first is due to the dissolution or vaporization of a part of the mineral and metallic substances that compose the soil of certain vineyards. These dissolutions and vaporizations brought on by the continual action of air, heat, and atmospheric humidity, mix with the elements in the sap, enter with it into plants, and remain suspended in all the parts that compose it. Such is, without a doubt, the principle of the *goût de terroir naturel* that we designate in certain wines by the name of gun flint, truffles, violets, raspberries, et cetera. These tastes are inherent in the nature of the soil and independent of the will or work of men; moreover, they are more often seen as a quality than as a vice in the wine.[17]

The authors of the passage (Chaptal, Rozier, Parmentier, and d'Ussieux) provide an authoritative voice promoting terroir: in fact, Chaptal and Parmentier are still known today (the former for "chaptalization," the process of adding sugar to wine must to increase alcohol content, the latter for his role in promoting potatoes as food to ward off famine in France). Their description of terroir is strikingly modern; they envision it not only as a normal element of the earth's contribution to the wine, but as a positive aesthetic aspect. The flavors that issue from the wine are both caused by the wine, and result from the minerals in the soil, appearing as delicate fragrances (violets, raspberries) and prestigious flavors (truffles).

Such descriptions acknowledge that different types of terrain naturally produce subtle flavor variations, incarnating fruits, flowers, and minerals (e.g., the modern-sounding gun flint in the above passage). Moreover, at least a handful of eighteenth-century authors created a lexical distinction between diverse types of terroir to account for the negative sense of the word in some contexts while making it a positive, "natural," part of appreciating wine in others. Chaptal, Rozier, Parmentier, and d'Ussieux, for example, qualify *goût artificiel de terroir* as the unpleasant smells that can be produced in vines and wine as a result of certain plants or trees (e.g., aristolochia, corolla, verbena, etc.) growing in the vicinity of the vineyard, use of the wrong kind of fertilizer, effects of smoke coming from a lime kiln or charcoal stove, and so forth.[18] This classification promoted the continued ambivalence felt toward the word while suggesting that terroir was making progress toward becoming a "normalized" part of wine consumption.

<h2 style="text-align:center">THE PRE-REVOLUTION BOURGEOIS
ATTRACTION TO THE EARTH</h2>

There were other noteworthy signs signaling a change in ethos and the evolution of terroir in relation to French identity. One cannot complete the pre-Revolutionary portrait of agriculture, cuisine, and land without invoking the role of the *sociétés d'agriculture.* The *sociétés* were regional gentlemen's clubs that met monthly to discuss agricultural themes. These groups joined innovation, practicality, and ritual to the aesthetics of Rousseau and his adherents, setting the stage for terroir's return from banishment. The first *société d'agriculture* in France was founded in 1758 in Rennes by the economist and "physiocrat" (from the Greek-derived *physiocracy,* or government of/by nature) Jacques-Claude-Marie Vincent de Gournay.[19] The organization, based on an English model, was sponsored by Louis XV (and later by Louis XVI) to encourage and promote farming practices through rational debate and intellectual exploration. This, the founders hoped, would ultimately lead to higher agricultural yields. Paris followed suit in 1761, establishing the *Société royale d'agriculture de la généralité de Paris,* the most famous of the dozens of other societies of agriculture that sprang up around the country. After a brief hiatus during the Revolution years for political and economic reasons, the *sociétés* dropped the *royale* component in their names and returned in force at the beginning of the nineteenth century, expanding in new chapters throughout France.

The *sociétés* owed their genesis to positive depictions of the natural world by authors such as Rousseau, as well as to the work of botanists, naturalists, and physiocrats, including Duhamel du Monceau, Buffon, and François Quesnay. From the 1740s on, France began to reevaluate the economic importance of agriculture over commerce, and eminent voices such as that of Quesnay, along with Vincent de Gournay, and Anne-Robert-Jacques Turgot pronounced that France's real economic strength lay in the agricultural products of its land and not in foreign trade or the mercantilist practices that had dominated economic policy since the seventeenth century.[20] These individuals, at least at certain moments in the second half of the eighteenth century, wielded significant amounts of power (Turgot, for example, served as *contrôleur général des finances* under Louis XVI from 1774 to 1776). They were responsible not only for securing expenditures for agriculture and encouraging private property ownership, but also for conceiving a free-market economy based on France's agricultural wares. Their theories, in turn, sparked further interest in the *sociétés d'agriculture.*[21]

As far as the *sociétés* themselves went, the participants were generally members of the bourgeoisie and *noblesse terrienne* who met once a month to talk about new agricultural ideas, theories, and the implementation of practices. In the changing political landscape leading up to the Revolution, the *sociétés* solicited government financial support for their endeavors, since, as the logic went, modernizing agriculture would eventually add to France's coffers. Even if the financial returns envisioned by the physiocrats never came to fruition, the ideas fared extremely well and the *sociétés* themselves became increasingly popular. On the other hand, the groups were criticized for their lack of practicality: they quickly became known as meeting places for abstract philosophizing and affected reflection on agriculture's high-minded intellectual components instead of practical conversation.

Joseph Berchoux, known for creating France's modern definition of gastronomy, mocked the ambiance that dominated at many of the groups' meetings at the beginning of the nineteenth century. His satire *The Complete Course of Modern Agriculture (Cours complet d'agriculture moderne)* is presented as a dialogue that queries the concept of the *sociétés* and the period's agricultural practices in general.

> *Question:* What is modern agriculture?
>
> *Response:* It is the art of cultivating the earth with a pen, ink and paper [...]
>
> *Question:* Mustn't one have spent some time in the country to have an idea of fieldwork and the way to encourage the earth's fecundity?
>
> *Response:* The countryside is good for laborers, for pioneers, and for those caught up in old routines; but intellectuals, who practice transcendent agriculture, do not need to leave the great city gates [...] [they use] simple rural and poetic discourses that they write in the morning in slippers and a robe.
>
> *Question:* What must one do to become initiated in this science?

Response: One must learn by heart the *Georgics,* the *Bucolics, Le Poème des saisons, des mois, l'Homme des champs* [. . .][22]

Question: What must one do next?

Response: One must be well behaved, and must be accepted as a member in many *sociétés d'agriculture.*[23]

Although Berchoux's text was published after the Revolution, the parodic tone that it sets is a faithful representation of pre-Revolutionary criticisms of the *sociétés d'agriculture:* the real work was a secondary concern, while the primary occupation was romanticizing georgic and bucolic ideals. This critical take on the romanticizing of agriculture serves as proof that the terroir-related values that had appeared in Rousseau and elsewhere gained widespread traction in the years bookending the Revolution, and were mediated by literary depictions rather than deriving from a purely agricultural context.

In this regard, it is worth nothing that, along with conflict over the armchair farmer image, there were tensions between social classes at the meetings themselves. Arthur Young, who traveled across France in the late 1780s to learn about agricultural practices and visit the former estate of his sixteenth-century hero, Olivier de Serres, took exception to the boorish behavior of the upper-class members at one *société* meeting: "At a meeting of the society of agriculture in the country, where common farmers were admitted to dine with people of the first rank, this proud fool [the Bishop of Beauvais] made difficulties of sitting down in such company."[24] Young went on to lament that the *sociétés* lacked a serious, practical side and were instead bureaucratic institutions that did little to address concrete agricultural issues and get down to the nitty-gritty of things.[25] That said, even though the word *terroir* was rarely directly taken up in the pages of their proceedings, the popularity of the *sociétés* attests to the economic and social transformation of French identity: being linked to the earth was in vogue, as long as one didn't get too close.

Another important sign of the reversal of connotation with respect to terroir was the sudden popularity of the English garden, a prototype that rejected the aesthetics of reasoned order that had dominated Versailles. Its popularity was in part due to the valorization of the "natural movement" advocated by Rousseau. This emphasis on respect for "natural" rhythms in the English garden aesthetic conflicted with the artificial mastery over nature demonstrated in the French garden, which had been lauded in the seventeenth century for, to take one example, producing fruits and vegetables out of season and in climes to which they were not indigenous. In *Émile,* by contrast, Rousseau calls for natural flavors and produce grown in season, rejecting as inferior in ethics and in culinary value anything that does not occur according to the natural cycle: "It takes effort—and not taste—to disturb the order of nature, to wring from it involuntary produce which it gives reluctantly and with its curse. Such produce has neither quality nor savor."[26] This aesthetic persuasion was of course at diametric odds with the sorts experiments and pursuits encouraged by La Quintinie in the *potager du roi.*

This change of tastes played out in the physical organization of the garden. The French garden adhered to principles of symmetry, geometry, and regularity, epitomized in its ordered, elaborate fountains and the contrived, eye-popping patterns of its garden beds. The English garden was fashioned according to a "natural" conception, with lakes, ponds, and irregular lines formed of mixed horticultural choices. Rousseau had an English-style *jardin paysager* at Ermenonville, and throughout France the popularity of such gardens began to increase during the 1760s.[27] Marking another change from the aesthetics of the seventeenth century, writers like the theorist Jean-Marie Morel, in his *Théorie des jardins,* recommended that gardens be climate-specific, and that gardeners not attempt to adapt plants from other zones.[28] Morel stipulates that the gardener must account for nature, take stock of what he can and cannot change, and attempt to remain in harmony with the overarching natural appearance of the garden's own specific place. Tastes in clothing and architecture have varied between countries and climates throughout the centuries, he writes, but gardens and their productions should stay stable and fixed in place by the laws of nature.[29] Morel goes out of his way to contrast this pastoral aesthetic with the ideal state of agriculture, where rows and regularity were needed. His writing as a whole suggests that the flavors and behavior of plants and people are mapped to the specificity of place, and that natural conditions are manifested in terroir-determined expressions.[30]

Furthermore, Morel's brand of aesthetics was upheld by writers such as Jacques Delille, who, in his *Homme des champs, ou les géorgiques françaises* (1800), correlated the change in garden preferences with the kind of literary genius it took to represent such landscapes. In the seventeenth century, Delille explains in the preface to his book, René Rapin had composed a poem in four separate, symmetrical parts (flowers, meadows, waters, and forests) to describe the measured perfection of the French garden. This model, continues Delille, lacked taste, charm, and, insofar as it presented little challenge for the author, literary merit. Delille boasts that he and his contemporaries, one hundred years later, have chosen to mirror in their writing the chaotic twists and turns of nature, stylistically leaving behind the stodgy geometrical garden to incorporate in prose nature's irregularity, complexity, and beauty.[31]

Delille, in fact, was one of the precursors of the third wave of signs that terroir's fate was changing: the sudden popularity of garden manuals and the romanticizing of nature for nature's sake, which had fallen from grace in the first third of the seventeenth century. In the beginning pages of his 1774 work *L'Agriculture ou les Géorgiques françaises,* Pierre Fulcrand de Rosset pays homage to the king for having recognized the value of agriculture and, among other gestures, having encouraged the *sociétés d'agriculture:* "The agricultural societies formed in the provinces under your protection have excited, instructed, and guided cultivators."[32] De Rosset expresses how badly, in spite of the current king's patronage, agriculture had been disdained and neglected in France since the time of Henri IV, and that even antiquity's greatest writers had not been able to awaken France from a slumber of "luxury and idleness" *("luxe et oisivité").* He goes on to quote Voltaire, whose acceptance speech for membership in the Académie française had confirmed France's "unwarranted" derision for farming.[33] De Rosset's work, which employed the word *terroir* nineteen times in both positive and neutral senses, thus coincided with this larger movement and the beginnings of a global reversal of France's conception of agriculture.

Still, despite these positive signs, several other authors writing agricultural manuals or georgic poetry at the time carefully abstained from using the word *terroir* (Delille, for example, uses it only once in *L'Homme des champs*). One senses that, in spite of the change of fortune the concept saw throughout the eighteenth century, its connotations remained damaged by the pejorative pall the seventeenth century had cast upon it. Yet, despite its continued ambivalence, the notion of terroir became an important element in creating the provincial identities that fueled the Revolutionary spirit.[34] No better proof of terroir's pertinence in this regard exists than the National Constituent Assembly debates in 1789 and 1790, which sought to redefine the country physically in order to represent new, republican strategies and ideals.

TERROIR'S ROLE IN MAPPING POST-REVOLUTIONARY FRANCE

In 1789, after the Revolution, the debate began on how the Constitutional Committee (Comité de constitution) and the National Constituent Assembly

(Assemblée nationale constituante) ought to remap France and physically define the post-Revolutionary country. Members sought both to create a new, unified national identity and to establish a system that would facilitate effective governmental administration of the provinces. The solution was to design a system of departments, creating national unity by breaking down existing French regions in favor of spaces easily governed by a central Parisian government.

Terroir, climatic determinism, and theories on space and regional identity all played parts in this idea and its execution. Marie-Vic Ozouf-Marignier, who authored the definitive work on the genesis of the French system of *départements,* is clear about the centrality that spatial considerations assumed in decisions about the new administrative structure of France. On the topic of conceptualizing the new departments, she writes that "this way of envisioning the planning invokes the principle of spatial determinism, according to which the social organization must correspond to the territorial layout. The theoreticians of the eighteenth century think implicitly that in acting on the space, one can obtain a new social structure."[35] In other words, those setting out to remap France were convinced that geography and land, properly used, would contribute to the success of the republic. The point of dissension in these debates was not *if* space mattered, but rather *how* to make use of it or, alternatively, how to counteract the effects of regional landscape, climate, and terroir.

Put simply, Paris was the autonomous, rational "head," while the provinces and the rest of France could be considered as the body. There were two different conceptions of how these bodily departments should be drawn. Certain members of the National Constituent Assembly thought that the new departments should be mapped according to existing regional identities because to do anything different would conflict with nature, which had historically determined the customs and mores of given geographical regions. On the opposing side, other individuals set out to divide France into geometrically neutral areas, in order to break up regional identities and provincial powers, with the conviction that, in doing so, they would create a stronger, more unified French whole that shared a common interest and was organized through a rational *esprit d'ordre.* Between these two extremes, several framers and theoreticians viewed the question with ambivalence. The liberal political theoretician Nicolas de Condorcet, for example, spoke explicitly of the need to create one graphical and physical template for France that would apply to all sectors of the French population, no matter the difference in soil, climate, customs, and personalities of the inhabitants. Yet he also went on to accentuate the importance of respecting natural differences: "But one must at the same time acknowledge that we should take into account the physical geography in these different divisions, so as only to join areas between which communication is easy, and to which a resemblance in the climate and in the soil gives a common culture, habits, and customs: that is what nature prescribes."[36] Even a proponent of a more universal scheme for division expressed no doubt that different climates, soils, and terroirs influenced people in different ways. The question was merely how to accommodate the influence.

Emmanuel Joseph Sieyès was among the proponents of a rationalized redrawing of France. He remarked that "it would be quite essential to make a new territorial division with equal areas."[37] Sieyès advanced a plan for the geometric configuration of departments of uniform size that would cut indiscriminately across France in eighty-one squares, erasing the identity of former provinces and imposing a strictly rationalist vision of space. Octave Mirabeau, by contrast, was a strong advocate of a terroir-based depiction of France. When it came to framing the departments according to fixed, uniform dimensions or, alternatively, according to the character imprinted on people by the terroir, Mirabeau explicitly compared human beings and plants and evoked the necessity of respecting the terroir, arguing that "it follows that, since nature varies in its productions according to the climate, the exposition, and the kind of terrain, and that the personal qualities of men, whom we ought to consider as another terroir-determined plant, are as variable as other plants; it follows, I say, that the laws of action and of distribution, relative to the production and distribution of substances, ought to vary as well."[38] Mirabeau and others like him argued that nature must be respected in the formation of new departments because it had historically determined customs and behaviors in each region leading up to the Revolution. Therefore, Sieyès's division would be unworkable: "I would like a material, factual division, suitable to localities, to circumstances, and not in the least a mathematical division, almost ideal, and whose execution seems impracticable."[39] Mirabeau ultimately conceived the mathematically "ideal" division as being the result of an unobtainable, utopian conception.

When the departmental map of France was finally created in 1790, it was a mix between the logical prototype and a regional model that took into account natural borders and, in many cases, the dividing lines of the older provinces. As it turns out, ambivalence toward terroir prevailed: although different framers were not of the same mind, the overriding sentiment was that it would be too dangerous and disorderly to dismantle completely the identity of the provinces: "How can we win out against the feeling that attaches the denizen of the provinces as much to the name of the soil as to the soil itself?" queried one member of the assembly, staking regionalism firmly not only on the origin, but on the origin's appellation, the lexical symbol rooting the person to his or her identity.[40] As a result, the new map cut through old regions, but also took into account history, economic and demographic realities, and the natural boundaries created by rivers, mountains, and terroirs. It was ultimately a hybrid between the rational model proposed by Sieyès and the older pre-Revolutionary regional divisions of France. Yet, the fact that the debate existed in the first place, and the fact that the cartographical conception of France was so important in considering its identity, reflects how tightly bound the concepts of landscape, region, and terroir had become in the French imagination.

It is worth noting the irony of the mapping process, which was meant to dissolve differences and create unity. In fact, it both accentuated the importance of terroir and the provinces as a mental construct, and ultimately reinforced Paris as a center that transcended the departments. Alain Corbin points this out, explaining that with the division of the old regional provinces into new departments, provincial identity was both reframed and retrenched in the collective French mind. Paris was portrayed symbolically as the capital that sat above the country: it was both the head reuniting and mastering the fractious parts, its objectivity symbolized by its central position and its regard from the stable center of the circle toward the outlying regions, and the sun around which the departments revolved like planets. In his chapter "Paris-Province," in Pierre Nora's *Les Lieux de mémoire,* Corbin observes that the continued construction of an autonomous provincial character in the second half of the century had the unexpected consequence of heightening the role of Paris as a place that transcends and supersedes identity based on terroir: "All that encourages pride for the small region brings comfort to the Parisian difference, anchors the specificity of the image of that city which transcends regionalism: by the same token, all that contributes to promote the provinces tends to devalue the provinces."[41]

FRANCE AS A NATION OF TERROIR

A number of geographical gourmet maps sprang up immediately after the Revolution, and it is hard not to consider their appearance in juxtaposition to the efforts of those members of the National Constituent Assembly (and individuals such as Sieyrès) who sought to divide France according to a strict rationalist, "flavorless" conception. The existence of regional culinary representations of the country in fact incarnated a new way of framing identity and expressing nationalism. As with the creation of the departments, however, the phenomenon managed to reinforce terroirs and individualize regions while at the same time disassociating Paris from the rest of the country.

Already in the years leading up to the Revolution, the famous culinary writer Le Grand d'Aussy had defined France according to its regional productions, helping to establish a new way of thinking about nation. In the opening lines of his influential three-volume *History of the Private Life of the French* (*Histoire de la vie privée des français*), he explains the rationale for his project of defining France in terms of food and the productions of the soil: "because the different cantons of the kingdom did not produce the same things, the diversity of places necessarily led to a diversity in the way of life."[42] Le Grand d'Aussy maps France according to its agricultural productions, regions, and the characteristics of its people. Reiterating theories primarily from Bruyèrin-Champier's sixteenth-century Latin text *De Re Cibaria,* he explains where the women are prettiest (in the forests of the Auvergne), where the French are the most drunk (near Flanders), where the language is the most wild and people most prone to thievery (Brittany), and where the men are the fattest and care more about their next meal than about being properly dressed (Burgundy).[43] Although Le Grand d'Aussy recycled ideas from Bruyèrin-Champier, rendering the Latin into French, he also changed the context of the discussion from a text primarily concerned with agricultural production to a book attesting to how agricultural accounts might be used to understand and frame the French people in general.

The tendency to define France according to its agricultural production became more common in the first decade of the nineteenth century. The practice seems to have arisen from a need to understand the French nation in a new way during the chaos of the Napoleonic era, following the Revolution and the division of the country into departments. This is the sort of sentiment that the famous gastronome Grimod de la Reynière expressed in the preface of his *Manuel des amphitryons* (the term *amphitryon* is an allusion to the eponymous play by Molière, itself referring to a Greek myth about hospitality; in literary terms, it means the "host" of a dinner party), published in 1808. He highlights the three-hundred-year tradition of fine cuisine in France, recognizing it as a force that had survived the turmoil of the

Revolution thanks to certain luminary voices who conserved culinary traditions notwithstanding political adversity. These masters could teach this culinary heritage to those whose newly improved social situations and wealth had provided them the means to participate in fine culinary culture.[44] Coupled with this role as a sort of social anchor, cuisine logically provided a general means of classifying and framing France.

In 1803, in the *Almanach des gourmands,* Grimod de la Reynière proposes a new sort of map with graphic representations of France where identities would be based on regional food productions: "Thus, instead of the bell tower of Amiens, we would discern in that place a duck pâté; in Nérac, a terrine of red partridge; one of duck liver in Toulouse; pork feet and head cheese in Troyes; a jar of barberry conserves in Dijon; figs in Ollioules."[45] Six years later, in 1809, Charles Louis Cadet de Gassicourt responded by creating a *carte gastronomique* of France, spatially placing agriculture and gastronomy in a representation that presented the French culinary imagination with just the sort of distinctions proposed in the *Almanach des gourmands*. Such cartographic depictions of France's alimentary identity—less than twenty years after the map of the country had been redrawn into departments in 1790— went a long way toward creating both a nuanced national spirit (presenting France as a diverse agricultural country and a culinary paradise) and championing a notion of identity that deviated from the artificial, administratively oriented departments that Sieyès and others had lobbied to create in order to dissuade regional entities from defining post-Revolutionary France.

Identity through specificity of place was also reinforced at the table, by new rules of etiquette that prescribed proper consumption according to terroir. In other words, the regionalist dimension of France was actualized and reinforced each time the refined eater considered what was before him at the table. Certainly, this is true in terms of wine. Grimod de la Reynière and Gassicourt counsel the *amphitryon* to specify the wine according to the terroir it came from:[46]

24. The amphitryon and his stand-ins must always proclaim, at least one time, the name of the wine they offer, its terroir [. . .] if they have confidence in the trustworthiness of the merchant who sold it to them.

25. It would be to express oneself in an incongruous manner to offer Bordeaux, Burgundy, Champagne; one must announce Lafite, Saint-Émilion, Château Margaux, et cetera; Beaune, Chambertin, Pommard, et cetera; Ay, Sillery, Pierry, et cetera; but one must always have these names preceded by *wine of,* et cetera.[47]

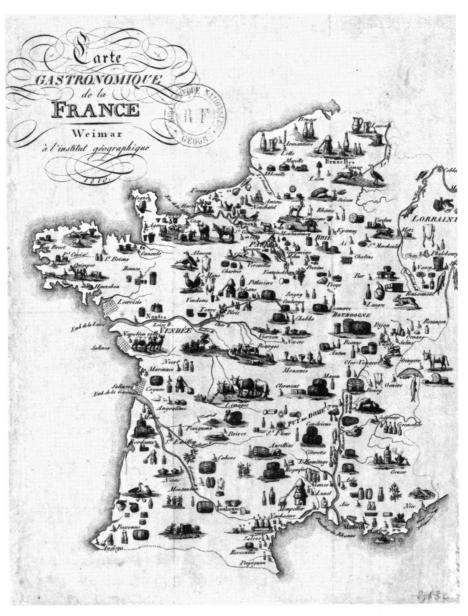

FIGURE 10. *Carte gastronomique* of France, created by Charles Louis Cadet de Gassicourt in 1809, showing the best food products according to region. Courtesy of the Bibliothèque Nationale Française.

Yet though these authors insist on the value of the provinces, they also make it clear that the tastes in Paris remain the best: there, they claim, one finds the best restaurants in the world and the best cooks.[48]

In fact, though there was a recognition of terroirs and an imperative to catalogue them at the table in polite company, there remained tension between Paris and the provinces. For Grimod de la Reynière, the most authoritative voice in French cuisine at the beginning of the eighteenth century, Paris remained vital—the heartbeat of good cuisine. Even if food was naturally better at its place of origin, the skill of preparation in Paris made for the best culinary experience.

> To return to the *charcutiers,* it is a recommendable profession, which holds a distinguished place in Paris among the culinary ranks. It is not their fault if the pig is much better in the departments of Aube and the Rhône than that of the Seine; and if the cheese, the heads, and the trotters of Troyes and the sausages of Lyon are better than those of Paris: but all that depends on the excellence of the work, which is better completed by them than anywhere else; and nowhere else can one eat sausages, minced pork livers, pigs' feet stuffed with trout, andouilles, and *boudins blancs* that are as delicate, as well confectioned, and finally as delicious than in France's capital, which we can consider as well as the "culinary capital of Europe."[49]

The Parisian chef and eater thus remained at the "center" of France, confectioning and judging Europe's finest culinary wares with insuperable skill and discretion. As before, Parisian eaters were presented as uniquely able to catalogue (and cook) the goods produced elsewhere in France with impartial taste, art, and science. Their objectivity was reflected in the method and measurements of cookbooks, but is also well documented in the world of connoisseurship, as appears in the above quote from Grimod de La Reynière, where the connoisseur is instructed to announce the wine and its region of origin. This dynamic was already well established (in the writing of Menon, for example): the best foods admittedly come from specific regions or terroirs of France, yet the best cooks perfect nature's wares with their art and technique, making food edible, safe, and enjoyable. It is a confirmation that the art and science of Paris reign supremely over the natural aesthetic identified with the terroirs of France.

Examples of this sentiment abounded after the Revolution. Julia Csergo, in her essay "The Emergence of Regional Cuisines," refers to a *député* from the Gironde who proposed creating a miniature garden of France laid out according to its departments that would showcase a regional specialty from each department (e.g., olive trees, fig trees, apple trees for cider, etc.): "Where unique products are lacking, or in gardens where the climate does not allow them to be grown, one would place a small column bearing an inscription marking a famous event or person suitable for distinguishing the particular *département* among the geographic squares."[50] The model would allow children to experience, learn about, and *live* France's regions from afar, all the while representing the space using the cartographic proportions and rational detachment that reflected the larger ambivalence that came with identifying oneself or defining oneself by the land. This perspective suggested both rational, human mastery over nature, in the superimposition and parceling of land into geographic quadrants, and at the same time, the brand of patriotism that comes with exploring the identity of a country through food. The first involves the detachment of a connoisseur, while the second implies living the nation through food. Both aspects bring terroir into focus, and yet "terroir," the word itself, remained absent from the pages of Grimod de la Reynière and Gassicourt. Even with the renewal of positive uses of the term in the years leading up to the Revolution, and with the concept of terroir built inexorably into the French imagination as a way of framing itself as a country, the word remained judiciously avoided, a phenomenon that would not be more or less completely reversed until the middle of the twentieth century.

Conclusion

TERROIR AND NATION: FROM GEOGRAPHIC
IDENTITY TO PSYCHOGEOGRAPHY

IN 1961, THE LITERARY CRITIC Roland Barthes evoked terroir as he summed up the power of food and drink in France in terms of culinary nationalism and nostalgia, two themes the preceding pages have traced back to the Renaissance. He explains that "food allows people (I am speaking here of French themes) to partake each day of the national past [...] it upholds the memory of the terroir in modern life [...]. One can say that, through their food, the French live to some extent the continuity of their nation."[1] Barthes identifies a quest in French society to recover the halcyon days of the country's worldwide preeminence, finding national identity and keeping terroir alive in an imaginary journey initiated by food and the senses. Despite the quote's relative modernity, the tradition of that journey began four hundred years earlier, when Grandgousier sat down in *Gargantua* to consume France physically and mentally in a selection of meats and sausages from the country's four corners, a practice that would have fit perfectly at Barthes's modern table in provenance if not in quantity.

And France repaid its debt: Rabelais's image has remained ingrained in the country's imagination as part of the modern pleasure of eating regional foods. In a 1930s Loire valley geography schoolbook, for example, children learned how they would one day imbibe the spirit of regional personalities like Rabelais by drinking wines from the area: "In drinking our wines, the friends of the grapevine will see floating in their glass a bit of the genius of our great Touraine personalities: Rabelais, Balzac, Descartes, Paul-Louis Courier, the Courteline, René Boylesve, and all of the others whose souls were steeped in our generous wines."[2] Just like the wines they drank in life, the textbook encouraged readers to conclude, the region's authors had been molded and shaped by the land, acquiring a specific Loire valley persona. The

FIGURE 11. This mid-twentieth-century advertisement for Amora Dijon Mustard brings to life mustard, French literature (in the form of La Fontaine, the well-known seventeenth-century author of animal fables), and Dijon terroir for consumers, particularly children.

young readers, in turn, were encouraged through the taste of the wines to appropriate the authors' essence (with perhaps a bit of their genius), combining themes of pleasure, literature, and geographical space in a discourse framing the uniqueness and individuality of France's terroirs and its people.

The preceding pages have demonstrated that from the Renaissance on, individuals in France discovered, essentialized, and developed a national and regional existence in relation to terroir and the local geographical features of the country. The following pages explore two reflections about what has preceded. First, they contend that the modern AOC system for food was formalized *after* terroir became inscribed as a method for understanding people, language, and literature. Second, they assert that more than just creating identity and expectations in food and people, terroir ultimately became a way of *living* the nation. Instead of culinary tourism aimed at eating and discovering foreign lands, the twentieth-century culmination of terroir in France became a sort of food-based "staycation," wherein the French experienced the diversity of their people and lands through regional food specialties.[3]

This culinary self-discovery recalls Guy Debord's concept of "pyschogeography," first presented in his 1955 *Introduction to a Critique of Urban Geography*. Debord explains that along with understanding the economic structures of society as shaped by objective nature, soil, and climate, one could plumb the depths of psychogeography, a notion which "sets for itself the study of the precise laws and special effects of the geographical environment, whether consciously organized or not, on the emotions and behavior of individuals."[4] As the term was used more frequently, its definition broadened, and it began to describe how people appeal to geographical constructions to experience emotions and memories, and how they mentally reify their identities through interactions with the landscape. In terms of terroir, instead of mapping the characteristics of the land outward toward expectations about flavor, the psychogeographic notion takes the process inward, using the taste of the culinary product to experience the land, "traveling" through food mentally to another place and perhaps, as with the Proustian madeleine, to another time. As was the case throughout the evolution of terroir, in many ways the modern phenomenon occurred in the realm of language before being formalized in that of food.

THE CONSUMPTION OF FRENCH
REGIONAL AUTHORS

In 1903, the then-prominent author and literary critic Remy de Gourmont published an article called "Intellectual Map of France" in which he proposed using climate and geology in identifying France's writers. He both drew on and outstripped premodern attempts at understanding literature through earthly origins, listing the kinds of genius by types of soil in a depiction that was equally if not more developed than anything that could be found in food and wine texts at the time.

De Gourmont describes how he would methodically categorize literary genius as a result of the soils and minerals the authors were raised upon. He gives his work an air of authority by tapping into a scientific terminology of geographical features and geological texts to speak about literature, bolstering it rhetorically with an example of how great soil produces great wine: "I would like such a map to be geologic and climatic as well as ethnographic: men are a product of the soil. The chalk of Artois cannot produce the same character as do the Paleozoic rocks of Brittany or the Jurassic terrain of Burgundy. Poets seem to be born abundantly in the Paleozoic terrains [. . .]. One would note as well the relationship between the kind of superior minds of a province and what they customarily drink. Wine seems very propitious in the formation of genius, evinced by rich Burgundy."[5] De Gourmont assimilates literature, cuisine, and science in a reflection that compares human beings directly to plants, and in which the literary aptitude of writers is correlated with the wines they drink. Both wines and intellects are determined by the soil, with those of Burgundy towering above the others.

Although he goes on to explain that he will not compose the entire intellectual map of France himself because the country's regions are just too varied and diverse to produce an easily chartable set of ethnotypes, de Gourmont does concede that it is possible to draw some primary conclusions supporting the assertion that writers, and people in general, derive their intelligence, emotions, and behavior from the soil they come from:

> One would [...] be tempted to attribute to primary terrain a special productivity in nonmusical, cerebral poets such as Chateaubriand and Renan: Brittany and the western tip of Normandy are composed of primary rocks. One of the most fecund terrains in men of high intellectualism would be the Jurassic: it is found in Burgundy and in part of the Lorraine. Tertiary terrain, which covers northern Normandy and a large part of the southwest, also seems apt to produce beautiful human work. Cretaceous soil produces mystical people, either in poetry, religion, or politics. Finally, volcanic terrain represents sterility, a sterility tempered by some flowerings: Pascal . . .[6]

The quote reveals how thematically wedded the discourse of terroir was to anthropological conceptions of human beings and to attempts in the early twentieth century to frame the French nation according to diversity of place. Five years before the first laws regulating the authenticity of agricultural regions and three decades before the INAO would create the AOC system in an attempt to regulate and classify different wines and foods, literary critics were already elaborating a set of expectations in terms of authors and their terroirs.

De Gourmont's idea gained traction not only in France, but also in French Canada, where a genre of literary regionalism and a series of novels glorifying rural customs, both dating back to the nineteenth century, became known as the *"littérature du terroir"* during the first years of the twentieth century (de Gourmont is one of the first individuals on record to employ the term).[7] Back in France, one of de Gourmont's more enthusiastic readers, Adolphe van Bever, took the idea even further, creating a multivolume anthology in 1909 called the *Poètes du terroir*.[8] The three tomes compiled a collection of poems of France's regions in alphabetical order (Berry, Bretagne, Champagne, Lorraine, Roussillon, etc.) in a chronology ranging from the sixteenth through the nineteenth century, most of them from relatively unknown authors. Van Bever argued that grouping by "terroir" was more important than chronology, since authors from different times but the same place were more alike than contemporaneous authors from different terroirs. Van Bever explicitly linked the influence of the terroir to poetic production, and the diversity of the poetic production to an idea of French national identity.

Van Bever's nationalist sentiments also brought to the fore a tension between Paris and the provinces that, as the above pages have shown, dates to the seventeenth century. In the first pages of *Poètes du terroir,* he revises the hierarchy to put the provinces on top: "Provincial supremacy hardly arose just yesterday, nor did we only then start thinking that this little homeland, terroir if you will, was the subsoil that unremittingly allowed the most beautiful flora of French genius to germinate, grow, and bloom."[9] Glorifying the provinces and using a plant metaphor to describe human beings, van Bever asserts that the influence of the soil and the countryside is personalized in France's great writers.[10] There is such a special relationship between soil and literary production, van Bever continues, that it is difficult for readers who do not share a terroir with a given poet to grasp the full message of the poems: one must be from a terroir or have become acquainted with it in order to understand it—and the literature it produces—easily.

As far as the skeptics, van Bever takes their criticism of the supposedly parochial nature of such works to task: "Will people say that those works of a clearly regional character are inferior because they occlude the breadth of our vision, and are incomprehensible to the noninitiated concerning the terroir they exalt? Does that mean that one must condemn a production for what it offers that is original and because it does not meet the demands of certain people?"[11] In a formulation that would be construed in the twenty-first century as an argument against uniformity and globalization, van Bever sets out to glorify the nuanced diversity of the zones of French national production, claiming that a linguistic monoculture leads to a national cultural poverty. In a sentiment recalling the Charles de Gaulle quote about the difficulty of governing a country that makes 246 types of cheese, van Bever constructs the value of the French nation according to variety and difference. The pleasure and challenges occasioned by the regional disparity one would encounter while reading regionally diverse authors are a part of savoring and comprehending the country's diverse cultural fabric.

In fact, in a movement diametrically opposed to the sort of uniformity in language that characterized the seventeenth-century Académie française, with its derision for regional speech, van Bever laments that France has lost in recent years many of the "three thousand patois and dialects" that "symbolized the power of the terroir."[12] He explains that although at one time practically each commune in France had its own dialect, this number had been greatly reduced through the confluence of several "negative" factors, including the standardization of primary school teaching, the centralization of administrative powers, and the multiplication of the means of communication, which limited diversity and favored uniformity. By reversing the seventeenth-century take on terroir, and offering pleasure in discovering the provinces through poetry, van Bever provides a compelling testimony that attitudes toward terroir have remained ambivalent over the centuries.

De Gourmont and van Bever thus exposed the influence of the land on language, proposing it both as a metric for categorizing literature and as a set of conceptual blocks with which to build the idea of the nation at the beginning of the twentieth century. Yet, although van Bever recommended savoring the land and nation through regional poetic writing, he was far from the strongest voice advocating for the psychogeographic experience. Colette constructed an especially intimate relationship between language, terroir, and wine, using the latter to transform the land into an experiential mode of existence. In 1932, three years before the inception of the INAO, Colette wrote that "the vine and wine are great mysteries. It is the only one among vegetables to convey to us the veritable flavor of the earth. How faithful is the translation! By way of the grapes, its smells express the secrets of the soil. The silex, through the vine, lets us know that it is living, fusible, nourishing. Ungrateful chalk cries tears of gold in wine."[13] Colette does not look to the geographical constitution of the origin to understand the wine, but rather advocates sampling the wine in order to "translate" the earth's mysteries and derive a cerebral and affective understanding of the ground. Employing the same human-plant metaphor that occurred as early as the sixteenth century in Montaigne, Colette likens plants to human beings, explaining that grapevines provide "translations of the earth" and cry "tears of gold."[14]

Marguerite Yourcenar further solidified the identity between humans, plants, and terroir, while perfectly representing the tendency toward sensorial transport in food and literature. Once again, the drinker no longer assesses the wine according to its terroir but rather accesses the hermetic world of terroir through the beverage. A passage from her novel *Mémoires d'Hadrien* (1951) in which the emperor Hadrian reflects on earthly pains and pleasures depicts Greek Samos wine as an initiator to the secrets of the earth: "Wine lets us in on the volcanic mysteries of the soil, on its hidden mineral richness: a glass of Samos wine drunk at noon in the sun, or on the contrary imbibed during a winter night in a state of fatigue which allows one immediately to feel in the depths of the diaphragm its warm flow, its unmistakable burning dispersion through the arteries, is an almost sacred sensation, sometimes too strong for the human head."[15] The discourse offers a sensual discovery presented as a personal, yet universal experience, reposing on the delivery of "sacred" mysteries that enter the intimate confines of the body. This literary account, like that of Colette, blends a description of humans and wine. Yet, here, instead of personifying the plants, human beings are virtually "plantified" through an initiation by the vine. The wine's warm-blooded vital force, containing the sun's energy and the mysteries of the soil, physically flows through the arteries like sap. Nature is both exalted and physically consumed in an experience that is sometimes too intense "for the human head."

LIVING THE LAND THROUGH SCIENTIFIC LITERATURE

This psychological partaking of regional identity and terroir was not only literary, but also scientific, in large part due to the efforts of Paul Vidal de la Blache, popularly known today as the father of the French school of geography. He founded the influential journal *Annales de géographie* in 1893, and had a wide following among scientists and intellectuals by the end of World War I.[16] His innovation was to link intimately the definition and scope of geography with human culture, asserting that one cannot understand a society's behavior without taking into account the geography of the land, and that one cannot appreciate the land without understanding the culture of a people.[17] In 1903, the same year that de Gourmont released his musings about literature in the "Carte intellectuelle de France," Vidal de la Blache published his landmark *Tableau de la géographie de la France,* a work that contemporary food scholars define as a key moment in terroir's modern genesis.[18]

Although, like early discourses on medical humors, Vidal de la Blache's methodology was built on a set of essentialist theories explaining human comportment according to landscape, the author explained the determinant power of the land in terms of political, social, and economic factors, providing a key to *how* people are determined by places. Vidal de la Blache's conviction was that the landscape conveyed Frenchness to its citizens, and that notion spread to writers and other intellectuals to become the province of popular opinion, and even a part of early twentieth-century schoolroom teaching.[19] More importantly, by instilling regional pride in foods and encouraging intimate relationships between people and agricultural products, Vidal de la Blache helped set the tenor for the discussions about creating agricultural appellations that would follow in the first decades of the twentieth century.

Once again, popular beliefs about the geographic influences of food on plants were extended to account for human behavior, but there was more at work than sober predictions of character based on landscape: Vidal de la Blache instilled a romantic psychogeographic tone in what was otherwise presented as a scientific text. The first pages of the *Tableau* lyrically explain that a country's physical history is in synch with the life of the individual: each person is "imprinted with the local saps and essence of the earth where he lives."[20] Speaking about variations of calcareous soil in the Burgundian landscape, Vidal de la Blache animates the earth with the same vibrancy that the *Théâtre d'agriculture* had three hundred years earlier, teasing out of a rock a description that borders on prose poetry: "It is the valleys that mark this calcareous region as clearly Burgundian. Although dry, these rocks impregnated by organic substances nevertheless possess marvelous properties of life. One can see a bushy thicket growing from the smallest of crags in the steep slopes; the loose stones set in banks by the fieldworkers nestle under a fine, crazy vegetation of lianas and thorns; between these rocks ripen the best wines. The nutritive substances of this terroir, concentrated, it is true, in a narrow space, communicate to plants a savory vigor, which is passed on to animals and to people."[21] Like de Gourmont, Vidal de la Blache equates the quality of humans to that of fine Burgundy wine. More importantly, his prose transforms geography into an animated, almost allegorical character through a series of oxymoronic counterpropositions. The calcareous soil is dry, hard, and dusty, but also teams with "organic substances" that are "ripening," "concentrated," "vigorous," and "savory." The austere, biblical image of parched land is imbued with sexual energy ("impregnated by organic substances"), enlivened by the personified thorns, and redeemed from otherwise bleak bareness by "crazy" lianas. In other words, the man commonly known as the "father of modern geography" describes the terroir of Burgundy with psychogeography bubbling forth. Within the romanticism of the prose, the reader discovers the landscape, and is mentally transported to Burgundy through the colorful richness of the text.

Psychogeographics infiltrated not only literary and scientific texts, but also twentieth-century cookbooks. Pre- and post-Revolutionary works such as *L'Histoire privée des français* by Le Grand d'Aussy and the *carte gastronomique* of Gassicourt already contained increasing culinary nationalism. But there was a real proliferation of the genre between 1903, when de Gourmont and Vidal de la Blache published their terroir-centric characterizations of France, and 1930. During this time, France put theory to practice and increasingly learned to experience its idea of nationhood through direct, hands-on experience with regional wines and dishes.[22]

The 1913 publication of *Les Bons Plats de France: Cuisine régionale,* written by Marthe Allard Daudet and published under the pseudonym "Pampille," was as much motivated by defining nationhood as by sharing regional recipes. As culinary historian and sociologist Priscilla Ferguson puts it, Pampille "aims at nothing less than defining France through its cuisine. That culinary country is not to be found in the extravagant creations of celebrated (male) chefs in fancy modern restaurants but rather in the unpretentious, familiar dishes made every day in ordinary kitchens by ordinary cooks. The building blocks of this culinary country, she shows us, are the dishes from the provinces, none of them creations of any individual, all of them products of the land itself."[23] The person cooking thus brings to life through dishes a piece of regional France that is experienced and enjoyed at each meal. Along with the nationalistic tone of the writing, defining country outward by its regional components, there was a clear psychogeographic appeal. Pampille implores her readers to discover the land and the regions (in person, if possible), writing that every grain of salt for the pot-au-feu recipe "contains an entire landscape."

More importantly, the sort of culinary tourism that Pampille promotes was taken up in earnest in the 1920s by Maurice Edmond Sailland (better known as "Curnonsky") and Marcel Rouff in their authoritative twenty-four-volume series *La France gastronomique,* published from 1921 to 1928. This series promoted French regional food as a part of national identity: "The marvelous diversity of our provinces [. . .] is found in regional dishes."[24] The theory of such works was put into practice with the rise of national tourism facilitated by the invention of the automobile and subsequent touring clubs and tourist guides, such as the famous *Guide rouge* of Michelin, directing the traveler to worthy culinary destinations. These guides encouraged French citizens to visit their regional neighbors, discovering the extent to which variety in the national cuisine could be the spice of their vacations and leisure life.[25]

Such modern versions of French terroir can help us to decipher how a segment of the population elected to frame itself and the country in the twentieth century, but they came about only after a long, varied evolution. From the culinary conception of nation in Rabelais to Du Bos's theories on painting and aesthetics, concerns about identity have intermingled with musings on food. From the mix of science and literature in the first manual on wine written in the French language by Jacques Gohory to the Académie française's obsession with impure language, sources have assimilated taste, place, and national character. Although buried in the past, these sources are still much a part of the present. Indeed, the premodern origins of terroir are just below the surface in the contemporary culture of food and wine. They issue forth daily as individuals continue to associate taste, identity, and place at the French table.

NOTES

INTRODUCTION

1. Mignon 1962, 57.

2. *Newsweek,* Oct. 1, 1962, p. 24.

3. *Dictionnaire de l'Académie française* 1694.

4. See Guy 2007, 118–58, for a description of the historical context leading to the establishment of these laws in the Champagne region of France. Guy's account provides a paradigmatic model applicable to agricultural regions outside Champagne as well.

5. Flavor expectations are important outside the realm of terroir as well. For the correlation between the expectations of a particular food's flavor and the eater's judgment of its quality, see Spence and Piqueras-Fiszman 2014, 10, as well as Lee, Frederick, and Ariely 2006.

6. The best translations in Italian are *suolo, terreno,* and *territorio.* Spanish offers *tierra, terreno, terruño,* and *comarca. Terroir's* closest translation in German, along with *Erdboden, Boden,* and *Ackerland,* is *Bodenständigkeit,* which signifies "rootedness" and is rather broad in its application outside the culinary world. See Vaudour 2002, 119–20.

7. Lewis and Short 1879, s.v. "territorium."

8. For more on farming in antiquity, see White 1970.

9. On the agricultural history in France, see Frémont 1997. For wine, see Dion 1959.

10. On the Cistercians, see Lukacs 2012, 70–75. See also Verdon 2002, especially 148–52 on the Andeli poem.

11. Quellier 2012, 143.

12. See Pinkard 2008, Pitte 1991, and Flandrin and Montanari 2000.

13. See Vaudour 2002, Wilson 1998, Robinson 2006, Robinson and Johnson 2013, and Dougherty 2012. For a broad historical account of terroir with an excellent bibliography, see Unwin 2012. For a cultural account of terroir, in addition to Trubek 2008, see Assouly 2004. Nossiter's 2009 account of terroir and wine is more

lyrical. For wine and terroir in a historical context, see Dion 1959. Finally, for an excellent historical account of wine's place in France's cultural, philosophical, and literary imagination from the Middle Ages to the present, including an extensive recent bibliography, see Argod-Dutard, Charvet, and Lavaud 2007.

14. Bourdieu 1984, 374–96.

15. Bruno Latour's *The Pasteurization of France* (1984) 1993 demonstrates the interconnectedness of what are often construed to be isolated systems of thought and practices inside and outside the world of science. In several respects this book seeks to bring to the fore a similar dynamic in terms of terroir and agriculture.

CHAPTER ONE

1. The literary opus of Rabelais exists in five volumes originally published from 1532 to 1564. I will use the English translation of Donald Frame in Rabelais 1999 unless otherwise noted. For the French version of Rabelais, I have used the critical edition of Jean Céard, Gérard Defaux, and Michel Simonin (Rabelais 1994a). Both the French and the English texts of Rabelais combine the five books of the series into one volume. The individual books appear in narrative order: *Gargantua, Pantagruel, Tiers livre, Quart livre,* and *Cinquième livre.* Other translations throughout this book are my own unless otherwise noted.

2. I will largely evoke the second and fifth volumes of Rabelais's work in this chapter, but other volumes, notably the fourth, are also important in identity- and food-related questions. For a historical account of French gastronomic mores, a discussion of Rabelaisian eating ethics, and a history of regional cuisine, see Pitte 1991; on food and table culture in the Renaissance, see also Jeanneret 1991. For an account of the importance of food in Rabelais's *Quart livre,* see Tomasik 2010 and Albala and Imhof 2004. For a comprehensive account of food in Renaissance Europe (without emphasis on Rabelais), see Albala 2002; see also Wheaton 1983, Mennell 1996, Montanari 1995, Flandrin and Montanari 2000. On the role of drinking in Rabelais, see Rigolot 1995; Renner 2007; Mabilleau, Cloué, and Viel 2002; Jeanneret 1983; Viel 2004a, 299–301; Viel 2001; Desrosier-Bonin 1992, 53–107; Demerson 2001; Screech 1980. For bacchic myth in Rabelais and religious satire, see Weinberg 1972, 45–92. See also Demerson 1972, 229–30.

3. Rabelais 1999, *Gargantua,* 12. My translation of a portion of second sentence (untranslated by Frame). Rabelais conflates human beings, territory, and food throughout his works. See for example Kinser's 1990 account of the significance of the sausage people in Rabelais's *Quart livre.*

4. This observation owes in part to Francis "Pim" Higginson. See Higginson 2001, 171. See also Tomasik 2010, esp. 29–32, 39–41. On p. 40, Tomasik quotes Pierre Belon to demonstrate that the richness of foods doubles as a demonstration of the richness of the French language, which is capable of providing a correspondingly extensive taxonomy. For the concept of how food and meals are used to build community culture and identity in Rabelais, see Chatelet 1977, 55–92.

5. See Rabelais 1999, *Pantagruel*, 311.

6. See Corriente 2008, 313.

7. See Rabelais 1999, *Gargantua*, prologue and chapter 5.

8. Rabelais 1999, *Gargantua*, 50.

9. Rabelais 1999, *Gargantua*, 36.

10. Rabelais 1823, I: 265, n32.

11. The conference was presented by Alain Lecomte, director of the Musée Rabelais, on June 27, 2014. It was entitled *Conférence sur l'empreinte de Rabelais dans le Chinonais*.

12. "Rabelais, in the sixteenth century, made no mistake in writing about 'this good Breton wine that does not grow in Brittany, but in the good countryside of Véron.'" Quoted from the Maison des Vins et du Tourisme du Véron, "Le terroir et les vins de Chinon," accessed March 5, 2013, www.lamaisondesvinsduveron.com /p12,le-terroir-et-les-vins-de-chinon.

13. See Plato's *Symposium*, 215a and 216d.

14. Rabelais 1999, *Gargantua*, 3. I have substituted "drinkers" for "topers" in the translation.

15. For some of the banquet's more "sober" aspects and their rhetorical importance in Rabelais, see Renner 2007. On the concept of the symposium as a historical Greco-Roman institution in Rabelais, see Jeanneret 1987, 141–50.

16. There is doubt concerning the authorship of the fifth volume, although Mireille Cuchon in her introduction to Rabelais 1994b, xvi–xvii, argues that Rabelais is indeed the author. Others have continued to argue against the volume's authenticity. For a relatively recent account of the debates, see Cooper 2001. Its authenticity is of little importance in this analysis, since whoever the author, the textual content and its popularity demonstrate how terroir and wine culture appeared in the context of the sixteenth century.

17. See for example Agricola 1546, on which see the editor's note in Rabelais 1994a, *Cinquième livre*, ch. 33, 1468, n1: "We see beginning in the sixteenth century a vogue for literature dealing with the underground and the creatures that are meant to populate it: see for example the treatise of Georges Agricola, *De ortu causis subterranearum*."

18. My translation of the first sentence (untranslated by Frame); Rabelais 1999, *Cinquième livre*, 685.

19. Rabelais 1999, *Cinquième livre*, 709.

20. The choice of Falernian wine here gets right to an ambivalence toward origin that pervades Rabelais. Wine from Falerno was once heralded as ancient Rome's finest, but in later times the falsification of Falernian wines was notoriously widespread. To say one was serving a "Falernian" wine was akin to saying that one would serve a rotgut substitute. For more on food and wine in antiquity, see McGovern, Flemming, and Katz 2004; Dalby 2003; and Davidson 1997.

21. Rabelais 1999, *Cinquième livre*, 710.

22. Rabelais 1999, *Cinquième livre*, 587. As M. A. Screech concurs, Bacchus, at least in this iteration, "is no mad god of drunken, earth-bound squalor; he symbolizes

that spiritually liberating power of joyful wine, which classical and Christian man drank as a conscious act of wise and ennobling humanity, encouraging eloquence and the quest of truth." Screech 1979, 454–55.

23. See Mahé 1988, 305, on the unifying role of Bacchus in the Renaissance.

24. The tradition of inspiration by means of wine was passed on to the poets of the Pléiade through Horace. In the first lines of Horace's Epistle 1.19, one finds the Renaissance—and early modern—leitmotif that no poem can endure or please people if it is written by a water-drinker. Horace credits the observation to Cratinus. For Bacchus and poetic inspiration in the Pléiade, see Cave 2009, 64–68.

25. "Hymne de Bacchus," in Ronsard 1993, 2:601, vv. 277–81.

26. For an account of the Renaissance reception of Anacreon, see O'Brien 1995.

27. On the Epicurean theme of *carpe diem* in the Pléiade, and its two central sources, see Azibert 1972. See Horace, *Odes,* Book I, Ode 11, "To Leuconoe," for the theme's origin.

28. Ode 16, "Le Cinquième Livre des odes," in Ronsard 1993, 1:900–901.

29. See, notably, Ronsard 1993, "Préface sur la Franciade touchant le poëme héroïque," 1:1187. For a series of essays on Virgil's influence in Renaissance France, see Usher and Fernbach 2012.

30. See Gale 2000, x. See also Putnam 1979, and the discussion of Slavitt 1990, xiv–xxiv.

31. Virgil's fourth-century CE commentator, the grammarian Maurus Servius Honoratus, was among the early voices to speak of the work's complexity and hidden underlying meanings. Servius's commentaries were well known by readers of Virgil in the French Renaissance.

32. Virgil 1999, 2:1–8.

33. Pickard-Cambridge (1953) 1968.

34. Virgil 1999, 2:53.

35. Peletier du Mans (1555) 1996, 231, lines 7–16. Cf. "Gayeté III," in Ronsard 1993, 1:532–34. In Peletier du Mans 1555 (1996), 230–31, n3, editor Jean-Charles Monferran comments on the popularity of depictions of the grape harvest in Renaissance poetry, including its occurrences in Des Périers, Belleau, and Baïf.

36. See Virgil 1999, 2:298–314. The term "naturalized mythology" belongs to both Henri Chamard and Natalie Mahé. Chamard 1939, 330, notes that Ronsard's Horacian odes contain a specifically French component, springing from nationalist inspirations: "This time, in spite of Horace, we are fully in terroir; the vision of the landscapes and scenes is so direct that it is hard to image that the poet had recourse to foreign sources."

37. "La Deffence et Illustration," in du Bellay 2003, 1:76, bk. 2, ch. 12, lines 41–44, 45–48, 57–59. The credit for this observation belongs to Storer 1923, 8. Cf. Virgil 1999, 2:136–76.

38. See Virgil 1999, 2:150–51.

39. See "Deffence," in du Bellay 2003, 1:23, bk. 1, ch. 4, lines 40–47, for the importance of human labor in cultivating the natural potential of language. The passage consistently applies an agricultural model and terms to language.

40. "Deffence" in du Bellay 2003, 1:23, bk. 1, ch. 4, lines 40–47.

41. Du Bellay 2003, 1:23–24.

42. For a slightly divergent, but not wholly irreconcilable view, see Hampton 2001, 155–69. Ronsard's explanation of the interaction between nature and the poet's art *(techne)* is also telling. In the 1550 preface to his odes, Ronsard speaks of the abundance and diversity that a poet ought to instill in his work if he is to be successful, specifying however that the final product must always resemble nature. See Ronsard 1993, 2:973. For questions of diversity and abundance in Ronsard, see Cave 1973, 178. See also Duport 2002, 301–3.

43. "Gayeté III," in Ronsard 1993, 1:532, vv. 9–16. As a separate remark, it is noteworthy that the wines of Brie supplied the Parisian population and, by the seventeenth century, more generally the French cabaret culture. They were generally considered of low quality at this point. The evolution of their status in the sixteenth century is not clear, since Serres (1600) 2001, 141, includes the wines of Brie in the same echelon of quality as the wines of Champagne and Burgundy.

44. Virgil, *Georgics* 3.2: *"Pastor ab Amphryso."* Noted in Chamard 1939, 289.

45. "A sa muse," Ode 36, Ronsard 1993, 1:926.

46. Peletier du Mans 2005, lines 309–10. Cf. Lucretius 2007, book 5, lines 1041–56.

47. *Devis sur la vigne, vin et vendanges,* Gohory 1549. The merging of the literary and the culinary in a "shared sense of culinary consciousness" occurs even more completely in other examples just a few years later, as Tomasik 2010, 41, points out, citing Belon 1555, who makes a direct reference to Rabelais to attest to the variety of dishes found in France. On Gohory, see Gorris-Camos 2008.

48. Argod-Dutard, Charvet, and Lavaud 2007, 351.

49. Gohory, 1549, n.p. See fifth page of ms, beginning with preface *"au lecteur,"* for Hesiod, twenty-first page for mention of Horace. Virgil is cited several times, and the *Georgics* specifically on the thirty-fifth page.

50. Gohory 1549, n.p., forty-first and forty-second pages, beginning with preface *"au lecteur."*

51. For more on terminology and discussion as to whether or not Gohory *does* present a wine-specific, quasi-modern vocabulary, see Henry 2007, 47–60.

52. See Daniel Pickering Walker (1958) 2000, 97. Du Bellay invokes Gohory directly in sonnet 72 of *Les Regrets.*

53. Gohory 1549, n.p., forty-ninth to fifty-first pages, beginning with preface *"au lecteur."*

54. "From this the wine sometimes smells of the terroir, manure, unpleasantly of the barrel, or cabbages that some plant in the area." Gohory 1549, n.p., fifteenth page, beginning with preface *"au lecteur."*

55. Estienne 1554. Estienne also published *La Guide des chemins de France* in 1552, an early version of what we know today as a tourist guidebook, which indicated in passing several local and regional alimentary productions and specialties. More importantly, in 1537 he published a work called *Vinetum,* a short topical guide that

served primarily to give the equivalent in French of Latin vine- and wine-related terms from Columella, Varro, Virgil, and Pliny, but also addressed techniques of pruning, grape varietals, and assessments of France's wine-producing regions (especially the ones in close proximity to Paris). The guide was never translated into French. For more, see Argod-Dutard, Charvet, and Lavaud 2007, 343–50.

56. Estienne and Liébault 1586, 340.

57. Estienne and Liébault 1586, 351.

58. Bruyérin-Champier (1560) 1998, translated as *L'Alimentation de tous les peuples et de tous les temps jusqu'au XVIe siècle.*

59. For more on the variety of the eating habits in regional France, where acknowledgments by dieticians, agronomists, naturalists, and authors of travel literature upheld that foods of different qualities were produced in different regions, see Hyman and Flandrin 1986.

60. Bruyérin-Champier (1560) 1998, 523.

61. Bruyérin-Champier (1560) 1998, 522.

62. Le Paulmier 1589.

63. "You can take pleasure at moments [in the reading of the work] as a distraction from the care that other more serious matters demand of you." Le Paulmier 1589, preface.

64. See Le Paulmier 1589, 25.

65. Le Paulmier 1589, 49. Le Paulmier goes on to indicate which terroirs are best (le Costentin), which give the strongest ciders (Auge), and which are likely to negatively mark the cider (Pays de Caux) because of the marl in the soil.

66. Le Paulmier 1589, 47, 78.

CHAPTER TWO

1. For a general account of Montaigne's relationship with nature, see Hoffman 2006. See also Bellenger 1978; Duval 1983; Micha 1964, 121–33; and Céard 1977. On the subject of Montaigne and food and wine, which I will treat indirectly in this chapter, see Coulon 2009, Bots 2004, De Souza Filho 2004, and O'Brien 2000. Although Montaigne does not speak specifically of terroir in relation to food, food comes up often in his work as a metaphor for language. See, for example, "On the Vanity of Words," vol. I, ch. 51, which incorporates artifice at the table with artifice in speech. Montaigne citations from here forward will specify the volume with a roman numeral followed by the chapter and page where necessary.

2. Montaigne 1991, "Of Smells," I, ch. 55. Unless otherwise noted, all of the English translations of Montaigne to follow are from this volume.

3. Montaigne 1991, I, ch. 55, 353.

4. "A woman smells nice when she smells of nothing, just as we say that the best perfume for her actions is for her to be quiet and discreet. And when people give off nice odours which are not their own we may rightly suspect them, and conclude that they use them to smother some natural stench." Montaigne 1991, I, ch. 55, 352.

5. Screech uses *soil* instead of *terroir,* but I will retain *terroir* from the French text. Montaigne, I, ch. 55, 353.

6. This stereotype remained intact for hundreds of years. The Emile Littré dictionary of 1872 defines *scythe* as the "name for people roaming the north of Europe and of Asia. Fig. Barbarian, rude man." Littré 1872.

7. In addition to the references on "nature" in Montaigne listed above in note 1, see Christodoulou 1979; Schneider 1996.

8. "To the Reader," Montaigne 1991, lxiii. "Au lecteur," Montaigne 1965, 3.

9. Montaigne 1991, I, ch. 31, "Des Cannibales," 231. "Fresh from the gods" *("Viri a diis recentes")* is from Seneca, Epistle 90. "Taught by nature" *("Hos natura modos primum dedit")* is from Virgil, *Georgics,* 2.208.

10. Montaigne 1991, I, ch. 31, 231.

11. For the corresponding aesthetics of purity and the natural in the context of food in Renaissance France, see the last chapter of Freedman 2008.

12. Montaigne 1991, I, ch. 31, 231–32. It is worth noting evidence that Bruyérin-Champier, referenced in the previous chapter, held the opposite view. He claims that uncultivated wine is never as good as the cultivated, all the while acknowledging that there is a "crowd of mad people who are wrong to maintain that negligence gives to wines a more noble taste and a more rich savor." Bruyérin-Champier (1560) 1998, 524.

13. Montaigne 1991, II, ch. 12, "An Apology for Raymond Sebond," 648. Climate theory was a political and medical construct in antiquity, and the fifth-century BCE Greek historian Herodotus evokes environmental determinism throughout his *Histories;* see for example 9.122. It was also developed in places ranging from Plato's *Laws* to Aristotle's *Politics.* Other important influences include Cicero, Vitruvius (notably in book 6 of his treatise on architecture), and Publius Flavius Vegetius, a fourth-century CE military theoretician. Passages reflecting Cicero's position on environmental determinism appear throughout his opus; see notably *De lege agraria,* 295.5, where Cicero argues that disposition is conditioned by environment rather than seed: "Men's characters are inserted in them not so much by origin and semen as by those things which nature itself endows to form our way of life whereby we are fed and live" *("Non ingenerantur hominibus mores tam a stripe generis ac seminis quam ex eis rebus quae ab ipsa natura nobis ad vitae consuetudinem suppeditantur, quibus alimur et vivimus");* quoted in Isaac 2004, 88. See also Vegetius, 1.1, 321; 1.2, 87; 3.10, 222.

14. See Lenoble 1969.

15. Montaigne 1991, II, ch. 12, "An Apology for Raymond Sebond," 648.

16. For Bodin's environmental determinism and its impact, see Lestrigant 1993, 255–75. A third influence in the tradition of French environmental determinism is Bernard Palissy. See Palissy (1580) 1844. Despite the preponderance of Bodin over Montaigne with respect to climatic determinism, the latter's remarks on the subject were taken up almost verbatim by Pierre Charron at the end of the century. See Charron 1601, bk. 1, ch. 38.

17. For Tacitus, see *Germania* (De Origine et situ Germanorum). For climatic determinism in Tacitus, see Krebs 2011, 159–60.

18. Bodin (1576) 1986, 667–68.

19. Hippocrates (1923) 2004, 23:133.

20. Bodin (1566) 1941, 334.

21. Bodin (1566) 1941, 335.

22. Bodin (1566) 1941, 335.

23. Bodin (1566) 1941, 335.

24. Bodin (1566) 1941, 344.

25. See Bodin (1576) 1986, bk. 5.

26. Bodin (1576) 1986, 52.

27. Vitruvius 1547, 8.3.

28. See for example the following passage from Bodin: "What's more, Vitruvius confirms more or less this opinion. In the northern countries, he says, nations produce tall populations, light skin, straight red hair, blue-green eyes, and hardy blood." Bodin (1566) 1941, 75. See Vitruvius 1547, 6.11–12.

29. Bodin (1576) 1986, bk. 5, ch. 1.

30. See Argod-Dutard, Charvet, and Lavaud 2007, 356.

31. The anecdote was reported by Joseph Scaliger. See de Serres 1873, preface by Paul Favre, ix. See also Vaschalde 1886, 84.

32. For example: ENSAAMA Ecole Nationale Supérieur d'Arts Appliqués et de Métiers d'Art Oliver de Serres; L'École Oliver de Serres de Roubaix; L'École Oliver de Serres-Carette, and so on.

33. De Serres was a Protestant. For the place of religion in sixteenth-century agricultural texts, see Duport 2002, for example p. 194: *"La Renaissance rend à l'activité agricole sa place première dans le projet divin."*

34. De Serres (1600) 2001, 274.

35. Despite this mostly pragmatic and non-aesthetic formulation for terroir, Florent Quellier, following Danièle Alexandre-Bidon, cites a passage from Olivier de Serres on the unpleasant taste that the earth can leave in water, an "inopportune terrestrial odor," to conclude that the taste of earth, appreciated in medieval times, was falling from favor. See Quellier 2007a, 79; Alexandre-Bidon 2005, 160–70; de Serres (1600) 2001, 1301. I would suggest that there is very limited evidence in de Serres to make this case conclusively.

36. De Serres notes this derision toward farming in the preface of *Le Théâtre:* "There are those who mock books on agriculture, referring us to the peasants who, they claim, are the only ones able to judge this discipline." De Serres (1600) 2001, 63.

37. De Serres (1600) 2001, 71.

38. De Serres (1600) 2001, 59.

39. De Serres (1600) 2001, 79–80.

40. The work's preface is not without an invocation of God, whom de Serres thanks for the infinite quantity and diversity of exquisite wares bestowed upon his children through the intermediary of Earth.

41. Boulaine and Moreau 2002, 37. See de Serres 2001, 89, for the exact quote. Italics belong to Boulaine and Moreau.

42. The personification owes a particular debt to Virgil's *Georgics* and, before that, to Lucretius. As Monica Gale specifies in her book on the Lucretian themes in the *Georgics,* for Virgil "several of the different soils have distinct 'personalities': in book two the rich soil is 'cheerful' (*laeta,* 184) while chalk is 'difficult' and 'grudging' (*difficiles, maligni,* 179), and salt or cold soils are qualified as 'wicked' (*malus,* 243, *sceleratum,* 256)." Gale 2000, 87. Gale goes on to explain in a footnote that although *laeta* ("fertile," "joyful") is common in agricultural contexts, in this series, because of an effect of "accumulation," it implies personification and personality.

43. De Serres derides mythological references as belonging to pagan ignorance: "Regarding the inventor of wine, we stop at the one marked by the scriptures, meaning Noah, leaving aside the imagination of pagans, whose ignorance has so led them astray that they have confusedly attributed this excellent beverage, some to Denys, son of Jupiter, named also Bacchus and Pater Liber for the freedom of the wine; others to Icarus, father of Erigonus, to Saturn, to Eumolpus, and to others that I let go with reason." De Serres 2001, 270.

44. De Serres 2001, 449, for the alfalfa reference; 884–85, for the reference to carnations.

CHAPTER THREE

1. For an account of the shift of power toward absolutism in the seventeenth century, see Bonney 1995; Bluche 1990. For a contrasting view of absolutism that depicts it as less "absolute," see Hurt 2002; Cosandey and Descimon 2002. For an article that lays out the opposition between the two theories regarding Louis XIV's absolutism and provides a complete bibliography, see Beik 2005.

2. Douglas (1966) 2002, x–xxi and 1–7, provides parameters and an extended definition of dirt, impurity, and contagion.

3. Nicot 1606. Other seventeenth-century sources attest to terroir as a term applying to municipal jurisdictions, in addition to the agricultural connotations stressed above in Nicot. See for example Frédéric Godefroy, *Dictionnaire de l'ancienne langue française et de tous ses dialectes du 9e au 15e siècle.*

4. Furetière (1690) 1978.

5. Furetière 1701.

6. Not all definitions were negative. Several exceptions to the term's predominantly negative usage help demonstrate the word's ambivalence. To give an example, the 1694 edition of the *Dictionnaire de l'Académie française* defines terroir negatively with reference to people but leaves the connotations with regard to wine neutral: "One says that wine smells of the terroir, that it has a taste of terroir, to say that there is a certain taste that comes from the quality of the terroir."

7. Fumaroli 1994, 648; for a more developed discussion see the entire chapter, "Le Parnasse de l'éloquence royale: L'Académie française sous Richelieu," 647–60.

8. Fumaroli 1994, 648.

9. Faret 1630.

10. Pellisson-Fontanier 1688, 17–18. For additional history of the Académie, see Guion 2012; Cerquiglini 2004; Delhez-Sarlet 1979. See also Shoemaker 2007, 193–96.

11. www.académie-française.fr/linstitution/les-missions.

12. Pellisson-Fontanier 1688 relates several anecdotes about the uneasiness that came with the *Académie*'s ambitious project of cleansing the French language. See, for example, pp. 39–40, where Pellison-Fontanier describes the popular classes (*le peuple*) and their suspicion of the hegemony enforced through language by the upper classes.

13. Estienne (1578) 1896, 27. For more on the concept, see Hampton 2001, 155.

14. In the first years of the seventeenth century, Guillaume du Vair wrote a treaty on eloquence remarking that the Scythes, trying to counterfeit Greek speech, exuded malice that smelled "nothing like Athenian terroir." Du Vair was not trying to convey that language should exude regional particularity. Rather, in its isolation, language should be untouched by the particularities of outside influences. Du Vair (1590) 1609, 119. For more on du Vair, see Fumaroli 1994, 498–519. For more on the Greeks and autochthony, see Blok 2009. See also Rosivach 1987.

15. Vaugelas 1647, n.p., preface.

16. Vaugelas 1647, n.p., preface.

17. Vaugelas 1647, n.p., preface.

18. Bellegarde (1697) 1712, 232.

19. Bellegarde (1697) 1712, 232. It should be noted that *goût* de *terroir* is the most common pejorative phrasing, while *goût* du *terroir* is usually more neutral, indicating the normative influence of earth on its produce. Both iterations are used in a negative way, however, during the seventeenth and eighteenth centuries, with *goût de terroir* being the most categorically negative.

20. Beauval 1688, 488.

21. Bouhours 1671, 78. Though *"couler de sa source"* is figurative language for "self-evident," I have elected to leave the literal sense in the translation as well, since it is part of the extended metaphor comparing water and speech.

22. See Giuliani 2008.

23. Muralt 1739, vol. 1, 7. Note that *"goût du terroir"* replaces *"goût de terroir"* here.

24. Perrault and Perrault 1721, 568.

25. Perrault and Perrault 1721, 568–69.

26. Elsewhere in their second volume, for example, the Perrault brothers nuance their use of "terroir." The word does not appear in a negative context, but instead identifies the heightened sense of smell and taste possessed by connoisseurs who know how "to discern the terroirs of all wines" or to indicate the area of the sea where a particular oyster has been harvested. This skill attested to the connoisseur's neutrality. He does not necessarily *like* the smell of terroir, but possesses acute senses that detect its imprint on the taste of food. Perrault and Perrault 1721, 541.

27. Buffier 1704, 177.

28. *Dictionnaire de l'Académie française* 1694. Jargon could also signify technical language, as it does today in both French and English.

29. Buffier 1704, 177–78.

30. Buffier 1704, 178.

31. For an excellent contextualization of Méré's place in the development of taste in the seventeenth century, see Moriarty 1988, 83–106.

32. "De l'éloquence et de l'entretien," in Méré 1701, 71.

33. Méré 1930, 114. Cf. "De l'éloquence et de l'entretien," in Méré 1701, 71–73.

34. On Renaissance authors, see Timothy Hampton, who writes that "what is important here is the way in which Estienne, like Aneau and many other writers on the topic, seeks to attach French to the soil of France, and to find 'Frenchness' in the relationship of language and land." Hampton 2001, 156.

35. Baillet 1685–86, 1:230.

36. For more on Baillet and the theory of climatic determinism, see Naves 1936.

37. Le Bovier de Fontenelle (1688) 1790, 281–82.

38. Le Bovier de Fontenelle (1688) 1790, 282.

39. Fontenelle's position on the "quarrel between the ancients and the moderns" is both complicated and nuanced. See Norman 2011, 40–47.

40. Saint-Évremond 1706, vol. 3, 55–64.

41. Saint-Évremond 1706, vol. 3, 56.

42. Saint-Évremond 1706, vol. 3, 62.

43. The same aesthetic in language is expressed seventy-five years later in François Ignace d'Espiard's *Esprit des nations,* where simple, noble language is pure and natural with no *"goût de terroir."* See Espiard 1753, 91.

44. Saint-Évremond 1852, 414.

45. "Discours de la conversation," in Méré 1692, vol. 1, 60. I have translated *"douceur"* with the word "blandness," though *douceur* in many contexts would mean sweetness. In the seventeenth century, however, it could also be used in opposition to spicy or piquant, or as a criticism to indicate that there was not enough salt. See the *Dictionnaire de l'Académie française* 1694.

46. Méré 1692, vol. 1, 60.

47. For a discussion on the use of artifice in cuisine in seventeenth- and eighteenth-century France, see Davis 2009.

48. L.S.R 1674, 1–2.

49. L.S.R 1674, 2.

CHAPTER FOUR

1. In fact, the qualifiers used to describe gardens were often the same as those applied to language and cuisine. For the example of language diversity, see Fumaroli 1994, 415. For gardens, see Mukerji 1997, 27. For diversity and food, see "Capturing the Variety of Nature," in Pinkard 2008, 60–64.

2. Garrigues 2001, 24, notes the metaphor.

3. See Lenoble 1969, a seminal work on the premodern French conception of nature. See also Thomas 1983.

4. De Serres (1600) 2001, 71.

5. De Serres (1600) 2001, 1157.

6. "Can he convert mountains into plains, and plains into mountains? He should thus console himself in God's providence, which distributed to each person that which he knew to be necessary." De Serres (1600) 2001, 62.

7. In addition to 2.109, see *Georgics* 1.50–61; Cato, *De Agri Cultura* 1; Varro, *Rerum Rusticarum* 1.6; Columella, *De Re Rustica* 1.4. For Virgil's discourse on limits and debt to Lucretius, see Gale 2000, 201.

8. Gale 2000, 71.

9. Mariage (1990) 1999, 49–50.

10. There are the four instances of the word in Mollet 1652, and it does not appear at all in Bonnefons 1651.

11. Preface to Boyceau 1638, book 2.

12. Two of the three books in Boyceau's treatise concentrate on beauty, order, and symmetry in the garden. See Mariage (1990) 1999, 65–68. For the cookbooks, see the priorities professed by Saint-Évremond in his letter to Olonne and by L. S. R., mentioned in the previous chapter and below.

13. Boyceau 1638, book 1, 2.

14. Mukerji 1997, 2; Garrigues 2001, 12–13; Baridon 2008, 4; Goldstein 2007, 24.

15. Elias 1983, 227.

16. Saint-Simon, *Mémoires.* Quoted in Elias 1983, 227.

17. See Garrigues 2001, 198.

18. For a good account of the expenses of the gardens of Versailles, see Garrigues 2001, ch. 6.

19. Baraton 2006, 182.

20. Scudéry and Lallemand (1669) 2002, 93.

21. For more on this, see Coffe and Baraton 2007, 148.

22. Mukerji 1997, 169.

23. This idea owes to Quellier 2007b.

24. Mukerji 1997, 64.

25. See Garrigues 2001, esp. 12.

26. For a period account of the fruits on Louis XIV's table, see Félibien 1674, 57–61.

27. Quintinie 1692, 1:63. Elsewhere when La Quintinie talks about wine, 1:296, terroir appears as more of a neutral descriptor, resembling more the matter-of-fact description proposed by Olivier de Serres than in this first passage, where it is decidedly negative. Such variations attest to the ambivalence of the term, which, although overridingly negative, was context dependent.

28. The negative connotations surrounding terroir would slowly began to evolve in the eighteenth century, but remained expressed in largely negative terms by agricultural authorities until the 1760s. See, for example, Alletz 1762, 457: "The qualities of a good wine are to be limpid, fine, dry, without a *goût de terroir,* and it must have power." After the 1760s, there is more sporadic use of *goût de terroir* as exclusively

negative, but it does persist. See, for example, Lenoir 1828, 128: "There are soils that exude, when they are wet, a disagreeable odor. The vines that grow there almost always produce wines infected by the *goût de terroir.*"

29. See Mukerji 1997, 266. Descartes's confidence in the overarching power of reason, for example, was widely criticized in that it did not attribute enough of a role to divine power. Criticism of Descartes took other pertinent forms as far as Versailles is concerned; La Quintinie, for example, was skeptical that Descartes's mechanical explanations could be relevant or correct in an application to the garden. See Baridon 2008, 113–17.

30. Though Descartes held that reason functioned unimpeded by climate, Descartes's biographer Adrien Baillet recounts that Descartes elected to leave France for a cooler country because he was, in part, concerned that the effects of the warmer climate would handicap his ability to reason. See Baillet 1693, 81.

31. Mukerji 1997, 266.

32. Gassendi's *Syntagma philosophicum,* which includes his treatise on Epicurus, was published posthumously in 1658. His work was known earlier by many learned scholars (Mersenne, Descartes, etc.). For more on Gassendi's reception, see Lennon 1993. It is worth noting that while Epicurus himself was less well known before Gassendi, Epicurean ideas were amply disseminated by Lucretius, who was widely read in France from circa 1550. See Fraisse 1962; Ford 2007.

33. François Bernier further enlarged the audience by making Gassendi's *Syntagma philosophicum* available in an abridged French version a generation after its initial publication. Bernier 1684b.

34. For agency, freedom and necessity in Gassendi, see Osler 1994 and Sarasohn 1996.

35. See Bernier 1684b, "De la saveur et de l'odeur," 163–80, for a description of how humans perceive taste and smell.

36. For smells, Bernier allows that perceptions are much more varied according to temperament in different people. Bernier 1684b, 177–78.

37. Bernier 1684a, 133.

38. Bernier 1684a, 133–34

39. Bernier 1684a, 138.

40. Flandrin 1986, 299.

41. See Ferguson 2004, 37, which picks up on the Cartesian influence as it existed in French cookbooks of the late eighteenth and nineteenth century in France: "The culinary writers' preoccupation with method also echoes what was long the totemic text of French culture, René Descartes's *Discours de la méthode.*" See also Hyman and Hyman 1996, which documents Cartesian buzzwords such as *méthode* and *règles* applied to culinary practices in the seventeenth century. They do not specify the exact origin of the following reference, which is most likely unknown or anonymous: "According to a contemporary (*of the cookbook author LSR*), with all of these novelties, the *Cuisinier français* 'won the glory [of having] given rules and a method' to an art that up until then did not have one." Hyman and Hyman 1996, 649. The word *méthode* appears twenty-three times in L. S. R.'s *L'Art de bien traiter.*

42. The remark belongs to Pinkard 2008, 61–62.

43. Massialot (1691) 1693, preface, n.p. Massialot allows that there are several paths to success in recipes and that everyone is free to "follow his method," diverging from what one might consider as a purely Cartesian ideology.

44. Menon 1753, ii.

45. See Davis 2009 and Davis 2012, chapter 1, for a compelling account of the use of techniques of disguise by chefs of this period in France.

46. Flandrin 1986, 299.

47. Massialot (1691) 1693, preface, n.p.

48. L.S.R. 1674.

49. Alquier (1670) 1728, 73–74.

CHAPTER FIVE

1. Saint-Évremond 1706, vol. 5, 16.

2. See Tallement des Réaux 1960, 412. The satire in question was purportedly burned.

3. De Serres (1600) 2001, 271; Le Paulmier 1589, 24; Estienne and Liébault (1578) 1637, 584, all speak of these wine-producing towns (especially Ay) as being among the best and associate them with royalty, proving that the choices of the Côteaux had previously been validated by earlier sources.

4. See Donneau de Visé (1665) 2013, 1–26, for Peter Shoemaker's historical contextualization. The moralist contemporary of Saint-Évremond, La Bruyère, evoked the Côteaux in his *Caractères* in the context of a social criticism; see La Bruyère (1688) 1995, "Des Grands," 352. See also Nicolas Boileau-Despréaux's third satire, "Le Repas ridicule," in Boileau-Despréaux (1665) 1966, vv. 112–16, 171.

5. Hope 1993, 10.

6. "And it is true, just as a good gourmet can quickly discern their origin, age, and other differences by means of the taste of wines, so can the person who knows cider point out by their taste all of the merits and imperfections, the age, the terroir, and other differences." Le Paulmier 1589, 49.

7. Donneau de Visé (1665) 2013, vv. 397–409.

8. Saint-Évremond 1707–14, II, "Lettre à M. le Comte d'Olonne," 118.

9. Saint-Évremond 1740, I, 32.

10. Dens 1981, 68.

11. Saint-Évremond 1966, I, 256–57.

12. Donneau de Visé (1665) 2013, 14.

13. One of the key French authors responsible for the new Paracelsan-inspired and chemistry-based approach to medical science was Nicolas Lémery. His *Cours de chimie, contenant la manière de faire les opérations qui sont en usage dans la médecine* . . . was published in 1675 and quickly translated into several languages. For a discussion on the evolution in medical knowledge and its reflection in seventeenth- and eighteenth-century cuisine, see Spary 2012, especially chapter 1, and Pinkard 2008,

64–71. For the ongoing influence of Galen in the perception of wine in early modern times, see Shapin 2012, esp. 60–63.

14. Framboisière 1669, 86.

15. See Flandrin 1982. La Framboisière was inspired in particular by Jean Liébault and Laurent Joubert, the first of whom he quotes almost verbatim. For a detailed discussion on wine-color preferences in Paris in the seventeenth and eighteenth century with respect to Champagne, see B. Musset 2008, 123–39.

16. Framboisière 1669, 85.

17. Framboisière 1669, 85.

18. Broekhuisen 1687.

19. Broekhuisen 1687, 372.

20. Broekhuisen 1687, 373.

21. Broekhuisen 1687, 373.

22. The reference occurs for the first time in the 1727 edition of the dictionary, edited by Basnage de Beauval and Brutel de la Rivière, and published by P. Huisson.

23. Lucretius 2007, bk. 2, vv. 38–40.

24. This physical account of taste and health, as opposed to a more chemical depiction based on salts and tartrates, demonstrates the uncertainty that reigned at the time in the medical world regarding how people actually tasted their food and derived nutriments from it. Curiously, and in a way that is very relevant to terroir, La Quintinie reflected at length on how plants derive nutriments from the soil, mocking the physical, mechanical model in vogue at the time, which Broekhuisen espouses here. See Baridon 2008, 113–17.

25. Bourdieu 1984,197.

26. Peter Shoemaker, introduction to Donneau de Visé (1665) 2013, 7.

27. Hope 1993, 11.

28. For an account of the literary tradition of bad taste in early modern France, see Tsien 2012.

29. See Corum 1998, ch. 3. See also Wood 2004.

30. Boileau-Despréaux (1665) 1966, "Satire III," vv. 89–93.

31. L.S.R explains: "It is not at all today this prodigious disgorgement of dishes, the abundance of spices and fricassees, the extraordinary mix of meats that constitutes good food, it is not these mixed pilings of diverse species, these mountains of roasts, these redoubled changing of flying plates, and desserts bizarrely served." L.S.R. (1674) 1995, 21.

32. Up until the nineteenth century, serving domestic rabbits as dinner fare was considered entirely bad form, especially if they had been fed on cabbage. See Marenco 1992, 73.

33. Boileau-Despréaux (1665) 1966, v. 119.

34. Boileau-Despréaux (1665) 1966, vv. 105–12. Curiously, numerous French agricultural and culinary dictionaries designate the tame "Cauchois" pigeon as tastier and more tender than the ringdove *("ramier")*.

35. Voltaire (1751) 1964, s.v. *"goût."*

36. Boileau-Despréaux (1665) 1966, lines 112–16.

37. Saint-Évremond 1999, 182.

38. *Sur nos comedies,* in Saint-Évremond 1966, 3:44.

39. Ibid., 45.

40. For a discussion on Saint-Évremond's complex relationship with the novel, see Lallemand 2005.

41. Saint-Évremond's thoughts on climatic determinism are nuanced elsewhere. See Moriarty 1988, esp. 110. See also Hope 1962, 61. Moriarty argues that Saint-Évremond renounced his views on climatic determinism in 1671 and offers the example of the "Lettre à Monsieur Le Maréchal de Créqui," in Saint-Évremond 1966, 4:127–28. I would argue that closer reading of this letter disproves this conclusion: Saint-Évremond merely argues that there are "polite" people in every country, not that climatic determinism does not exist.

42. The first thesis of note, by Daniel Arbinet (originally from Beaune), was published by the Faculty of Medicine in Paris in 1652 and was titled "Therefore the wine of Beaune is the most smooth to drink and the most healthful." Arbinet 1652.

43. Vallot, d'Aquin, and Fagon 1862, 222–23, 412–16.

44. Vallot, d'Aquin, and Fagon 1862, 222–23, 412–16.

45. "If the wine of Reims is more agreable and healthful than the wine of Burgundy: Question debated the 5th of May of the year 1700 at the *Écoles de Médicine de Reims*"; quoted in B. Musset 2008, 128. By comparison, Chaptal notes fewer than one hundred years later that in Burgundy, the red soils produce the best wines: "In Burgundy, the black or red earth, light or friable, is reputedly the best." Chaptal 1819, 27.

46. B. Musset 2007, 128.

47. Charles Coffin was the most well known. See B. Musset 2007, esp. 83–87, and Sabatier 1998.

48. See B. Musset 2007 for a full account of this phenomenon, including a variety of statistics.

49. See Arnoux 1728, 18, 29.

50. See B. Musset 2007, 83–87.

51. Exports of Champagne to Paris and Versailles from Épernay alone went from 960 bottles in 1708 to 62,085 bottles in 1727. See B. Musset 2007, 86.

52. Voltaire (1736) 1877, 87.

53. Vallot, d'Aquin, and Fagon 1862, 222–23, 412–16.

54. Maucroix 1710, 385.

CHAPTER SIX

1. For an account of the history of citizenship in France, see Weil 2002. For a modern historical account of citizenship based on territory in France, juxtaposed to blood descent in Germany, see Brubaker 1992. For a historical account of the creation of the French national identity and the evolving internal image of and expectations for its citizens, see Beaune 1993.

2. The best account contextualizing the life and political values of the Count Boulainvilliers is Ellis 1988.

3. See Montesquieu (1748) 1989, bks. 14–18. For Buffon's climatic determinism, see Buffon 1837, 4: 437–56, "Of the Degeneration of Animals." Montesquieu and Buffon deployed ideas regarding the environment in very different ways: in Montesquieu's case, by proposing that the laws be modeled on climate theory (see Rahe 2009), and in Buffon's case, by explaining "degeneration" from perfection in the human race as an effect of the climate (see Roger 1997, 164–83).

4. "The most useful book that has ever been written on these matters in any European nation." Voltaire 1788b, 67. To date, the most complete account on Du Bos is Lombard 1913.

5. To take stock of the extent of general controversy raised by the matter through references to and quotes from a number of contemporaries who weighed in on the matter, see Lombard 1913, chs. 5 and esp. 6.

6. Arendt 1968, 42; Foucault 2003, esp. lecture 7; Nicolet 2003; Ellis 1988. See also Nichols 2010.

7. See Boulainvilliers 1732, 30–32. For the particularities of Boulainvilliers's vision of Clovis, see 34–35.

8. Boulainvilliers wrote that the conquering Franks possessed over the subjugated Gauls "a formal distinction such as that between a master and slave." Boulainvilliers 1732, 41.

9. For an excellent detailed account of the underpinnings of Boulainvilliers's beliefs, see chapter 1, "The Franks and the State of France," in Ian Wood's excellent *The Modern Origins of the Early Middle Ages* 2013, 19–36.

10. The 1732 edition advertises that the theories advanced by the book were widely known even before its publication: "There are certain manuscripts whose excellence causes them to multiply in such a surprising way that often the person who believes themselves to possess the only copy finds other copies in different places [. . .] the writings of the deceased M. de Boulainvilliers are of this sort." Boulainvilliers 1732, unnumbered first page.

11. Boulainvilliers 1732, 251. See also 227.

12. Boulainvilliers 1732, 337.

13. Boulainvilliers 1732, 251.

14. Boulainvilliers 1732, 337.

15. "For what could the French have done, as it is elsewhere noted, new conquerors of lands without men to cultivate them, or men without lands to feed them and subsist themselves?" Boulainvilliers 1732, 38.

16. "An attachment to agriculture sapped the noble will to fight." Boulainvilliers 1732, 316. See also 64, where Boulainvilliers explains that the Franks were intended not to undertake the "onerous charges" of manual labor but to be prepared for war.

17. Montesquieu (1748) 1989, book 30, ch. 10, last paragraph: "M. le comte de Boulainvilliers and M. l'abbé Dubos each created a system, one of which seems to me to be a conspiracy against the Third Estate and the other against nobility [. . .] you should remain between the two." See de Dijn 2008, 20–33.

18. Du Bos (1719) 1770, 141.

19. Du Bos 1734, vol. 1, 1–3.

20. Quoted in Lombard 1913, 151.

21. For theories of polygenesis (biological differences in human "races," with each race developing from distinct genetic origins) versus monogenesis (a single origin of humanity), see Curran 2011, 74–116, 139–45.

22. See Buffon 1837, vol. 4, "Of the Degeneration of Animals," 437.

23. See Lombard 1913, 245–47: he explains that Du Bos wrote of having read the issue of *Nouvelles de la République des Lettres* in which Pierre Bayle published Broekhuisen's theories. Du Bos repeatedly makes reference to Bodin and specifically quotes Fontenelle, opining that the author should have developed his theories regarding the effects of climates on human ideas. Du Bos (1719) 1770, 156–57.

24. Du Bos (1719) 1770, 273.

25. Du Bos (1719) 1770, 273.

26. Du Bos (1719) 1770, 275.

27. Du Bos (1719) 1770, 281.

28. Du Bos (1719) 1770, 283.

29. Du Bos (1719) 1770, 250.

30. Du Bos (1719) 1770, 250–51.

31. Du Bos (1719) 1770, 283.

32. The term "democratization" in this context belongs to Luc Ferry. For Ferry on Du Bos, see Ferry 1990, ch. 2.

33. Du Bos (1719) 1770, 310.

34. There is a long history in French literature of discussion on the nature and qualities of marl, one that first gained prominence with Bernard Palissy in the sixteenth century. For Palissy's discussion on the nature, cause, and effects of marl, see Palissy (1580) 1844, 325–57.

35. Montesquieu 1899, "La Différence des génies," in *Pensées,* no. 2265.

36. Montesquieu (1721) 1964, "Lettre persane 121."

37. Montesquieu 1892, 152–53, "Essai sur les causes." For analysis, see Volpilhac-Auger 2000.

38. Montesquieu 1892, 117. For more on this manuscript, which draws from several of Montesquieu's earlier writings, see Volpilhac-Auger 2000.

39. In addition to Curran 2011, 74–116, 139–45, see Dobie 2010, 35–43.

40. La Mettrie (1748) 1921, 72–73.

41. Du Bos (1719) 1770, 311–12.

42. See Carrier 1993, 122. See also Prettejohn 2005, 15; Tanner 2005, ch. 1.

43. See Woodfield 1973.

44. Winckelmann 1781, 40.

45. For more on this evolution, see Sabatier 1998, 48–52.

46. B. Musset 2007, 124.

47. "Red wine is the least heady, the most stomach-worthy, and the one that ordinarily goes best with all temperaments; it fortifies, dispels melancholia, resists

venom, incites urination and women's menstrual cycle, it dispels gas, and helps with gangrene, it settles, it is good for contusions, for dislocations." N. Lémery (1698) 1760, 789.

48. On the evolving role of the chef in Enlightenment France, especially with respect to medicine and dietetics, see Takats 2011, 116–140.

49. Lauréault de Foncemagne, "Dissertation préliminaire sur la cuisine moderne," in Menon 1749, xx–xxi.

50. Menon 1749, xx.

51. Menon 1749, xxi.

52. Menon 1749, xxii.

53. For an explanation of how the purification ethic described in this quote played into the early institution of the restaurant in Paris during the 1760s and 1770s, in which part of the chef's job was to "cleanse nature" and "civilize raw materials," see Spang 2001, 41.

54. Menon 1749, xx.

55. The ongoing comparison between the arts and cuisine is made in Menon 1749, i–xiii.

56. Menon 1749, ix.

CHAPTER SEVEN

1. "Rousseau loves to describes the joys of a harvest, the pleasures of the vineyard, the superiority of the *terroir* to the city." Gopnik 2011, 89. Gopnik uses the word *terroir* to characterize the variety of views, ethics, and rural idealism promoted by Rousseau. For the Ermenonville anecdote, see Pinkard 2008, 237.

2. On Rousseau and nature, and specifically on Rousseau's advocating of nature as a standard for behavior in the face of the destabilizing force of the advent of modern science, see L. Cooper 1999; Horowitz 1987. For nature, Rousseau, and aesthetics related to food, see Pinkard 2008, 192, 236–37. See also Bonnet 1979, 117–50.

3. For more on Montesquieu, see chapter 6. See also Buffon 1837, 4:437; Chardin 1771, 86.

4. Voltaire 1788, bk. 3, 66, "Letter to Frederick, December 8, 1772."

5. Rousseau 2010, 643.

6. Rousseau 2010, 643.

7. Rousseau does not mention the French slave trade in the Antilles, and has an ambivalent discourse on slaves and slavery in general, although he is clear in denouncing it in *Du contrat social*. See Miller 2008, 67–69.

8. Rousseau 2010, 644. The editors of this translation elected to substitute *soil* for the word *terroir*. I have replaced *terroir* for the context of this discussion.

9. See Bell 2001, chapter 5.

10. Darnton 1984, 242.

11. See Fougère 1997, 199–210; Brunel 1906, 85.

12. Rousseau 1961, 605.

13. Rousseau 1997, 496.

14. Brennan 1997, 198.

15. This phenomenon was largely regional: according to Roger Dion, the lower classes of urban areas had access to wine. This was either through the cabarets or through the *guignettes,* drinking establishments outside city borders that served untaxed wine. Dion 1959, 459, 505–11. For a more recent treatment, see Quellier 2007a, 53–57; and Plack 2009.

16. Diderot and d'Alembert 1751–72, s.v. *"vin."*

17. Chaptal, Rozier, Parmentier, d'Ussieux 1801, 340–41.

18. Chaptal, Rozier, Parmentier, d'Ussieux 1801, 341–42.

19. On the physiocrats, see Steiner 2003.

20. See the introduction to Passy 1912 for more on the conditions and historical context leading to the institution of the agricultural societies.

21. See Steiner 1998.

22. The *Poème des saisons,* written by Jean-François de Saint-Lambert and published in 1769, describes the natural cycle and work of the countryside. Voltaire heralded it as a work of genius. The *Poème des mois* was a reactionary work published by Jean-Antoine Roucher in 1779. Jacques Delille published *L'Homme des champs ou les Géorgiques françaises* in 1800 while in exile in Switzerland due to the Revolution.

23. Berchoux 1815, 277–282.

24. Young 1906, 180, n1.

25. See Fabbroni 1780.

26. Rousseau 2010, 519; Rousseau 1969, 679–80.

27. Conroy 1982, 92.

28. Morel 1776, 45. For a recent discussion on the changing significance of the garden in eighteenth-century France and various conceptualizations of nature accompanying the phenomenon, see Ehrard 2013.

29. Morel 1776, 190.

30. This "natural aesthetic" contrasts with the iron-fisted vision of the Abbé Pluche, who compared the legislation of the people to the gardening of plants, advocating complete authority and autonomy on the part of the gardener, who should keep people in line like plants, cultivating them both avidly to obtain the production he desires. Pluche (1732) 1752, 3. See also Conroy 1982, 95–98.

31. Delille 1800, preface, n.p.

32. Rosset 1774, 6.

33. Rosset 1774, 14.

34. One example of this appears in Louis-Sébastien Mercier rallying against an unfair tax system that levied the same tax on the poorer wine-producing regions, such as Brie, as on the more prestigious *crus,* such as Champagne and Burgundy. "The cask of excellent Burgundy, of delicious Champagne, pays no more for entrance than does the cask of Brie, and the wine that rips the throat of the pruner is taxed at the same rate as the nectar that perfumes the mouth of the member of the State Council." L. S. Mercier 1783, vol. 8, 205.

35. Ozouf-Marignier 1989, 23.

36. Condorcet 1788, 188–90, quoted in Ozouf-Marignier 1989, 28.

37. Sieyès 1789, 42–44, quoted in Ozouf-Marignier 1989, 38.

38. Mirabeau 1775, 53–54.

39. Ozouf-Marignier 1989, 51.

40. Baron de Jessé, October 19, 1789, quoted in Ozouf-Marignier 1989, 48.

41. Courbain 1992, 784.

42. Le Grand d'Aussy (1782) 1815, 15.

43. Le Grand d'Aussy (1782) 1815, 130, 15, 16, 18.

44. Grimod de la Reynière 1808.

45. Grimod de la Reynière 1807.

46. See the listing "Amphitryon" in *Dictionnaire de L'Académie française* 1932–35, 8th ed.

47. Grimod de la Reynière and Gassicourt 1828, 365.

48. Grimod de la Reynière, in the *L'Almanach des gourmands* 1807, goes to no uncertain lengths to establish the best regions for veal, pork, etc.

49. Grimod de la Reynière and Gassicourt 1828, 83–84.

50. Csergo 1999, 503.

CONCLUSION

1. Barthes 1979, 171.

2. Rougé, Dupuis, and Millet 1936, quoted in Thiesse 1997, 46.

3. On culinary tourism, see Long 2010, 21–50.

4. Debord 1955, quoted in Bauder and Engel-Di Mauro 2008, 23. The OED classifies the term as the "study of the influence of geographical environment on the mind, behaviour, etc.; geography considered in regard to its psychological effects." *Oxford English Dictionary* 2007, 3rd ed. For a relatively contemporary discussion of the term, see Hart 2004.

5. De Gourmont (1903) 1905, 186.

6. De Gourmont (1903) 1905, 192.

7. There was also a literary journal called *Terroir,* which made its debut in 1909. De Gourmont uses the term *littérature du terroir* as early as 1893, in his *Les Canadiens de France,* 190. The more common term, coined in the last part of the nineteenth century, *"roman du terroir,"* became prevalent in the years leading up to 1920; its exact origins are unknown. For more on the French Canadian regional movement, see Blodgett 2004.

8. Van Bever quotes de Gourmont directly, using the author-terroir quote given above. See van Bever (1909) 1918, vii.

9. De Gourmont had also opined that France's wealth in human diversity and genius owed more than a little to the provinces: "The less dense a population is, the more beautiful is the human plant, more beautiful in the sense of stronger, richer in vigor [*sève,* or sap]. Paris possesses unfavorable conditions to produce a man of

genius; that variety comes from the countryside; it is born, one would say, directly from arable soil and forest land." De Gourmont (1903) 1905, 185.

10. For accounts on French food and nationalism, see Ferguson 2010; Claflin 2007; Csergo 2007.

11. Van Bever (1909) 1918, xiii.

12. Van Bever (1909) 1918, vii. Van Bever provides here an oddly prescient insight later presented by Weber 1976 (translated into French as Weber 1983), who holds that regional identities and dialects were more important in France before agricultural modernization at the end of the nineteenth century, which brought an end to regional languages and rural, place-specific ways of life.

13. Colette (1932) 1986, 51.

14. Despite the novelty in Colette's romanticized methodology, a tradition of travel literature that explores France through its food itself dates, at least in some form, to the seventeenth century. The most important early point of reference in the tradition is *Voyage d'Encausse,* a spirited, coauthored piece of seventeenth-century travel literature, written half in prose and half in verse that Yves Giraud refers to as a *"gastronomico-mondain"* touristic journey. Chapelle and Bachaumont (1661) 2007, 12. See also Gillet 1985.

15. Yourcenar (1951) 1974, 14.

16. For a general account of Vidal de la Blache's influence, see Guiomar 1986.

17. In his *Tableau de la géographie de la France,* Vidal de la Blache examines the geography of France region by region, focusing on the underlying geologic structures but also celebrating differences in regional character, including food and drink, along the way. See Trubek 2008, 23. See also Robic 1994, Robic 1999, and Robic 2000.

18. See Guy 2007, 43–44, 136–39; Trubek 2008, 22–24.

19. Pitte 2006, 2 points out: "Already in 1884, Philéas Gilbert devised the great imperialist dream: to create a school dedicated to the universal gastronomic synthesis [. . .], where each country would appear with its alimentary productions." The exact reference is Gilbert 1884, 81–82.

20. Vidal de la Blache (1903) 1908, 3.

21. Vidal de La Blache (1903) 1908, 118.

22. Csergo 1999, 506.

23. The observation owes to Ferguson 2010, 102.

24. Curnonsky and Rouff 1921–28, 1:8.

25. On the evolution of French national culinary tourism in the nineteenth and twentieth centuries, see Csergo 2011.

PRIMARY SOURCES

Adanson, Algaé. 1827. *La Cuisinière de la campagne et de la ville.* Paris: Audot.

Agricola, Georgius. 1546. *De ortu et causis subterraneorum* [On the origin and causes of subterranean things]. Basel.

Alberti, Leon Battisti. 1553. *L'Architecture et l'art de bien bastir de Léon Baptiste Albert.* Translated by Jean Martin. Paris: Jacques Kerver.

Alletz, Pons Augustin. 1762. *L'Agronome: Ou Dictionnaire portatif du cultivateur.* Vol. 2. Paris: Savoye.

Alquier, François-Savinien d'. (1670) 1728. *Les délices de la France, avec une description des provinces et des villes du royaume.* Leide: Théodore Haak.

Arbinet, Daniel. 1652. *Donc le vin de Beaune est le plus suave à boire et le plus salubre.* Paris: Faculty of Medicine.

Arnoullet, Olivier. 1542. *Livre fort excellent de cuisine.* Lyon.

Arnoux, Claude. 1728. *Dissertation sur la situation, de Bourgogne, sur les vins qu'elle produit, sur la manière de cultiver les vignes, de faire le vin, et de l'éprouver.* London: S. Jallason.

B.D.R. 1698. *Apologie des œuvres de Monsieur de St. Evremont.* Paris: Jacques Collombat.

Baïf, Jean-Antoine de. 1975. "Le Premier des Météores." In *Premier livre des poèmes de Baïf,* edited by G. Demerson, 205–12. Grenoble: Presses Universitaires.

Baillet, Adrien de. 1685–86. *Jugements des savants sur les principaux ouvrages des auteurs.* 9 vols. Paris: A. Dezallier.

———. 1693. *La Vie de Monsieur Descartes.* Paris: Veuve Mabre Cramoysi.

Baranger, Léon, and André Simon. 1926. *Almanach du franc buveur.* Paris: Chamontin.

Baumgarten, Alexander Gottlieb. 1739. *Metaphysica.* Halle: Carl Hemmerde.

Beaujeu, Pierre Quiqueran de. 1551. *De Laudibus Provinciae.*

Beauval, Henri Basnage de. 1688. *Histoire des ouvrages des sçavans.* Vol. 3. Paris.

Beguillet, François. 1770. *Œnologie ou Discours sur la meilleure méthode de faire le vin et de cultiver la vigne.* Dijon: Defay.

Belleau, Remy. 1556. *Les Odes d'Anacreon Teien, traduites de grec.* Paris: André Wechel.

———. 1867. "Hymne à Bacchus." In *Œuvres complètes,* edited by A. Gouverneur, 43–44, Paris: A. Franck.

———. 1954. "Description des vendanges." In *La Bergerie,* edited by Doris Delacourcelle. Genève: Droz.

———. 1995. *Œuvres poétiques.* Edited by Guy Demerson. Paris: Champion.

Bellegarde, Jean Baptiste Morvan. (1697) 1712. *Réflexions sur le ridicule et sur les moyens de l'éviter, où sont représentez les différens caractères et les moeurs des personnes de ce siècle.* Paris: Henri Schelte.

Belon, Pierre. 1555. *La Histoire de la nature des oyseaux.* Paris: Guillaume Cavellet.

———. 1558. *Remonstrances sur le défaut de labour et culture des plantes.* Paris.

Berchoux, Joseph de. 1805. *La Gastronomie, poème, suivi des poésies fugitives de l'auteur.* Paris: Giguet et Michaud.

———. 1815. "Cours complet d'agriculture moderne, par demandes et par réponses." In *Voltaire ou le Triomphe de la Philosophie Moderne, Poème en huit chants avec un epilogue suivi de diverses pièces en vers et en prose.* Lyon: Pelzin.

Bernier, François. 1684a. "La Nouvelle Division de la terre par les différentes espèces ou races d'hommes qui l'habitent." *Journal des sçavans,* 24 April: 133–39.

———. 1684b. *Abrégé de la philosophie de Gassendi.* Lyon: Anisson, Posuel, et Rigaud.

Bodin, Jean. (1566) 1941. *La Méthode de l'histoire.* Edited by Pierre Mesnard. Paris: Belles Lettres.

———. (1576) 1986. *Les Six Livres de la République.* Edited by Christiane Frémont, Marie-Dominique Couzinet, and Henri Rochais. Paris: Fayard.

———. 1768. *De la legislation; ou du gouvernement politique des empires: Extrait des Six Livres de la République.* London, Paris: Cailleau.

Boileau-Despréaux, Nicolas. (1665) 1966. *Art poétique, Satire III.* Paris: Gallimard, Éditions de la Pléiade.

———. 1966. *Œuvres complètes.* Edited by F. Escal. Paris: Gallimard.

Bonnefons, Nicolas de. 1651. *Jardinier français.* Paris: Des-Hayes.

———. 1654. *Les Délices de la campagne.* Paris: Des-Hayes.

Bouhours, Dominique. 1671. *Les Entretiens d'Ariste et d'Eugène.* Paris: S. Mabre-Cramoisy.

Boulainvilliers, Henri de. 1732. *Essai sur la noblesse de France, contenans une dissertation sur son origine et abaissement.* Amsterdam.

Boyceau, Jacques. 1638. *Traité du jardinage.* Paris: Michel Van Lochom.

Breton, Robert. 1539. *Economium Agriculturae.* Paris: C. Wechel.

Brillat-Savarin. (1825) 1975. *Physiologie du goût.* Edited by Roland Barthes. Paris: Hermann.

Broekhuisen, Benjaminus. 1687. *Rationes philosophico-medicae, theoretico-practicae* [Philosophical-medical theoretical-practical reasonings]. The Hague: M. Uytwerf.

Bruno, G. [Augustine Fouillée.] 1877. *Le Tour de la France par deux enfants.*

Bruyérin-Champier, Jean. (1560) 1998. *De Re Cibaria.* Translated by Sigurd Amundsen as *L'Alimentation de tous les peuples et de tous les temps jusqu'au XVIe siècle.* Paris: L'Intermédiaire des chercheurs et des curieux.

Buffier, Claude. 1704. *Examen des préjugez vulgaires.* Paris: Jean Mariette.

Buffon, George-Louis Leclerc de. 1837. *Histoire naturelle générale et particulière avec la description du cabinet du roy.* Paris: Furne.

César, Constantin. 1543. *Les Vingt Livres de Constantin César, auxquels sont traités les bons enseignements d'agriculture.* Translated by Antoine Pierre. Poitiers: Enguilebert de Marnef Freres.

Chapelle, Claude Emmannuel Luillier, and François Le Coigneux de Bachaumont. (1661) 2007. *Voyage d'Encausse.* Edited by Yves Giraud. Paris: Champion.

Chaptal, Jean-Antoine-Claude. 1819. *L'Art de faire le vin.* Paris: Deterville.

Chaptal, Jean-Antoine-Claude, François Rozier, Antoine Augustin Parmentier, and Louis d'Ussieux. 1801. *Traité théorique et pratique sur la culture de la vigne: Avec l'art de faire le vin, les eaux-de-vie, esprit-de-vin, vinaigres simples et composés.* Vol. 1. Paris: Delalain.

Chardin, Jean. 1771. *Voyages de Monsieur le Chevalier Chardin en Perse et autres lieux de l'Orient.* Vol. 3. Amsterdam: Jean Louis de Lorme.

Charron, Pierre. 1601. *De la sagesse.* Paris.

Chatelet, Noëlle. 1977. *Le Corps à corps culinaire.* Paris: Seuil.

Chenaye-Aubert, François-Alexandre de la. 1750. *Dictionnaire des aliments, vins et liqueurs.* Paris.

Chesnaye, Nicole de la. 1507. *La Nef de santé avec le gouvernail du corps humain et la condannacion des bancquetz à la louenge de la diepte et sobriété.* Paris: Vérard.

Colette. (1932) 1986. *Prisons et paradis.* Paris: Fayard.

Colonna, Francesco. 1546. *Hypnerotomachie, ou Discours du songe de Poliphile.* Paris: Jacques Kerver.

Condorcet, J. A. N. de Caritat, marquis de. 1788. *Essai sur la constitution et les fonctions des assemblées provinciales.* Paris.

Courtépée, Abbé Claude. 1775. *Description générale et particulière du duché de Bourgogne.* Dijon: L. N. Frantin.

Curnonsky [Maurice Edmond Sailland] and Marcel Rouff. 1921–28. *La France gastronomique.* 28 vols. Paris: F. Rouff.

Daneau, Lambert. 1582. *Traité contre les Bacchanales du Mardigras.* Paris.

Debord, Guy. (1955) 2008. "Introduction to a Critique of Urban Geography." In *Critical Geographies: A Collection of Readings,* edited by Harald Bauder and Salvatore Engel-Di Mauro. Kelowna: Praxis (e)Press. Accessed November 25, 2014. www.praxis-epress.org/availablebooks/introcriticalgeog.html.

De la Faye, Antoine. 1580. *Traité et remonstrance contre l'yvrognerie.* La Rochelle: P. Hautlin.

De la Mothe La Vayer, François. (1636) 1809. *De la contrariété d'humeurs qui se trouve entre certaines nations, et singulièrement entre la française et l'espagnole, ou de l'antipathie des français et des espagnols.* Paris: Beausseaux.

Delille, Jacques. 1800. *L'Homme des champs, ou Les Géorgiques françoises.* Strasbourg: Levrault.

De Serres, Olivier. (1600) 2001. *Le Théâtre d'agriculture et mesnage des champs.* Arles: Actes Sud.

———. 1804. *Théâtre d'agriculture.* Paris: Madame Huzard.

———. 1873. *Théâtre d'agriculture.* Edited by Paul Favre. Paris: L. Favre.

Des Périers, Bonaventure. 1856. "Chant de vendanges." In *Oeuvres françoises,* edited by L. Lacour, 92. Paris: P. Jannet.

Dictionnaire de l'Académie française. 1694. Paris: Jean Baptiste Coignard.

Diderot, Denis de, and Jean Le Rond D'Alembert. 1751–72. *Encyclopédie, ou dictionnaire raisonné des sciences, des arts, et des métiers.* 28 vols. Paris: Briasson, David, Le Breton, Durand.

Donneau de Visé, Jean. (1665) 2013. *Les Costeaux ou les marquis friands.* Edited by Peter Shoemaker. Paris: Modern Humanities Research Association.

Du Bartas, Guillaume de Saluste. (1581) 1994. *La Sepmaine.* Edited by Y. Bellenger. Paris: Société des Textes Français Modernes.

Du Bellay, Joachim. 1996a. *Défense et illustration de la langue française.* Paris: Gallimard.

———. 1996b. *Divers Jeux rustiques.* Paris: Gallimard.

———. 2003. *Oeuvres complètes.* Edited by Marie-Dominique Legrand, Michel Magnien, Daniel Ménager, and Olivier Millet. 2 vols. Paris: Champion.

Du Bos, Jean-Baptiste. (1719) 1770. *Réflexions critiques sur la poésie et sur la peinture.* 3 vols. Paris: Pissot.

———. 1734. *Histoire critique de l'établissement de la monarchie française dans les Gaules.* 3 vols. Amsterdam: François Changuion.

Dulaure, Jacques-Antoine. 1785. *Nouvelle Description des curiosités de Paris.* Paris: Lejay.

Du Vair, Guillaume. (1590) 1609. *De l'éloquence françoise et des raisons pourquoy elle est demeurée si basse.* Paris: François Arnoullet.

Espiard, François Ignace d'. 1753. *L'Esprit des nations.* Paris: Beauregard, Gosse, Van Daalen.

Estienne, Charles. 1537. *Vinetum.* Paris: Apud Franciscum Stephanum.

———. 1545. *De dissectione partium corporis humani libri tres.* Paris: Apud Simonem Colinaeum.

———. (1552) 1565. *La Guide des chemins de France.* Paris: Charles Estienne.

———. 1554. *Praedium rusticum.* Paris: Charles Estienne.

Estienne, Charles, and Jean Liébault. (1578) 1637. *L'Agriculture ou la maison rustique.* Paris: Jacques Du-Puys.

Estienne, Henri. (1578) 1896. *La Précellence du langage français.* Edited by Edmond Huguet. Paris: Armand Colin.

Fabbroni, Giovanni. 1780. *Reflexions sur l'état actuel de l'agriculture, ou, Exposition du véritable plan pour cultiver ses terres avec le plus grand avantage.* Paris: Nyon l'Aîné.

Faret, Nicolas. 1630. *L'Honnête Homme ou l'art de plaire à la cour.* Paris: Toussaint du Bray.

Félibien, André. 1674. *Les Divertissements de Versailles donnés par le roi à toute sa cour au retour de la conquête de la Franche-Comté en l'année mille six cent soixante-quatorze.* Paris: Coignard.

Fontenelle, Bernard le Bovier de. (1688) 1790. *Digression sur les Anciens et les Modernes.* Paris: Jean-François Bastien.

Fouillée, Augustine. *See* Bruno, G.

Fourier, Charles. 1966–68. *Oeuvres complètes.* 12 vols. Paris: Anthropos.

Framboisière, Nicolas Abraham de la. 1669. *Le Gouvernement nécessaire à chacun pour vivre longuement en santé.* Lyon: Beauviollin.

Furetière, Antoine. (1690) 1978. *Le Dictionnaire universel.* The Hague: A. and R. Leers.

————. 1701. *Le Dictionnaire universel.* The Hague: A. and R. Leers.

Gallo, Augustino. 1572. *Secrets de la vraye agricvltvre, et honestes plaisirs qv'on reçoit en le mesnagerie des champs.* Translated by François de Belle-Forest. Paris: Nicolas Chesneau.

Gassendi, Pierre. 1658. *Syntagma philosophicum.* Lyon.

Gauchet, Claude. 1583. *Le Plaisir des champs.* Paris: Chesneau.

Gilbert, Philéas. 1884. *L'Art culinaire.* Vol. 2. Paris.

Godinot, Jean. 1722. *Manière de cultiver la vigne et de faire le vin en Champagne.* Reims: Barthelemy Multeau.

Gohory, Jacques. 1549. *Devis sur la vigne, vin et vendanges.* Paris: Sertenas.

Gourmont, Remy de. 1893. *Les Canadiens de France.* Paris: Firmin-Didot.

————. (1903) 1905. "Carte intellectuelle de France." *Epilogues: Réflexions sur la vie, 3e série, 1902–1904.* Paris: Société du Mercure de France.

Grimod de la Reynière, Alexandre-Balthazar-Laurent. (1803) 1807. *Almanach des gourmands: Ou calendrier nutritif, servant de guide dans les moyens de faire excellente chère . . . par un vieux amateur.* Vol. 5. Paris: Chaumerot.

————. 1808. *Manuel des amphitryons: Contenant un traité de la dissection des viandes à table, la nomenclature des menus les plus nouveaux pour chaque saison, et des élémens de politesse gourmande.* Paris: Capelle et Renand.

Grimod de la Reynière, Alexandre-Balthazar-Laurent, and Charles-Louis Cadet de Gassicourt. 1828. *Le Gastronome français, ou, L'Art de bien vivre.* Paris: Charles-Béchet.

Herodotus. 1998. *Histories.* Translated by R. Waterfield. Oxford: Oxford University Press.

Hesiod. 1999. *Theogony and Works and Days.* Translated by M. L. West. Oxford: Oxford University Press.

Hippocrates. (1923) 2004. *Air, Water, Places.* Translated by W. H. S. Jones. Cambridge, MA: Loeb.

————. 1996. *Airs, eaux, lieux.* Translated and edited by Jacques Jouanna. Paris: Les Belles Lettres.

L. S. R. 1674. *L'Art de bien traiter: Divisé en trois parties: Ouvrage nouveau, curieux, et fort galant, utile à toutes personnes, et conditions, exactement recherché, et mis en lumière, par L. S. R.* Paris: Jean Du Puis.

————. (1674) 1995. "L'Art de bien traiter." In *L'Art de la cuisine française au XVIIe* *siècle*. Paris: Payot.

La Bruyère, Jean de. (1688) 1995. *Les Caractères*. Edited by E. Bury. Paris: Bordas.

La Mettrie, Julien Offray de. 1748. *L'Homme-plante*. Potsdam: Frederic Voss.

————. (1748) 1921. *L'Homme-machine*. Paris: Bossard.

La Varenne, François-Pierre de. 1651. *Le Cuisinier français*. Paris: Pierre David.

Le François, A. 1781. *Méthode abrégée et facile pour apprendre la géographie*. Paris: Belin.

Le Grand d'Aussy, Pierre Jean-Baptiste. (1782) 1815. *Histoire de la vie privée des français: Depuis l'origine de la nation jusqu'à nos jours*. Paris: PH.-D. Pierres.

Lémery, Louis. 1706. *Traité des aliments*. Paris: Cusson and Witte.

Lémery, Nicolas. 1675. *Cours de chimie, contenant la manière de faire les opérations qui sont en usage dans la médecine*. Paris.

————. (1698) 1760. *Dictionnaire universel des drogues simples*. Paris: d'Houry.

Lenoir, B. A. 1828. *Traité de la culture de la vigne et de la vinification*. Paris: Rousselon.

Le Paulmier, Julien. 1589. *Traité du vin et du sidre*. Caen: Le Chandelier.

Levinus. 1561. *De habitu et constitutione corporis*. Anvers: Simonis.

Liger, Louis. 1701. *Oeconomie generale de la campagne, ou nouvelle maison rustique*. Amsterdam: Henri Desbordes.

Liger, Louis, and Jean-François Bastien. 1798. *La Nouvelle Maison de l'agriculture*. Paris: Deterville.

Littré, Émile. 1872. *Dictionnaire de la langue française*. Paris: Hachette.

Lucretius. 1963. *The Philosophy of Epicurus: Letters, Doctrines, and Parallel Passages from Lucretius*. Translated by G. K. Strodach. Evanston: Northwestern University Press.

————. 2007. *The Nature of Things*. Translated by A. E. Stallings. London: Penguin Classics.

Magny, Olivier. (1559) 1876. "Hymne de Bacchus." In *Les Odes d'Olivier Magny*, edited by E. Courbet, 2: 56. Paris: A. Lemerre.

Massialot, Français. (1691) 1693. *Le Cuisinier royal et bourgeois*. Paris: Charles de Sercy.

Maucroix, François de. 1710. *Oeuvres posthumes: Lettres*. Paris: Étienne.

Menage, Gilles, et al. 1750. *Dictionnaire étymologique de la langue française*. Vol. 1. Paris: Librairie Briasson.

Menon. 1749. *La Science du maître d'hôtel cuisinier*. Paris: Paulus-du-Mesnil.

————. 1753. *La Cuisinière bourgeoise, suivie de l'office, à l'usage de tous ceux qui se mêlent de dépenses de maisons: Contenant la manière de dissequer, connaitre et servir toutes sortes de viandes*. Paris: Foppens.

Mercier, Louis-Sébastien. 1783. *Le Tableau de Paris: Nouvelle édition corrigée et augmentée*. 8 vols. Amsterdam.

Méré, Antoine Gombaud, chevalier de. 1692. *Les Oeuvres du Monsieur le Chevalier de Méré*. Vol. 1. Paris: Pierre Mortier.

————. 1701. *Oeuvres posthumes*. Paris: M. Uytwerf.

————. 1930. *Oeuvres complètes du chevalier de Méré*. Vol. 3. Edited by Charles-Henri Boudhors. Paris: F. Roches.

Michelet, Jules. 1846. *Le Peuple.* Paris: Hachette.

——. (1861) 1962. "Tableau de la France." *Histoire de France.* Paris: Albin Michel.

Mirabeau, Victor de Riqueti, marquis de. 1775. *Lettres sur la législation ou l'ordre légal, dépravé, rétabli et perpétué.* Vol. 3. Berne: La Société typographique.

Mollet, Claude. 1652. *Théâtre des jardinages.* Paris.

Montaigne, Michel de. 1965. *Essais.* Edited by P. Villey and Verdun L. Saulnier. 3 vols. Paris: PUF.

——. 1991. *Essays.* Translated by Michael Screech. New York: Penguin Classics.

Montesquieu, Baron de. (1721) 1964. "Lettres persanes." In *Œuvres complètes,* edited by Daniel Oster. Paris: Seuil.

——. (1748) 1989. *The Spirit of Laws.* Translated and edited by Anne M. Cohler, Basia Carolyn Miller, and Harold Samuel Stone. Cambridge: Cambridge University Press.

——. (1748) 2008. *De l'esprit des loix.* Edited by Catherine Volpilhac-Auger. 4 vols. Oxford: Voltaire Foundation.

——. 1892. *Mélanges inédits de Montesquieu.* Paris: G. Gounouilhou.

——. 1899. "La Différence des génies." In *Pensées et fragments inédits de Montesquieu,* n. 2265. Bordeaux: Gounouilhou.

——. 1955. *Essai sur les causes:* Vol. 3. *Oeuvres complètes.* Edited by A. Masson. Paris: Nagel.

Morel, Jean-Marie. 1776. *Théorie des jardins.* Paris: Pissot.

Muralt, Béat Louis de. 1739. *Lettres fanatiques.* 2 vols. London.

Musset, Victor-Donatien. 1810. *Bibliographie agronomique ou dictionnaire raisonné des ouvrages sur l'économie rurale et domestique et sur l'art vétérinaire.* Paris: D. Colas.

Nemeitz, J. C. 1727. *Séjour à Paris, instruction fidèle pour les voyageurs de condition.* Leiden: Jan van Abcoude.

Nicole, Pierre. (1671) 1996. *La Vraie Beauté et son fantôme.* Paris: Champion.

Nicot. 1606. *Thrésor de la langue française.* Paris.

Palissy, Bernard. (1563) 1996. *Recepte véritable.* Edited by Frank Lestringant and Christian Barataud. Paris: Macula.

——. (1580) 1844. "De la marne." In *Oeuvres complètes,* 325–57. Paris: Dubochet.

——. (1580) 2000. *Discours admirable de la nature des eaux et fontaines tant naturelles qu'artificielles.* Clermont-Ferrand: Paleo.

Patin, Guy. 1632. *Traité de la conservation de santé, par un bon régime et légitime usage des choses requises pour bien et sainement vivre.* Paris: Jean Jost.

Peletier du Mans, Jacques. 1555. *L'Art poétique.* Lyon: Jean de Tournes.

——. (1555) 1996. *L'Amour des amours.* Edited by Jean-Charles Monferran. Paris: Société des Textes Français Modernes.

——. 2005. "Louanges." In *Œuvres complètes,* edited by Sophie Arnaud, Stephen Bamforth, and Jan Miernowski, 105. Paris: Champion.

Pellisson-Fontanier, Paul. 1688. *Histoire de l'Académie française.* The Hague.

Perrault, Claude, and Pierre Perrault. 1721. *Oeuvres diverses de physique et de mécanique.* Vol. 2. Paris: Pierre van der Aa.

Picot, Jean. 1804. *Histoire des Gaulois . . . jusqu'a leur mélange avec les Francs et jusqu'aux commencemens de la monarchie française; suivie de détails sur le climat de la Gaule, sur la nature de ses productions.* Génève: J.-J. Paschoud.

Pidoulx, Pierre. 1540. *Grand Cuisinier de toute cuisine.* Paris.

Pio, J.-B. 1514. *In Carum Lucretium poetam commentarii a J. B. Pio editi, codice lucretiano diligenter emendato: Nodis omnibuset difficultatibus apertis . . . Venundatur ab Ascensio et Joanne Parvo.* Edited by N. Bérauld, J. Petit Josse Bade. Paris.

Plantina. 1998. *On Right Pleasure and Good Health.* Edited and translated by Mary Ella Milham. Tempe: Medieval and Renaissance Texts and Studies.

Pluche, Abbé. (1732) 1752. *Le Spectacle de la nature.* Vol. 2. Paris: Étienne et fils.

Poisson, Raymond. 1665. *L'Après-souper des auberges.* Paris: Gabriel Quinet.

Pollion, Marc Vitruue. 1647. *Architecture, ou L'Art de bien bastir.* Paris: Jean Martin.

Quintinie, Jean de la. 1692. *Instruction pour les jardins.* 2 vols. Paris.

Rabelais, François. 1711. *Oeuvres de François Rabelais.* Edited by Jacob Le Duchat and Bernard de La Monnoye. Paris: H. Bordesius.

———. 1823. *Œuvres de Rabelais: Ed. variorum, augmentées de pièces inédites, des songes drolatiques de Pantagruel . . . ; et d'un nouveau commentaire historique et philologique.* Edited by Charles Esmangart and Eloi Johanneau. 9 vols. Lausanne: Dalibon.

———. 1994a. *Les Cinq Livres.* Edited by Jean Céard, Gérard Defaux, and Michel Simonin. Paris: Livre de Poche.

———. 1994b. *Oeuvres complètes.* Edited by Mireille Huchon. Paris: Gallimard.

———. 1999. *The Complete Works of Rabelais.* Translated by Donald Frame. Berkeley: University of California Press.

———. 2009. *Traité de bon usage du vin.* Translated from the Czech by Marianne Canavaggio. Paris: Allia.

Régnier, Mathurin. 1729. "Le Souper ridicule." In *Œuvres complètes.* Paris: Lequien.

Ronsard, Pierre de. 1993. *Œuvres complètes,* 2 vols., *Bibliothèque de la Pléaide,* edited by Jean Céard, Daniel Ménager, and Michel Simonin. Paris: Gallimard.

Rosset, Pierre Fulcrand de. 1774. *L'Agriculture ou les Géorgiques françaises.* Paris: Moutard.

Rousseau, Jean-Jacques. 1961. "La Nouvelle Héloise." In *Œuvres complètes.* Edited by Bernard Gagnebin and Marcel Raymond. Vol. 2. Paris: Gallimard.

———. 1969. "Émile, ou, De l'éducation." In *Œuvres complètes.* Edited by Bernard Gagnebin and Marcel Raymond. Vol. 4. Paris: Gallimard.

———. 1975. "Fragments politiques." In *Œuvres complètes.* Edited by Bernard Gagnebin and Marcel Raymond. Vol. 3. Paris: Gallimard.

———. 1997. *Julie, or the New Heloise.* Translated and annotated by Philip Stewart and Jean Vaché. Hanover, NH: Dartmouth College Press.

———. 2010. "Emile, or On Education." In *The Collected Writings of Rousseau.* Translated and annotated by Christopher Kelly and Allan Bloom. Vol. 13. Hanover, NH: Dartmouth College Press.

Sailland, Maurice Edmond. *See* Curnonsky.

Saint-Évremond. 1706. *Les Véritables Oeuvres de Monsieur Saint-Évremond.* 5 vols. Edited by M. des Maizeaux. London: Tonson.

———. 1740. *Oeuvres de Monsieur de Saint-Évremond.* 10 vols. N.p.: N. pub.

———. 1852. *Oeuvres choisies de Saint-Évremond: Précédées d'une notice sur la vie et ses ouvrages.* Paris: Librairie de Firmin Didot.

———. 1966. *Œuvres complètes.* 4 vols. Edited by René Ternois. Paris: Marcel Didier.

———. 1998. *Entretiens sur toutes choses.* Edited by David Bensousson. Paris: Desjonquères.

———. 1999. "Autour d'Alexandre le Grand: Extraits de deux lettres adressées à Mme Bourneau." In *Racine, Œuvres complètes,* edited by George Forestier, 182. Paris: Gallimard, Éditions de la Pléiade.

Saint-Lambert, Jean-François de. 1769. *Les Saisons.* Amsterdam.

Scudéry, Madeleine de, and Marie-Gabrielle Lallemand. (1669) 2002. *La Promenade de Versailles.* Paris: Champion.

Serres, Michel. 1985. *Les Cinq Sens.* Paris: Grasset.

Sévigné, Madame de. 1974. *Correspondance, 1675–1680.* 2 vols. Edited by Roger Duchêne. Paris: Gallimard, Bibliothèque de la Pléiade.

Sieyès, Emmanuel-Joseph. 1789. *Instructions envoyées par M. le duc d'Orléans pour les personnes chargées de sa procuration aux assemblées de bailliages, relatives aux États Généraux.* Paris.

Taine, Hippolyte. 1864. *Histoire de la littérature anglaise.* 5 vols. Paris: Hachette.

Tallement des Réaux, Gédéon. 1960. *Historiettes.* Vol. 1. Edited by Antoine Adam. Paris: Gallimard.

Thevet, Andre. 1575. *Cosmographie universelle.* 2 vols. Paris: Guillaume Claudière.

Tocqueville, Alexis de. (1856) 1952. *Ancien Régime et la Révolution.* Paris: Gallimard.

Vallot, Antoine, Antoine d'Aquin, and Guy Crescent Fagon. 1862. *Journal de la santé du roi Louis XIV de l'année 1647 à l'année 1711.* Edited by J.-A. Le Roi. Versailles: A. Durand.

Vaschalde, Henry. 1886. *Olivier de Serres, seigneur du Pradel.* Paris: Éditions Plon.

Vaugelas, Claude Favre de. 1647. *Remarques sur la langue française: Utiles à ceux qui veulent bien parler et bien escrire.* Paris: J. Camusat.

Viard, Alexandre. 1806. *Le Cuisinier impérial.* Paris: Barba.

Vidal de la Blache, Paul. (1903) 1908. *Le Tableau de la géographie de la France.* Paris: Hachette.

Villiers, Jacques de. 1665. *Les Costeaux ou les marquis frians.* Paris.

Vinet, Elie. 1607. *La Maison champestre et agriculture.* Paris: Robert Fouet.

Virgil. 1973. *Les Géorgiques.* Translated by Maurice Rat. Paris: Garnier-Flammarion.

———. 1999. *Georgics.* Translated by H. Rushton Fairclough. Cambridge, MA: Harvard University Press, Everyman's Library.

Vitruvius. 1547. *Architecture ou Art de bien bâtir.* Translated by Jean Martin. Paris: J. Gazeau.

Voltaire. (1736) 1877. "Le Mondain." In *Oeuvres complètes de Voltaire,* vol. 10. Paris: Garnier.

———. (1746) 1879. "Discours de réception à l'Académie française." In *Œuvres complètes de Voltaire,* Mélanges II. Paris: Garnier.

———. (1751) 1964. *Dictionnaire philosophique.* Paris: Flammarion.

———. 1788a. *Lettres du roi de Prusse et de M. de Voltaire.* In *Oeuvres complètes de Voltaire,* vol. 54. Basel: Jean-Jaques Tourneisen.

———. 1788b. *Le Siècle de Louis XIV.* Vol. 1. Paris: Dusmenil.

Watelet, Claude-Henri. 1774. *Essai sur les jardins.* Paris: Prault.

Winckelmann, Johann Joachim. 1781. *Histoire de l'art.* 3 vols. Translated by M. Huber. Leipzig.

Yourcenar, Marguerite. (1951) 1974. *Mémoires d'Hadrien.* Paris: Gallimard.

SECONDARY SOURCES

Albala, Ken. 2002. *Eating Right in the Renaissance.* Berkeley: University of California Press.

———. 2003. *Food in Early Modern Europe.* Westport, CT: Greenwood Press.

———. 2005. "To Your Health: Wine as Food and Medicine in the Sixteenth Century." In *Alcohol: A Social and Cultural History,* edited by Mack Holt. Oxford: Berg.

Albala, Ken, and Robin Imhof. 2004. "Food in Rabelais." In *The Rabelais Encyclopedia,* edited by Elizabeth Chesney Zegura. Westport, CT: Greenwood Press.

Alcover, Madeleine. 1970. *La Pensée philosophique et scientifique de Cyrano de Bergerac.* Geneva: Droz.

Alexandre-Bidon, Danièle. 2005. *Une Archéologie du goût: Céramique et consommation.* Paris: Picard.

Ambrosoli, Mauro. 1997. *The Wild and the Sown: Botany and Agriculture in Western Europe, 1350–1850.* Cambridge: Cambridge University Press.

Andreani, Matthieu. 2012. "Présentation d'un corpus sonore: Enquêtes orales sur le légendaire sarrasin en France." *Les Carnets de la phonothèque,* blog of the Maison Méditerannéenne des Sciences de l'Homme–Phonothèque. August 8. http:// phonotheque.hypotheses.org/7372.

Arendt, Hannah. (1951) 1968. *The Origins of Totalitarianism.* Vol. 2, *Imperialism.* New York: Harcourt, Brace, and Jovanovich.

Argod-Dutard, Françoise, Pascal Charvet, and Sandrine Lavaud, eds. 2007. *Voyage aux pays du vin.* Paris: Robert Laffont.

Arnaud, Sophie. 2005. *La Voix de la nature dans l'œuvre de Jacques Peletier du Mans.* Paris: Champion.

Assouly, Olivier. 2004. *Les Nourritures nostalgiques: Essai sur le mythe du terroir.* Arles: Actes Sud.

———. 2007. "Le Motif de la simplicité comme enjeu de la gastronomie." In *Gastronomie et identité culturelle française,* edited by Françoise Hache-Bissette and Denis Saillard, 275–90. Paris: Nouveau Monde.

Atkinson, Geoffroy. 1960. *Le Sentiment de la nature et le retour à la vie simple, 1690–1740.* Geneva: Droz.

Azibert, Mireille Marie Louise. 1972. *L'Influence d'Horace et de Cicéron sur les arts de rhétorique première et seconde sur les arts poétiques du seizième siècle en France.* Pau: Marrimpouey.

Bakhtin, Mikhaïl. 1984. *Rabelais and His World.* Bloomington: Indiana University Press.

Baraton, Alain. 2006. *Le Jardinier de Versailles.* Paris: Grasset.

Baridon, Michel. 2008. *A History of the Gardens of Versailles.* Translated by A. Masson. Philadelphia: University of Pennsylvania Press.

Barthes, Roland. 1961. "Pour une psycho-sociologie de l'alimentation contemporaine." *Annales: Économies, Sociétés, Civilisations* 16, no. 5: 977–86.

———. 1979. "Toward a Psychosociology of Contemporary Food Consumption." In *Food and Drink in History,* edited by R. Forster and O. Ranum, 166–73. Baltimore: Johns Hopkins University Press.

Basset, Karine-Larissa. 2002–4. "Le Légendaire Sarrasin en France." Aix-en-Provence: Maison Méditerannéenne des Sciences de l'Homme–Phonothèque. Audio archive of forty-eight interviews recorded between 1996 and 2004; sixty-six hours. Available online at http://phonotheque.mmsh.univ-aix.fr/Record .htm?idlist = 35&record = 19110845124919380279.

Bauder, Harald, and Salvatore Engel-Di Mauro, eds. 2008. *Critical Geographies: A Collection of Readings.* Kelowna: Praxis (e)Press. Accessed November 25, 2014. www.praxis-epress.org/availablebooks/introcriticalgeog.html.

Bayard, Françoise. 1990. "Les Caves des financiers français au début du XVIIᵉ siècle." In *Le Vin des historiens: Actes du 1er symposium Vin et Histoire,* edited by Gilbert Garrier, 143–52. Suze-la-Rousse: Université du Vin.

Beaune, Colette. 1993. *Naissance de la nation française.* Paris: Gallimard.

Beik, William. 1985. *Absolutism and Society in Seventeenth-Century France: State Power and Provincial Aristocracy in Languedoc.* Cambridge: Cambridge University Press.

———. 2005. "The Absolutism of Louis XIV as Social Collaboration." *Past and Present* 188, no. 1 (August): 195–224.

Belin, Christian. 1995. *L'Œuvre de Pierre Charron, 1541–1603: Littérature et théologie de Montaigne à Port-Royal.* Paris: Champion.

Bell, David. 2001. *The Cult of Nation in France: Inventing Nationalism, 1680–1800.* Cambridge: Harvard University Press.

Bell, David, and Gill Valentine. 1997. *Consuming Geographies: We Are What We Eat.* Routledge: New York.

Bellenger, Yvonne. 1978. "Nature et naturel dans quatre chapitres des *Essais.*" In *Bulletin de la Société internationale des amis de Montaigne* 25, no. 6: 37–49.

———. 1988. "Les Paysages de montagne: L'Evolution des descriptions du début à la fin du XVI siècle." In *Le Paysage à la Renaissance,* edited by Yves Giraud, 121–33. Fribourg: Editions Universitaires Fribourg Suisse.

Benay, Jacques. 1964. "L'Honnête Homme devant la nature ou la philosophie du chevalier du Méré." *PMLA* 79, no. 1 (March): 22–43.

Benrekassa, Georges. 1983. *La Politique et sa mémoire.* Paris: Payot.

Bérard, Laurence, and Philippe Marchenay. 1995. "La Construction sociale des produits du terroir." *Terrain* 24: 153–64.

Berry, Alice Fiona. 1975. "Apollo versus Bacchus: The Dynamics of Inspiration (Rabelais's Prologues to *Gargantua* and to the *Tiers Livre*)." *PMLA* 90, no. 1 (January): 88–95.

Bideaux, Michel, Redmond O'Hanlon, and Jean-Michel Picard, eds. 1995. *Rabelais-Dionysus: Vin, carnaval, ivresse: Actes du colloque de Montpellier, 26–28 mai 1994.* Marseille: J. Laffitte.

Blodgett, E.D. 2004. "Francophone Writing." In *The Cambridge Companion to Canadian Literature,* edited by Eva-Marie Kröller, 49–58. Cambridge: Cambridge University Press.

Blok, Josine. 2009. "Gentrifying Geneology: On the Genesis of the Athenian Autochthony Myth." In *Antike Mythen: Medien, Transformationen und Konstruktionen,* edited by Ueli Dill and Christine Walde, 251–75. Berlin: Walter de Gruyter.

Blowen, Sarah, Marion Demoissier, and Jeanine Picard, eds. 2002. *Recollections of France: Memories, Identities, and Heritage in Contemporary France.* New York: Berghahn Books.

Bluche, François. 1986. *Louis XIV.* Paris: Fayard.

———. 1990. *Louis XIV.* Translated by Mark Greengrass. Oxford: Oxford University Press.

Bonal, François. 1995. *Dom Pérignon: Vérité et légende.* Langres: D. Guéniot.

Bonnet, Jean-Claude. 1979. "Le Système de la cuisine et du repas chez Rousseau." In *Jean Jacques Rousseau et la médecine naturelle,* edited by Serge A. Thériault, 117–50. Montréal: Les Éditions Univers.

Bonney, Richard. 1988. *Society and Government in France under Richelieu and Mazarin, 1624–1671.* New York: St. Martin's Press.

———. 1995. *The Limits of Absolutism in Ancien Régime France.* Aldershot, UK: Variorum.

Bots, Wim. 2004. "Montaigne, du boire et du manger." In *Le Boire et le manger au XVIe siècle,* edited by Marie Viallon, 47–53. Saint-Étienne: Publications de l'Université de Saint-Étienne.

Boulaine, Jean, and Moreau, Richard. 2002. *Olivier de Serres et l'évolution de l'agriculture.* Paris: l'Harmattan.

Boulerie, Florence. 2007. "Le Vin des savants." In *Voyage au pays du vin: Histoire, anthologie, dictionnaire,* edited by Françoise Argod-Dutard, Pascal Charvet, and Sandrine Lavaud. Paris: Robert Laffont.

Bourdieu, Pierre. 1984. *Distinction: A Social Critique of the Judgement of Taste.* Cambridge, MA: Harvard University Press.

Bourgeois, Armand. 1897. *Le Vin de Champagne sous Louis XIV et Louis XV, d'après des lettres et des documents inédits*. Paris: Bibliothèque d'Art de la Critique.

Brennan, Thomas. 1997. *Burgundy to Champagne: The Wine Trade in Early Modern France*. Baltimore: Johns Hopkins University Press.

Brown, James W. 1984. *Fictional Meals and Their Function in the French Novel, 1789–1848*. Toronto: University of Toronto Press.

Brubaker, Rogers. 1992. *Citizenship and Nationhood in France and Germany*. Cambridge, MA: Harvard University Press.

Brunel, Lucien. 1906. *Extraits: Jean-Jacques Rousseau*. Paris: Hachette.

Busson, Henri. 1957. *Le Rationalisme dans la littérature française de la Renaissance*. Paris: Vrin.

Calder, Ruth. 1996. "Molière, Misanthropy, and Forbearance: Eliante's 'Lucretian' Diatribe." *French Studies* 50, no. 2: 138–43.

Candau, Joël. 2000. *Mémoire et expériences olfactives: Anthropologie d'un savoir-faire sensorial*. Paris: PUF.

Capitan, Colette. 1993. *La Nature à l'ordre du jour, 1789–1793*. Paris: Kimé.

Carrier, David. 1993. *Principles of Art History Writing*. University Park: Pennsylvania State University Press.

Casabianca, Denis de. 2008. *Montesquieu: De l'étude des sciences à l'esprit des lois*. Paris: Honoré Champion.

Cave, Terence. 1970. "The Triumph of Bacchus and Its Interpretation in the French Renaissance: Ronsard's *Hinne de Bacus*." In *Humanism in France at the End of the Middle Ages and in the Early Renaissance*, edited by A. H. T. Levi, 249–70. Manchester: Manchester University Press.

———, ed. 1973. *Ronsard the Poet*. London: Methuen.

———. 1979. *The Cornucopian Text: Problems of Writing in the French Renaissance*. Oxford: Clarendon.

———. 2009. "Ronsard's Bacchic Fresco." In *Retrospectives: Essays in Literature, Poetics, and Cultural History by Terence Cave*, 50–75. Leeds: Modern Humanities Research Publications and Maney Publications.

Céard, Jean. 1977. *La Nature et les prodiges: L'Insolite au XVIe siècle en France*. Genève: Droz.

Cerquiglini, Bernard. 2004. *La Genèse de l'orthographe française, XIIe–XVIIe siècles*. Paris: Unichamp-Essentiel.

Chamard, Henri. 1939. *Histoire de la Pléiade*. Paris: H. Didier.

Charbonneau, Frédéric. 2008. *L'École de la gourmandise de Louis XIV à la Révolution*. Paris: Desjonquères.

Chauvigné, Auguste. 1891. "Géographie historique du pays de Véron." *Bulletin historique et descriptive* 6: 389–96.

———. 1909. *Monographie de la commune de Vouvray et de son vignoble*. Tours: Péricat.

Cholvy, Gérard. 1988. *Histoire du Vivarais*. Paris: Privat.

Christodoulou, K. 1979. "Art et nature chez Montaigne." *Bulletin de la Société Internationale des Amis de Montaigne* 5, nos. 31–32: 27–32.

Claflin, Kyri Watson. 2007. "Le 'Retour à la terre' après la Grande Guerre: Politique agricole, cuisine, et régionalisme." In *Gastronomie et identité culturelle française: Discours et représentations, XIXᵉ–XXIᵉ siècles*, edited by F. Hache-Bissette and Denis Saillard, 215–37. Paris: Éditions du Nouveau Monde.

Clark, Priscilla. 1975. "Thoughts for Food 1: French Cuisine and French Culture." *French Review* 49, no. 1: 32–41.

Classen, Constance, David Howes, and Anthony Synnott. 1994. *Aroma: The Cultural History of Smell*. New York: Routledge.

Clermontel, Danièle, and Jean-Claude Clermontel. 2009. *Chronologie scientifique, technologique et économique de la France*. Paris: Publibook.

Coates, Clive. 1997. *Côte d'Or: A Celebration of the Great Wines of Burgundy*. Berkeley: University of California Press.

Coffe, Jean-Pierre, and Alain Baraton. 2007. *La Véritable Histoire des jardins de Versailles*. Paris: Plon.

Conroy, Peter. 1982. "Le Jardin polémique chez J.-J. Rousseau." *Cahiers de l'Association internationale des études francaises* 34: 91–105.

Cooper, Laurence. 1999. *Rousseau, Nature, and the Problem of the Good Life*. University Park: Pennsylvania State University Press.

Cooper, Richard. 2001. "L'Authenticité du *Cinquième Livre:* État présent de la question." In *Le Cinquiesme Livre*, Études rabelaisiennes 40, 9–22. Geneva: Droz.

Corbin, Alain. 1982. *Le Miasme et la jonquille: L'Odorat et l'imaginaire social, XVIIIe-XIXe siècles*. Paris: Aubier Montaigne.

———. 1992. "Paris-Province." In *Les Lieux de mémoire*, edited by Pierre Nora. Vol. 3. Paris: Gallimard.

———. 2001. *L'Homme dans le paysage*. Paris: Les Éditions textuelles.

Corriente, Frederico. 2008. *Dictionary of Arabic and Allied Loanwords: Spanish, Portuguese, Catalan, Galician, and Kindred Dialects*. Leiden: Brill.

Corum, Robert T., Jr. 1998. *Reading Boileau: An Integrative Study of the Early Satires*. West Lafayette, IN: Purdue University Press.

Cosandey, Fanny, and Robert Descimon. 2002. *L'Absolutisme en France: Histoire et historiographie*. Paris: Éditions du Seuil.

Cosgrove, Denis. 1998. *Social Formation and Symbolic Landscape*. Madison: University of Wisconsin Press.

Coulon, Christian. 2009. *La Table de Montaigne*. Paris: Arléa.

Courcelles, Dominique de, ed. 2006. *Nature et paysages: L'Emergence d'une nouvelle subjectivité à la Renaissance*. Paris: École des Chartes.

Courtois, Jean-Patrice. 2004. "Le Physique et le moral dans la théorie du climat chez Montesquieu." In *Lectures de l'Esprit des lois*, edited by Thierry Hoquet and Céline Spector, 101–20. Bordeaux: PUF.

———. 2007. "Le Climat chez Montesquieu et Rousseau." In *L'Événement climatique et ses representations, XVIIe-XIXe siècle*, edited by Emmanuel Le Roy Ladurie, Jacques Berchtold, and J.-P. Sermain, 157–80. Paris: Desjonquères.

Crouzet, Denis. 2005. *Les Guerriers de Dieu: La Violence au temps des troubles de religion, v. 1525–v. 1610*. Collection Époques. Paris: Champ Vallon.

Csergo, Julia. 1998. "Tables provençales au XVIIe siècle: Spécialités locales et régionalisme alimentaire." In *Boire et manger au XVIIe siècle au temps de la marquise de Sévigné: Actes du 2ième symposium Vin et Histoire 16 et 17 Octobre 1996*, edited by Gilber Garrier, 111–36. Suze-La-Rousse: Université du Vin.

———. 1999. "The Emergence of Regional Cuisines." In *Food*, edited by Jean-Louis Flandrin and Massimo Montanari, 500–15. New York: Columbia University Press.

———. 2007. "Du discours gastronomique comme 'propagande nationale': Le Club des Cent, 1912–1930." In *Gastronomie et identité culturelle française: Discours et représentations, XIXe–XXIe siècles*, edited by F. Hache-Bissette and Denis Saillard, 177–201. Paris: Éditions du Nouveau Monde.

———. 2011. "La Gastronomie dans les guides de voyage: De la richesse industrielle au patrimoine culturel, France XIXe–début XXe siècle." In *In Situ* 15. doi: 10.4000/insitu.722. Accessed November 13, 2012.

Curran, Andrew. 2011. *The Anatomy of Blackness: Science and Slavery in an Age of Enlightenment*. Baltimore: Johns Hopkins University Press.

Dalby, Andrew. 2000. *Empire of Pleasures*. London: Routledge.

———. 2003. *Food in the Ancient World from A to Z*. London: Routledge.

Daled, Pierre F. 2005. *Le Matérialisme occulté et la genèse du sensualisme*. Paris: Vrin.

Darmon, Jean-Charles. 1998. *Philosophie épicurienne et littérature au XVIIe siècle*. Paris: PUF.

Darnton, Robert. 1984. *The Great Cat Massacre and Other Episodes in French Cultural History*. New York: Viking.

Davidson, James. 1997. *Courtesans and Fishcakes: The Consuming Passions of Ancient Athens*. London: Harper Collins.

Davis, Jennifer. 2009. "Masters of Disguise: French Cooks between Art and Nature, 1651–1793." *Gastronomica* 9, no. 1: 36–49.

———. 2012. *Defining Culinary Authority: The Tranformation of Cooking in France, 1650–1830*. Baton Rouge: Louisiana State University Press.

De Dijn, Annelien. 2012. *French Political Thought from Montesquieu to Tocqueville*. Cambridge: Cambridge University Press.

DeJean, Joan. 2005. *The Essence of Style: How the French Invented High Fashion, Fine Food, Chic Cafés, Style, Sophistication, and Glamour*. New York: Free Press.

Delaisement, Gérard. 1990. *Papillon de Lasphrise: Poète de Touraine*. Tours: C.L.D.

Delhez-Sarlet, Claudette. 1979. "L'Académie française au temps du Cardinal de Richelieu." *Marche romane* 29, no. 2: 41–60.

Demerson, Guy. 1973. "'Extraicts de haulte mythologie': La Mythologie classique dans les 'Mythologies Pantagruélicques' de Rabelais." *Bulletin de l'Association Guillaume Budé* 25, no. 25: 227–45.

———. 2001. "Trinch ou les hiéroglyphes de la boisson." In *Le Cinquiesme Livre*. Études rabelaisiennes, 40. Edited by Franco Giacone, 127–46. Geneva: Droz.

Dens, Jean-Pierre. 1981. *L'Honnête Homme et la critique du goût*. Lexington, KY: French Forum.

De Rosa, Raffaella. 2010. *Descartes and the Puzzle of Sensory Representation.* New York: Oxford University Press.

De Souza Filho, José Alexandrino. 2004. "La Civilisation à la française vue d'un point de vue culinaire: Le Cas Montaigne." In *Le Boire et le manger au XVIᵉ siècle,* edited by Marie Viallon-Schoneveld, 55–74. Saint-Étienne: Publications de l'Université de Saint-Étienne.

Desrosier-Bonin, Diane. 1992. *Rabelais et l'humanisme civile.* Études rabelaisiennes, 27. Geneva: Droz.

Detienne, Marcel. 1986. *Dionysus à ciel ouvert.* Paris: Hachette.

Dion, Roger. 1959. *Histoire de la vigne et du vin en France.* Doullens: Imprimerie Sévin.

———. 1990. *Le Paysage et la vigne: Essais de géographie historique.* Paris: Bibliothèque Historique Payot.

Dobie, Madeleine. 2010. *Trading Places: Colonization and Slavery in Eighteenth-Century France.* Ithaca: Cornell University Press.

Doody, Aude. 2007. "Virgil the Farmer? Critiques of the *Georgics* in Columella and Pliny." *Classical Philology* 102, no. 2 (April): 180–97.

Dougherty, Percy. 2012. "Introduction to the Geographical Study of Viticulture and Wine Production." In *The Geography of Wines, Regions, Terroirs and Techniques,* edited by Percy Dougherty. London: Springer Dordecht.

Douglas, Mary. (1966) 2002. *Purity and Danger.* London: Routledge.

Dubois, Claude-Gilbert. 1996. "La 'Nation' et ses rapports avec la 'République' et la 'royauté.'" In *Jean Bodin: Nature, Histoire et Politique,* edited by Yves Charles Zarka, 91–113. Paris: PUF.

Duport, Danièle. 2000. "La 'Science' d'Olivier de Serres et la connaissance du 'naturel.'" *Réforme, Humanisme, Renaissance* 50: 85–95.

———. 2002. *Le Jardin et la nature: Ordre et variété dans la littérature de la Renaissance.* Geneva: Droz.

Duval, Edwin. 1983. "Lessons of the New World: Design and Meaning in Montaigne's 'Des Cannibales' and 'Des Coches.'" *Yale French Studies* 64: 99–104.

Ehrard, Jean. 2013. "Nature et jardins dans la pensée française du 18ᵉ siècle." *Dix-huitième siècle* 45, no. 1: 365–77.

Elias, Norbert. 1983. *The Court Society.* Translated by Edmund Jephcott. New York: Pantheon.

Eliav-Feldon, Mariam, Benjamin Isaac, and Joseph Ziegler, eds. 2009. *The Origins of Racism in the West.* Cambridge: Cambridge University Press.

Ellis, Harold. 1986. "Genealogy, History, and Aristocratic Reaction in Early Eighteenth-Century France: The Case of Henri de Boulainvilliers." *Journal of Modern History* 58, no. 2: 414–51.

———. 1988. *Boulainvilliers and the French Monarchy: Aristocratic Politics in Early Eighteenth-Century France.* Ithaca: Cornell University Press.

Eze, E. C. 1997. *Race and the Enlightenment.* Oxford: Oxford University Press.

Faisant, Claude, Josiane Rieu, and James Dauphiné. 1998. *Mort et resurrection de la Pléiade.* Paris: Champion.

Ferguson, Priscilla Parkhurst. 2004. *Accounting for Taste: The Triumph of French Cuisine.* Chicago: University of Chicago Press.

———. 2010. "Culinary Nationalism." *Gastronomica* 10, no. 1 (Winter): 102–9.

Ferry, Luc. 1990. *Homo Aestheticus: L'Invention du goût à l'âge démocratique.* Paris: Grasset.

Fink, Béatrice. 1995. *Les Liaisons savoureuses.* Saint-Étienne: Publications de l'Université de Saint-Étienne.

Fitzpatrick, Joan, ed. 2013. *Renaissance Food from Rabelais to Shakespeare: Culinary Readings and Culinary Histories.* Surrey: Ashgate.

Flandrin, Jean-Louis. 1981. "Différences et différenciation des goûts: Réflexion sur quelques exemples européens entre le 14ᵉ et le 18ᵉ siècle." In *Oxford Symposium Proceedings,* edited by Alan Davidson, 191–207. London: Prospect Books.

———. 1982. "Médecine et habitudes alimentaires anciennes." In *Pratiques et discours alimentaires à la Renaissance, Actes du colloque de Tours 1979,* edited by Jean-Claude Margolin and Robert Sauzet, 85–96. Paris: Maisonneuve et Larose.

———. 1983. "La Diversité des goûts et des pratiques alimentaires en Europe du 16ᵉ au 18ᵉ siècle." *Revue d'histoire moderne et contemporaine* 30 (January-March): 66–83.

———. 1986. "La Distinction par le goût." In *Histoire de la vie privée,* edited by Philippe Ariès and Georges Duby. Vol. 3. Paris: Seuil.

———. 1992. *Chronique de Platine: Pour une gastronomie historique.* Paris: Odile Jacob.

Flandrin, Jean-Louis, and Massimo Montanari, eds. 2000. *Food: A Culinary History.* Translated by Clarissa Botsford, Arthur Goldhammer, Charles Lambert, Frances M. López-Morillas, and Sylvia Stevens. New York: Penguin.

Forbes, Patrick. 1967. *Champagne.* New York: Reynal.

Ford, Caroline. 1993. *Creating the Nation in Provincial France: Religion and Political Identity in Brittany.* Princeton: Princeton University Press.

———. 2001. "Landscape and Environment in French Historical and Geographical Thought: New Directions." *French Historical Studies* 24, no. 1: 125–34.

———. 2004. "Nature, Culture and Conservation in France and Her Colonies, 1840–1940." *Past and Present* 183, no. 1: 173–98.

Ford, Philip. 2007. "Lucretius in Early Modern France." In *The Cambridge Companion to Lucretius,* edited by Stuart Gillespie and Philip Hardie, 227–41. Cambridge: Cambridge University Press.

Forster, Robert, and Orest Ranum, eds. 1979. *Food and Drink in History.* Translated by Patricia Ranum. Baltimore: John Hopkins Press.

Foucault, Michel. 2003. "Society Must Be Defended." In *Lectures at the Collège de France, 1975–1976.* Translated by David Macey. New York: Macmillan.

Fougère, E. 1997. "Le Vin dans *La Nouvelle Heloïse:* In vino veritas." *Dix-huitième Siècle* 29: 199–210.

Fournol, Etienne-Maurice. 1970. *Bodin, prédécesseur de Montesquieu: Étude sur quelques théories politiques de la "République" et de "L'Esprit des lois."* Paris: Slatkine.

Fraisse, Simone. 1962. *L'Influence de Lucrèce en France au seizième siècle: Une conquête du rationalisme.* Paris: A. G. Nizet.

Franklin, Alfred, ed. (1874) 1984. *Les Rues et les cris de Paris au XIIIᵉ siècle.* Paris: Les Editions de Paris.

Freedman, Paul. 2005. "Spices and Late-Medieval European Ideas of Scarcity and Value." *Speculum* 80, no. 4: 1209–27.

———. 2008. *Out of the East: Spices and the Medieval Imagination.* New Haven: Yale University Press.

Frémont, Armont. 1997. *France: Géographie d'une société.* Paris: Flammarion.

Fumaroli, Marc. 1994. *L'Âge de l'éloquence.* Paris: Albin Michel.

Gade, Daniel. 2004. "Tradition, Terroir, and Territory in French Viniculture: Cassis, France, and Appellation Contrôlée." *Annals of the Association of American Geographers* 94, no. 4: 848–67.

Gale, Monica. 2000. *Virgil on the Nature of Things: The Georgics, Lucretius and the Didactic Tradition.* Cambridge: Cambridge University Press.

Garrier, Gilbert. 1995. *Histoire sociale et culturelle du vin.* Paris: Bordas.

———, ed. 1998. *Boire et manger au XVIᵉ siècle au temps de la marquise de Sévigné: Actes du 2ième symposium Vin et Histoire 16 et 17 Octobre 1996.* Suze-la-Rouse: Université du Vin.

Garrigues, Dominique. 2001. *Jardins et jardiniers de Versailles au Grand Siècle.* Paris: Editions Champ Vallon.

Gauter, J.-F. 2003. *Le Vin: De la mythologie à l'œnologie, l'esprit d'une civilisation.* Bordeaux: Éditions Féret.

Gendre, André. 1997. *L'esthétique de Ronsard.* Paris: SEDES.

Gigante, Denise. 2005. *Taste: A Literary History.* New Haven: Yale University Press.

Gillet, Philippe. 1985. *Par mets et par vins, voyages et gastronomie en Europe, XVIᵉ–XVIIIᵉ siècle.* Paris: Payot.

Giuliani, P. 2008. "Le Sang classique entre histoire et littérature, hypothèses et propositions." *XVIIᵉ siècle* 2, no. 239: 223–42.

Goldstein, Claire. 2007. *Vaux and Versailles: The Appropriations, Erasures, and Accidents That Made Modern France.* Philadelphia: University of Philadelphia Press.

Goldstein, Darra, and Kathrin Merkle, eds. 2005. *Culinary Cultures of Europe: Identity, Diversity and Dialogue.* Strasbourg: Council of European Publication.

Gopnik, Adam. 2011. *The Table Comes First: Family, France, and the Meaning of Food.* New York: Random House.

Gorrichon, Martine. 1976. *Les Travaux et les jours à Rome et dans l'ancienne France: Les Agronomes latins inspirateurs d'Olivier de Serres,* thèse- HF gé 32 4, École Normale Supérieure de Tours.

———. 2000. "Sources latines d'Olivier de Serres." *Réforme, Humanisme, Renaissance* 50, no. 50: 45–58.

Gorris-Camos, Rosanna. 2008. "Dans le labyrinthe de Gohory: Lecteur et traducteur de Machiavel." In *Géographie et politique au début de l'âge moderne,* edited by Paolo Carta, 195–229. Paris: ENS.

Guermès, Sophie. 1997. *Le Vin et l'encre: La Littérature française du XIIIe au XXe siècle.* Paris: Mollat.

Guiomar, Jean-Yves. 1986. "*Le Tableau de la géographie de la France* de Vidal de La Blache." In *La Nation,* 569–97. Vol. 2 of *Les Lieux de mémoire,* edited by Pierre Nora. Paris: Gallimard.

Guion, Béatrice. 2012. "Langue et nation: L'Invention du 'Siècle de Louis le Grand.'" *Revue Française d'Histoire des Idées Politiques* 2, no. 36: 347–63.

Guy, Kolleen. 2007. *When Champagne Became French.* Baltimore: Johns Hopkins University Press.

———. 2010. "Imperial Feedback: Food and the French Culinary Legacy." *Contemporary French and Francophone Studies* 14, no. 2 (March): 149–57.

———. 2011. "Silence and Savoir-Faire in the Marketing of Products of the Terroir." *Modern and Contemporary France* 19, no. 4: 459–75.

Hampton, Timothy. 2001. *Literature and Nation in the Sixteenth Century: Inventing Renaissance France.* Ithaca: Cornell University Press.

Hart, Joseph. 2004. "A New Way of Walking." *Utne Reader,* July–August. Accessed July 23, 2013, www.utne.com/2004–07–01/a-new-way-of-walking.aspx#axzz2a3V6IFwE.

Henderson, Jeffrey, ed. 1992. *Lucretius on the Nature of Things.* Cambridge, MA: Loeb.

Henry, François. 2007. "Mots propres, stile, et jargon peculier dans les domaines de la vigne et du vin: Vocabulaire ou terminologie?" In *Le Français préclassique* 10: 47–60.

Higginson, Francis "Pim." 2001. "Eating Your Way Out: The Culinary as Resistance in Ferdinand Oyono's *Le Vieux Nègre et la Médaille.*" In *French Food: On the Table, on the Page, and in French Culture,* edited by Lawrence R. Schehr and Allen S. Weiss. Hove, UK: Psychology Press.

Hinnewinkel, Jean-Claude. 2004. *Les Terroirs viticoles, origines et devenirs.* Bordeaux: Féret.

Hoffman, George. 2006. "Montaigne and the Investigation of Nature." In *The Cambridge Campanion to Montaigne,* edited by Ullrich Langer. Cambridge: Cambridge University Press.

Hope, Quentin M. 1962. *The "Honnête Homme" as Critic.* Bloomington: Indiana University Press.

———. 1993. "Saint-Évremond and the Pleasures of the Table." *Papers on French Seventeenth Century Literature* 20: 9–36.

Hornblower, Simon, and Antony Spawforth, eds. 1996. *The Oxford Classical Dictionary.* Oxford: Oxford University Press.

Horowitz, Asher. 1987. *Rousseau, Nature, and History.* Toronto: University of Toronto Press.

Howes, David, ed. 2005. *Empire of the Senses: The Sensual Culture Reader.* Oxford: Berg.

Hudson, Nicholas. 1996. "From 'Nation' to 'Race': The Origin of Racial Classification in Eighteenth-Century Thought." In *Eighteenth-Century Studies* 29, no. 3: 247–64.

Hulubei, Alice. 1938. *L'Églogue en France au XVIe siècle.* Paris: Droz.

Hurt, John J. 2002. *Louis XIV and the Parlements: The Assertion of Royal Authority.* Manchester: Manchester University Press.

Hyman, Philip, and Jean-Louis Flandrin. 1986. "Regional Tastes and Cuisines: Problems, Documents, and Discourses on Food in Southern France in the Sixteenth and Seventeenth Centuries." *Food and Foodways* no. 3: 221–52.

Hyman, Philip, and Mary Hyman. 1983. "Les Cuisines régionales à travers des livres de recettes." *Dix-huitième Siècle* 15: 65–74.

———. 1997. "Imprimer la cuisine." In *Histoire de l'alimentation,* edited by Jean-Louis Flandrin and Massimo Montanari, 643–45. Paris: Fayard.

Isaac, Benjamin. 2004. *The Invention of Racism in Classical Antiquity.* Princeton: Princeton University Press.

Jackson, John Brinckerhoff. 1994. *A Sense of Place, a Sense of Time.* New Haven: Yale University Press.

Jacquet, Olivier. 2008. "Territoire politique socialiste et terroir viticole." *Cahiers d'histoire, Revue d'histoire critique* 103: 24–36.

Jacquet, Olivier, and Gilles Laferté. 2006. "Le Contrôle républicain du marché: Vignerons et négociants sous la Troisième République." *Annales: Histoire, Sciences Sociales* 61, no. 5 (September–October): 1147–70.

Jeanneret, Michel. 1983. "Alimentation, digestion, réflexion dans Rabelais." *Studi Francesci* 81: 405–16.

———. 1987. *Des mets et des mots: Banquets et propos de la table à la Renaissance.* Paris: J. Corti.

———. 1989. "Banquets poétiques et métaphores alimentaires." In *Ronsard en son quatrième centaire,* edited by Yvonne Bellanger, Jean Céard, Daniel Ménager, and Michel Simonin, 2: 73–80. Genève: Droz.

———. 1991. *A Feast of Words: Banquets and Table Talk in the Renaissance.* Translated by Jeremy Whiteley and Emma Hughes. Chicago: Chicago University Press.

Jenkyns, Richard. 1998. *Virgil's Experience: Nature and History; Times, Names, and Places.* Oxford: Clarendon Press.

Johnson, Monte Ransome. 2003. "Was Gassendi an Epicurean?" *History of Philosophy Quarterly* 20, no. 4: 339–60.

Johnson, W. R. 2000. *Lucretius and the Modern World.* London: Gerald Duckworth.

Joukowsky, Françoise. 1988. "Qu'est-ce qu'un paysage ?" In *Le Paysage à la Renaissance,* edited by Yves Giraud, 55–65. Fribourg: Editions Universitaires Fribourg Suisse.

Kerényi, Carl. 1979. *Dionysus: Archetypal Image of Indestructible Life.* Translated by Ralph Manheim. Princeton: Princeton University Press.

Kinser, Samuel. 1990. "What Makes Sausage People Fight." In *Rabelais's Carnival: Text, Context, Metatext,* 93–110. Berkeley: Univesity of California Press.

Kladstrup, Don, and Petie Kladstrup. 2005. *Champagne.* New York: Harper Collins.

Korsmeyer, Carolyn. 1999. *Making Sense of Taste: Food and Philosophy.* Ithaca: Cornell University Press.

Krebs, Christopher. 2011. *A Most Dangerous Book: Tacitus's "Germania" from the Roman Empire to the Third Reich.* New York: Norton.

Lachiver, Marcel. 1990. "Autour du vin clairet." In *Le Vin des historiens: Actes du 1er symposium Vin et Histoire,* edited by Gilbert Garrier, 135–42. Suze-la-Rousse: Université du Vin.

Ladurie, Emmanuel Le Roy. 2002. *Histoire des paysans français: De la peste noire à la Révolution.* Paris: Seuil.

Lallemand, Marie-Gabrielle. 2005. "Saint-Évremond et le roman." In *Saint-Évremond au miroir du temps: Actes du colloque du tricentenaire de sa mort, Caen–Saint Lô (9–11 octobre 2003),* edited by Suzanne Guellouz, 121–36. Tübingen: Narr.

Lange, Frederick. 1925. *The History of Materialism.* New York: Harcourt, Brace, and Co.

Latour, Bruno. (1984) 1993. *The Pasteurization of France.* Translated by Alan Sheridan and John Law. Cambridge: Harvard University Press.

Laudun, Rachel. 2004. "Slow Food: The French Terroir Strategy and Culinary Modernism." In *Food, Culture and Society* 7, no. 2: 133–44.

Laumonier, Paul. 1932. *Ronsard, poète lyrique: Étude littéraire et historique.* Paris: Slatkine.

Laurioux, Bruno. 2006. *Gastronomie, humanisme et société à Rome au milieu du XVe siècle: Autour du* De honesta voluptate *de Platina.* Florence: Sismel, Edizioni del Galluzzo.

Lavondés, A. 1900. *Olivier de Serres: Seigneur du Pradel.* Paris: La Cause.

Lee, Leonard, Shane Frederick, and Dan Ariely. 2006. "Try It, You'll Like It: The Influence of Expectation, Consumption, and Revelation on Preferences for Beer." *Psychological Science* 17, no. 12: 1054–58.

Lennon, Thomas. 1993. *The Battles of Gods and Giants: The Legacies of Descartes and Gassendi, 1655–1715.* Princeton: Princeton University Press.

Lenoble, Robert. 1969. *Esquisse d'une histoire de l'idée de nature.* Paris: Albin Michel.

Lequenne, Fernand. 1983. *Olivier de Serres: Agronome et soldat de Dieu.* Paris: Berger- Levrault.

Lestrigant, Franck. 1982. "Europe et la théorie des climats dans la seconde moitié du XVIe siècle." In *La Conscience européenne au XVe et au XVI siècle,* 206–26. Paris: Ecole Normale Supérieure des Jeunes Filles.

———. 1993. *Écrire le monde à la Renaissance: Quinze Études sur Rabelais, Postel, Bodin et la littérature géographique.* Caen: Paradigme.

———. 2003. *Sous la leçon des vents: Le Monde d'Andre Thevet, cosmographe de la Renaissance.* Paris: Presses Universitaires de France.

Leushuis, Reinier, ed. 2008. *Esprit généreux, esprit pantagruélicque: Essays by His Students in Honor of François Rigolot.* Genève: Droz.

Leveel, Pierre. 2005. "Rabelais et la géographie." *Bulletin de l'Association des Amis de Rabelais et de La Devinière* 6, no. 4: 341–49.

Lewis, Charlton T., and Charles Short. 1879. *A Latin Dictionary.* Oxford: Clarendon.

Liaroutzos, Chantal. 1998. *Le Pays et la mémoire: Pratiques et représentations de l'espace français chez Gilles Corrozet et Charles Estienne.* Paris: Champion.

Lombard, Alfred. 1913. *L'Abbé du Bos, un initiateur de la pensée moderne, 1670–1742.* Paris: Hachette.

Long, Lucy, ed. 2010. *Culinary Tourism.* Lexington: University of Kentucky Press.

López Férez, J. A. 1994. "Los escritos hipocráticos y el nacimiento de la identidad europea." In *The Birth of European Identity: The Europe-Asia Contrast in Greek Thought 490–322 B.C.,* edited by H. A. Khan, 90–123. Nottingham: Nottingham University Press.

Lukacs, Paul. 2012. *Inventing Wine.* New York: Norton.

Mabilleau, Eric, Jean-Marie Cloué, and Claude Viel. 2002. "Le Vin dans l'œuvre de Rabelais." *Bulletin de l'Association des Amis de Rabelais et de La Devinière* 6, no. 1: 79–87.

Mackenzie, Louisa. 2011. *The Poetry of Place: Lyric, Landscape, and Ideology in Renaissance France.* Toronto: University of Toronto Press.

Mahé, Nathalie. 1988. *Le Mythe de Bacchus dans la poésie lyrique de 1549 à 1600.* Berne: P. Lang.

Marenco, Claudine. 1992. *Manières de table, modèles de mœurs: 17ème–20ème siècle.* Cachan: Éditions de l'E.N.S-Cachan.

Margolin, Jean-Claude. 2004. "Vagabondage culinaire et métaphores gastronomiques à travers la France du XVIe siècle." In *Le Boire et le manger au XVIe siècle,* edited by Marie Viallon, 31–46. Saint-Étienne: Publications de l'Université de Saint-Etienne.

Margolin, Jean-Claude, and Robert Sauzet, eds. 1982. *Pratiques et discours alimentaires à la Renaissance: Actes du colloque de Tours 1979.* Paris: Maisonneuve et Larose.

Mariage, Thierry. (1990) 1999. *The World of André Le Nôtre.* Translated by Graham Larkin. Philadelphia: University of Pennsylvania Press.

Mason, Adrienne. 2006. "'L'Air du climat et le goût du terroir': Translation as Cultural Capital in the Writings of Mme Du Châtelet." In *Emilie Du Châtelet: Rewriting Enlightenment Philosophy and Science,* edited and introduced by Judith P. Zinsser and Julie Candler Hayes, 124–41. Oxford: Voltaire Foundation.

McGovern, Flemming, and Solomon Katz, eds. 2004. *The Origins and Ancient History of Wine: Food and Nutrition in History and Anthropology,* Vol. 1, *Food and Nutrition in History and Anthropology.* London: Routledge.

Mennell, Stephen. 1996. *All Manners of Food: Eating and Taste in England and France from the Middle Ages to the Present.* Chicago: University of Illinois Press.

Mercier, Guy. 1995. "La Région et l'état selon Friedrich Ratzel et Paul Vidal de la Blache." *Annales de Géographie* 104, no. 583: 211–35.

Micha, Alexandre. 1964. *Le Singulier Montaigne.* Paris: Nizet.

Mignon, Ernest. 1962. *Les Mots du Général de Gaulle.* Illustrations by Jacques Faizant. Paris: Fayard.

Miller, Christopher. 2008. *The French Atlantic Triangle: Literature and Culture of the Slave Trade.* Durham, NC: Duke University Press.

Monferran, Jean-Charles. 1995. "De quelques lunes du XVIe siècle: L'Amour des amours de Jacques Peletier du Mans, La Sepmaine de Du Bartas." *Revue d'Histoire littéraire de France* 5: 675–89.

Montanari, Massimo. 1995. *La Faim et l'abondance: Histoire de l'alimentation en Europe.* Translated by Monique Aymard. Paris: Seuil.

Moriarty, Michael. 1988. *Taste and Ideology in Seventeenth-Century France.* Cambridge: Cambridge University Press.

Mornet, Daniel. 1907. *Le Sentiment de la nature en France de J.-J Rousseau à Bernardin de Saint-Pierre: Essai sur les rapports de la littérature et des mœurs.* New York: Burt Franklin.

Mottoule, Mathilde. 2006. *Vatel ou l'origine d'un mythe.* Paris: Fayard.

Mukerji, Chandra. 1997. *Territorial Ambitions and the Gardens of Versailles.* Cambridge: Cambridge University Press.

Musset, Benoît. 2007. "La Représentation du vin de Champagne en bouteilles dans les petits appartements du roi à Versailles." In *Le Verre et le vin de la cave au XVIIe à nos jours,* edited by Christophe Bouneau and Michel Figeac, 81–94. Pessac: MSHA.

———. 2008. *Vignobles de Champagne et vins mousseux: Histoire d'un mariage de raison 1650–1830.* Paris: Fayard.

Nappa, Christopher. 2005. "The Riddles of Bacchus." In *Reading after Actium: Vergil's "Georgics," Octavian, and Rome,* 68–114. Ann Arbor: University of Michigan Press.

Naves, Raymond. 1936. "Un Adversaire de la théorie des climats au XVIIe siècle: Adrien Baillet." *Revue d'histoire littéraire de la France* 43, no. 3: 430–33.

Nelson, Stephanie. 1998. *God and the Land: The Metaphysics of Farming in Hesiod and Vergil.* Oxford: Oxford University Press.

Nichols, Robert. 2010. "Henri de Boulainvilliers and the Interpretation of Racism." Paper presented at the Western Political Science Association 2010 Annual Meeting. Available at the Social Science Research Network, http://papers.ssrn.com /sol3/papers.cfm?abstract_id = 1580723. Accessed August 30, 2013.

Nicolet, Claude. 2003. *La Fabrique d'une nation: La France entre Rome et les Germains.* Paris: Perrin.

Nora, Pierre, ed. 1984–92. *Les Lieux de mémoire.* 3 vols. Paris: Gallimard.

Norman, Larry. 2011. *The Shock of the Ancient.* Chicago: University of Chicago Press.

Nossiter, Jonathan. 2009. *Liquid Memory.* New York: Farrar, Straus and Giroux.

O'Brien, John. 1995. *Anacreon Redivivus: A Study of Anacreontic Translation in Mid-Sixteenth-Century France.* Ann Arbor: University of Michigan Press.

———. 2000. "At Montaigne's Table." *French Studies* 54, no. 1: 1–16.

O'Hanlon, Redmond, Michael Bideaux, and Pierre Sauzeau, eds. 2000. *Bacchanales: Actes des colloques 1996–1998 organisés à Montpellier par l'Association Dionysos.* Montpellier: Université Paul Valéry.

Ory, Pascal. 1992. "La gastronomie." In *Les Lieux de mémoire,* edited by Pierre Nora, vol. 3, 743–69. Paris: Gallimard.

———. 1998. *Le Discours gastronomique des origines à nos jours*. Paris: Gallimard, Collection Archives.

Osler, Margaret. 1994. *Divine Will and the Mechanical Philosophy: Gassendi and Descartes on Contingency and Necessity in the Created World*. Cambridge: Cambridge University Press.

Ozouf-Marignier, Marie-Vic. 1989. *La Formation des départements: La Représentation du territoire français à la fin du 18ᵉ siècle*. Paris: École des Hautes Études en Sciences Sociales.

Passy, Louis. 1912. *Histoire de la Société nationale d'agriculture: 1761–1793*. Paris: Renouard.

Pickard-Cambridge, Sir Arthur. (1953) 1968. *The Dramatic Festivals of Athens*. Oxford: Clarendon.

Pinkard, Susan. 2008. *A Revolution in Taste: The Rise of French Cuisine*. Cambridge: Cambridge University Press.

Pitte, Jean-Robert. 1991. *Gastronomie française: Histoire et géographie d'une passion*. Paris: Fayard.

———. 2006. *Géographie culturelle*. Paris: Fayard.

Pitte, Jean-Robert, and Robert Duleau, eds. 1998. *Géographie des odeurs*. Paris: L'Harmattan.

Pitte, Jean-Robert, and Massimo Montanari, eds. 2009. *Frontières alimentaires*. Paris: CNRS.

Plack, Noelle. 2009. *Common Land, Wine and the French Revolution: Rural Society and Economy in Southern France, c. 1789–1820*. Surrey, UK: Ashgate.

Poliakov, Léon. 1971. *Le Mythe aryen: Essai sur les sources du racisme et des nationalismes*. Paris: Calmann-Lévy.

Potts, Denys. 2002. *Saint-Évremond: A Voice from Exile: Newly Discovered Letters to Madame de Gouville and the Abbé de Hautefeuille, 1697–1701*. Oxford: Legenda, European Humanities Research Centre, Oxford University.

Poulain, Jean-Pierre. 1997. "Goût du terroir et tourisme vert à l'heure de l'Europe." *Ethnologie française* 27, no. 1: 18–26.

———. 2002. *Sociologies de l'alimentation*. Paris: PUF.

Prettejohn, Elizabeth. 2005. *Beauty and Art, 1750–2000*. Oxford: Oxford University Press.

Putnam, M. C. J. 1979. *Virgil's Poem of the Earth: Studies in the Georgics*. Princeton: Princeton University Press.

Quellier, Florent. 2007a. *La Table des Français: Une Histoire culturelle (XVᵉ–début XIXᵉ siècle)*. Rennes: Presses Universitaires de Rennes.

———. 2007b. "Les Fruits de la civilité françoise: L'Engouement des élites du 17ᵉ siècle pour le jardin fruitier-potager." *Polia: Revue de l'art des jardins* 8 (Autumn): 25–39.

———. 2012. "Le Discours sur la richesse des terroirs au XVIIᵉ siècle et les prémices de la gastronomie française." *Dix-septième siècle* 254, no. 1: 141–54.

Quint, David. 1983. *Origin and Originality in Renaissance Literature*. New Haven: Yale University Press.

Rahe, Paul Anthony. 2009. *Montesquieu and the Logic of Liberty.* New Haven: Yale University Press.

Renner, Bernd. 2007. "From the 'Bien Yvres' to Messere Gaster: The Syncretism of Rabelaisian Banquets." In *At the Table: Metaphorical and Material Cultures of Food in Medieval and Early Modern Europe,* edited by Timothy Tomasik and Juliann Vitullo, 167–85, Arizona Studies in the Middle Ages and the Renaissance, no. 18. Turnhout, Belgium: Brepols.

Revel, Jean-François. 1985. *Un Festin en paroles: La Sensibilité gastronomique de l'antiquité à nos jours.* Paris: Suger.

Rigolot, François. 1995. " 'Service divin, service du vin': L'Équivoque dionysiaque." In *Rabelais-Dionysus: Vin, carnaval, ivresse: Actes du colloque de Montpellier, 26–28 mai 1994,* edited by Michel Bideaux, Redmond O'Hanlon, and Jean-Michel Picard. Marseille: Editions J. Laffitte.

———. 1996. *Les Langages de Rabelais.* Geneva: Droz.

———. 2002. "La Théorie méliorative de l'imitation." In *Ronsard, figure de la variété, en mémoire d'Isidore Silver,* edited by Colette H. Winn, 87–98. Travaux d'humanisme et de Renaissance, no. 368. Geneva: Droz.

Robic, Marie-Claire. 1994. "National Identity in Vidal's *Tableau de la géographie de la France:* From Political Geography to Human Geography." In *Geography and National Identity,* edited by David J.M. Hooson, 58–70. Oxford: Blackwell.

———. 1999. "L'Identité nationale et ses enjeux: À propos du *Tableau de la géographie de la France* de P. Vidal de la Blache." *Treballs de la Societat Catalana de Geografia* 48: 125–37.

———, ed. 2000. Le Tableau de la géographie de la France *de Paul Vidal de la Blache: Dans le labyrinthe des formes.* Paris: Committée de travaux historiques et scientifiques.

Robinson, Jancis. 2006. *The Oxford Companion to Wine.* Oxford: Oxford University Press.

Robinson, Jancis, and Hugh Johnson. 2013. *A World Atlas to Wine.* London: Beazley.

Roche, Daniel. 1998. "Le Vin, le pain, le gout." In *Clio dans les vignes, mélanges offerts à Gilbert Garrier,* edited by Jean-Luc Mayaud, 271–85. Lyon: Presses Universitaires de Lyon.

Roger, Jacques. 1997. *Buffon: A Life of Natural History.* Translated by Sarah Lucille Bonnefoi. Ithaca: Cornell University Press.

Rosivach, Vincent J. 1987. "Autochthony and the Athenians." *Classical Quarterly,* new ser. 37: 294–306.

Rouby, Catherine, Benoist Schaal, Danièle Dubois, Rémi Gervais, and A. Holley, eds. 2002. *Olfaction, Taste, and Cognition.* Cambridge: Cambridge University Press.

Rougé, Jacques-Marie, André Dupuis, and Émile Millet. 1936. *Aux beaux pays de Loire.* Tours: Arrault.

Sabatier, Gérard. 1998. "Une Révolution de palais: Le Remplacement des vins de Champagne par ceux de Bourgogne à la table de Louis XIV en 1694." In *Boire et* *manger au XVIIe siècle au temps de la marquise de Sévigné, Actes du IIe symposium Vin et Histoire,* edited by Gilber Garrier, 43–58. Suze-la-Rousse: Université du Vin.

Saillard, Denis. 2007. "Discours gastronomique et discours identitaires 1890–1950." In *Gastronomie et identité culturelle française: Discours et représentations, XIXe–XXIe siècles,* edited by Françoise Hache-Bissette and Denis Saillard, 233–50. Paris: Éditions du Nouveau Monde.

Sarasohn, Lisa. 1996. *Gassendi's Ethics: Freedom in a Mechanistic Universe.* Ithaca: Cornell University Press.

Schab, Frank, and Robert Crowder, eds. 1995. *Memory for Odors.* New Jersey: Lawrence Erlbaum.

Schäfer, Sabine. 1996. *Das Weltbild der Vergilischen* Georgika *in seinem Verhältnis zu* De rerum natura *des Lukrez.* Frankfurt: Peter Lang.

Schmidt, Albert-Marie. 1938. *La Poésie scientifique en France au seizième siècle.* Paris: Albin Michel.

Schneider, Bettina. 1996. *Nature und Art in Montaignes Essais.* Tübingen: Papers on French Seventeenth Century Literature.

Schosler, Jorn. 1978. La Position sensualiste de Jean-Jacques Rousseau." *Revue romane* 18, no. 1: 63–87.

Screech, M. A. 1979. *Rabelais.* Ithaca: Cornell University Press.

———. 1980. "The Winged Bacchus: Pausanias, Rabelais and Later Emblematists." *Journal of the Warburg and Courtauld Institutes* 43: 259–62.

Seaford, Richard. 2006. *Dionysos.* New York: Routledge.

Sedley, David. 1998. *Lucretius and the Transformation of Greek Wisdom.* Cambridge: Cambridge University Press.

Shapin, Steven. 2012. "The Tastes of Wine: Towards a Cultural History." *Rivista di Estetica* 51, no. 3: 49–94.

Shoemaker, Peter. 2007. *Powerful Connections: The Poetics of Patronage in the Age of Louis XIII.* Newark: University of Delaware Press.

Silver, Isidore. 1961. *Ronsard and the Hellenic Renaissance in France.* Vol. 1. St. Louis: Washington University Press.

Siraisi, Nancy. 1997. *Clock and the Mirror: Girolamo Cardano and Renaissance Medicine.* Princeton: Princeton University Press.

———. 2007. *History, Medicine, and the Traditions of Renaissance Learning.* Ann Arbor: University of Michigan Press.

Slavitt, David. 1990. *Eclogues and Georgics of Virgil.* Baltimore: Johns Hopkins University Press.

Smith, P. H. 1984. *The Anti-Courier Trend in Sixteenth-Century French Literature.* Geneva: Droz.

Spang, Rebecca. 2000. *The Invention of the Restaurant: Paris and Modern Gastronomic Culture.* Cambridge, MA: Harvard University Press.

Spary, E. C. 2012. *Eating the Enlightenment: Food and Sciences in Paris.* Chicago: University of Chicago Press.

Spence, Charles, and Betina Piqueras-Fiszman. 2014. *The Perfect Meal: The Multisensory Science of Food and Dining.* Oxford: Wiley Blackwell.

Spurr, M. S. 1986. "Agriculture and the *Georgics.*" *Greece and Rome* 33, no. 2: 164–87.

Staszak, Jean-François, and Marie-Dominique Couzinet. 1998. "À quoi sert la 'théorie des climats'? Éléments d'une histoire du déterminisme environnemental." *Corpus* 34: 9–43.

Steiner, Philippe. 1998. *Sociologie de la connaissance économique: Essai sur les rationalisations de la connaissance économique, 1750–1850.* Paris: PUF.

———. 2003. "Physiocracy and French Preclassical Political Economy." In *A Companion to the History of Economic Thought,* edited by Jeff E. Biddle, Jon B. Davis, Warren J. Samuels, 61–78. Malden, MA: Blackwell.

Stengel, Kilien. 2008. *Chronologie de la gastronomie et de l'alimentation.* Nantes: Éditions du temps.

Storer, Walter Henry. 1923. *Virgil and Ronsard.* Paris: Librairie Ancienne Edouard Champion.

Takats, Sean. 2011. *Expert Cook in Enlightenment France.* Baltimore: Johns Hopkins University Press.

Tanner, Jeremy. 2005. *The Invention of Art History in Ancient Greece: Religion, Society and Artistic Rationalisation.* Cambridge: Cambridge University Press.

Thacker, Christopher. 1979. *The History of Gardens.* Berkeley: University of California Press.

Thiesse, Anne-Marie. 1991. *Écrire la France: Le Mouvement littéraire régionaliste de langue française entre la belle époque et la liberation.* Paris: PUF.

———. 1997. *Ils apprenaient la France: L'Exaltation des régions dans le discours patriotique.* Paris: Éditions de la Maison Sciences de l'Homme.

———. 1999. *Création des identités nationales: Europe, XVIIIᵉ–XXᵉ siècle.* Paris: Seuil.

Thomas, Keith. 1983. *Man and the Natural World: A History of the Modern Sensibility.* New York: Pantheon.

Thomas, Richard. 1982. *Lands and Peoples in Roman Poetry: An Ethnographic Tradition.* Cambridge: Cambridge Philological Society.

Tobin, Ronald. 1985. *Littérature et gastronomie: Huit études.* Paris: Papers on French Seventeenth Century Literature.

Tomasik, Timothy J. 2001. "Certeau à la Carte: Translating Discursive Terroir in the Practice of Everyday Life and Cooking." *South Atlantic Quarterly* 100 (Spring): 517–40.

———. 2010. "Fishes, Fowl, and *La Fleur de toute cuysine:* Gaster and Gastronomy in Rabelais's *Quart Livre.*" In *Renaissance Food from Rabelais to Shakespeare: Culinary Readings and Culinary Histories,* edited by Joan Fitzpatrick, 25–51. Burlington, VT: Ashgate.

Tomasik, Timothy J., and Juliann Vitullo, eds. 2007. *At the Table: Metaphorical and Material Cultures of Food in Medieval and Early Modern Europe.* Turnhout, Belgium: Brepols.

Torero-Ibad, Alexandra. 2009. *Libertinage, science et philosophie dans le matérialisme de Cyrano de Bergerac.* Paris: Honoré Champion.

Trubek, Amy. 2008. *The Taste of Place: A Cultural Journey into Terroir*. Berkeley: University of California Press.

Tsakiropoulou-Summers, Tatiana. 2001. "Lambin's Edition of Lucretius: Using Plato and Aristotle in Defense of *De Rerum Natura*." *Classical and Modern Literature* 21, no. 2: 45–70.

Tsien, Jennifer. 2012. *The Bad Taste of Others: Judging Literary Value in Eighteenth-Century France*. Philadelphia: University of Pennsylvania Press.

Tuan, Yi-Fu. 1974. *Topophilia: A Study of Environmental Perception, Attitudes, and Values*. Englewood Cliffs, NJ: Prentice-Hall.

Unwin, Tim. 2012. "Terroir: At the Heart of Geography." In *The Geography of Wines, Regions, Terroirs and Techniques,* ed. Percy Dougherty. London: Springer Dordecht.

Usher, Phillip John, and Isabelle Fernbach, eds. 2012. *Virgilian Identities in the French Renaissance*. Gallica, 27. Rochester, NY: Woodbridge.

Van Bever, Adolphe, ed. (1909) 1918. *Les Poètes du terroir du XVe siècle au XX siècle*. 3 vols. Paris: G. Crès.

Varriano, John. 2010. *Wine: A Cultural History*. London: Reaktion.

Vaudour, Emmanuelle. 2002. "The Quality of Grapes and Wine in Relation to Geography: Notions of *Terroir* at Various Scales." *Journal of Wine Research* 13, no. 2: 117–41.

———. 2003. *Les Terroirs viticoles: Définitions, caractérisation et protection*. Paris: Dunod.

Verdon, Jean. 2002. *Boire au moyen âge*. Paris: Perrin.

Vernant, Jean-Pierre, and Albert Henrichs. 1982. "Changing Dionysiac Identities." In *Self Definition in the Graeco-Roman World,* edited by B. F. Meyer and E. P. Sanders, 137–60 and 213–16. London: SCM.

Viel, Claude. 2001. "Gastronomie rabelaisienne: La Fouace." *Bulletin de l'Association des Amis de Rabelais et de La Devinière* 5, no. 10: 686–88.

———. 2004a. "Gastronomie rabelaisienne: Vins aromatiques, hypocras, hydromel." *Bulletin de l'Association des Amis de Rabelais et de La Devinière* 6, no. 3: 299–301.

———. 2004b. "Rabelais médecin et naturaliste." *Bulletin de l'Association des Amis de Rabelais et de La Devinière* 6, no. 3: 286–92.

Volpilhac-Auger, Cathérine. 2000. "La Dissertation sur la différence des génies: Essai de reconstition." *Revue Montesquieu* 4: 226–37.

Vroon, Piet. 1997. *Smell*. Translated by Paul Vincent. New York: Farrar, Straus, and Giroux.

Vyverberg, Henry. 1989. *Human Nature, Cultural Diversity, and the French Enlightenment*. New York: Oxford.

Walker, Daniel Pickering. (1958) 2000. *Spritiual and Demonic Magic: From Ficino to Campanella*. University Park: Penn State Press.

Weber, Eugen. 1976. *Peasants into Frenchmen: The Modernization of Rural France, 1880–1914*. Stanford, CA: Stanford University Press.

————. 1983. *La Fin des terroirs: La Modernisation de la France rurale, 1870–1914*. Translated by Antoine Berman and Bernard Géniès. Paris: Fayard.

Weil, Patrick. 2002. *Qu'est-ce qu'un Français? Histoire de la nationalité française depuis la Révolution*. Paris: Grasset.

Weinberg, Florence M. 1972. *The Wine and Will: Rabelais' Bacchic Christianity*. Detroit: Wayne State University Press.

West, Stephanie. 2000. "Herodotus in the North? Reflections on a Colossal Cauldron." *Script Classica Israelica* 19: 15–34.

West-Sooby, John, ed. 2004. *Consuming Culture: The Arts of the French Table*. Newark: University of Delaware Press.

Wheaton, Barbara. 1983. *Savoring the Past: The French Kitchen and Table from 1300 to 1789*. Philadelphia: University of Pennsylvania Press.

White, K. D. 1970. *Roman Farming*. London: Thames and Hudson.

Wilson, James E. 1998. *Terroir: The Role of Geology, Climate, and Culture in the Making of French Wines*. Berkeley: University of Califonia Press.

Wilson, Margaret. 1991. "Descartes on the Origin of Sensation." *Philosophical Topics* 19, no. 1: 293–323.

Wilson-Okamur, David Scott. 2010. *Virgil in the Renaissance*. Cambridge: Cambridge University Press.

Wolikow, Claudine. 1998. "Vins, vignes, vignerons en France aux XVIIe–XVIIIe siècles." In *La Terre et les paysans en France et en Grande-Bretagne de 1600–1800*, edited by Hélène Fréchet, 253–76. Paris: Editions du Temps.

Wood, Allen G. 2004. "Boileau, régnier et le repas ridicule." *Papers on French Seventeenth Century Literature* 31, no. 61: 511–22.

Wood, Ian. 2013. *The Modern Origins of the Early Middle Ages*. Oxford: Oxford University Press.

Woodfield, Richard. 1973. "Winkelmann and the Abbé Du Bos." *British Journal of Aesthetics* 13, no. 3: 271–75.

Young, Arthur. 1906. *Arthur Young's Travels in France during the Years 1787, 1788, 1789*. Edited by Matilda Bethem-Edwards. London: G. Bell and Sons.

INDEX

absolutism: and the connotations of terroir, 54, 55, 72, 76; debates about, 11–12, 114–15. *See also* political theory

Académie française, 54, 56, 58, 174n12; *Dictionnaire de l'Académie Française,* 2, 63, 173n6, 174n28

advertisements, 4*fig.,* 16*fig.,* 131*fig.,* 155*fig.*

aesthetics: culinary aesthetics, 71–72, 87–92, 131–32, 134; emergence of terroir as aesthetic construct, 29, 34, 35–36, 55–56, 77–78; environmental determinism and, 114–15, 127; garden aesthetics, 12, 78–79, 136, 143–45; and terroir in Du Bos, 119–20, 126–28. *See also* beauty; order/disorder; purity/impurity; taste (discernment)

agricultural literature: eighteenth-century, 140–41, 145, 176–77n28; literary influences on, 10, 29; sixteenth-century, 29–35, 37, 169–70n55. *See also* garden literature; *Théâtre d'agriculture; other specific authors and titles*

agricultural metaphors, 67; in the Pléiade poets, 26, 27–29, 39, 168n39. *See also* humans-as-plants metaphors

agriculture and agricultural terroir, 5, 6–7; agricultural appellations, 2–3, 155, 157, 161; cultivated vs. wild foods, 40; in de Serres, 50, 51–52, 74–76, 77; eighteenth-century attitudes toward, 117–18, 134, 136–37, 141–43, 145; impact of modernization on regional differences, 186n12; and post-Revolutionary national iden-

tity, 149–50; seventeenth-century attitudes toward, 51–52, 73–78, 81, 117–18; *sociétés d'agriculture,* 134, 141–43, 145; techniques employed at Versailles, 80, 81*fig.,* 136; *terroir* as agricultural term, 50, 55–56, 77, 145; upper-class disdain for, 117–18, 145, 172n36,50; vs. gardens and gardening, 74. *See also* culinary terroir; *Georgics;* plants; soils; viticulture; wines and wine drinking

L'Agriculture et la maison rustique (Estienne and Liébault), 32–34, 50, 51, 178n1

L'Agriculture ou les Géorgiques françaises (Rosset), 145

air, as element of terroir, 8, 41, 66, 121, 122, 124, 126

Airs, Waters, and Places (Hippocrates), 43

Alembert, Jean Le Rond d', 60, 108. *See also Encyclopédie*

Alexandre (Racine), 105–6, 127

Alexandre-Bidon, Danièle, 172n35

Alletz, Pons Augustin, 176–77n28

Almanach des gourmands (Grimod de la Reynière), 150

Alquier, François-Savinien d', 91–92

Anacreontic poetry, 23, 24. *See also* Pléiade poets

Andeli, Henri, 5

Annales de géographie (journal), 160

AOCs *(appellations d'origine contrôlées),* 2–3, 155, 157, 161

"Apology for Raymond Sebond" (Montaigne), 40–42

Cato, 75

Chamard, Henri, 168n36

Champagne wines, 28, 110–12, 178n3, 180n51; the Champagne–Burgundy debate, 107–12, 113, 128; Saint-Évremond's preference for, 11, 94, 95, 96

Chapelle, Claude Emmanuel Luillier, 186n14

Chaptal, Jean-Antoine-Claude, 140–41, 180n45

Chardin, Jean, 115, 120, 133

Charron, Pierre, 171n16

chefs, 129–32, 133, 152, 183n53

Cicero, 41, 57, 113, 171n13

Les Cinq Livres. See Rabelais, François

Cinquième livre (Rabelais), 20–22, 167n16. *See also* Rabelais, François

class identity. *See* social status

cleanliness. *See* hygiene; purity

Clélie (Scudéry), 105, 127

Cleopatra (La Calprenède), 106–7

climat, 8–9, 137

climate: France's climate as superior, 91–92, 120. *See also* environmental determinism

Colette, 159, 186n14

colonialism, 125, 135

Columella, 5, 32, 50, 75, 169–70n55

Comment être autochtone . . . (Detienne), 115

Condorcet, Nicolas de, 146–47

connoisseurship. *See* culinary connoisseurship

cookbooks. *See* culinary literature; *specific authors and titles*

Corbin, Alain, 148

the Côteaux, 94–95, 96

Cours complet d'agriculture moderne (Berchoux), 142–43

Cours de chimie . . . (Lémery), 178–79n13

The Court Society (Elias), 9, 78

Csergo, Julia, 152–53

Cuchon, Mireille, 167n16

cuisine. *See* culinary *entries*; food *entries*

La Cuisinière bourgeoise (Menon), 89

Le Cuisinier français (La Varenne), 90, 177n41

Le Cuisinier royal et bourgeois (Massialot), 89, 90, 178n43

culinary connoisseurship, 3, 4, 8, 11, 17, 112; as the ability to discern terroir, 35, 174n26, 178n6; after Rousseau, 138–40; nineteenth-century developments, 148–53; Saint-Évremond as model connoisseur, 11, 93–97. *See also* taste (discernment)

culinary diversity, 1, 3, 14–15. *See also* regional foods

culinary literature, 77, 83; aesthetics in, 71–72, 87–92, 131–32; Cartesian influences in, 88, 177n41; eighteenth-century, 129–32, 133; modern, as psychogeography, 162–63; nineteenth-century, 148–53; seventeenth-century, 71–72, 77, 83, 87–92, 179n31. *See also specific authors and titles*

culinary metaphors, 71–72, 126–27, 128, 166n4, 170n1; seasoning metaphors, 70–71, 75, 104

culinary purity, 54, 69–72, 95–96, 129; exotic foods as impure, 130–31, 131*fig.*, 133, 183n53

culinary terroir, 2–3, 6–7, 8, 11, 12; gastronomic tourism and guides, 148–53, 155–56, 162–63, 186n14. *See also* culinary connoisseurship; culinary literature; culinary purity; food *entries*; regional foods and wines; wines and wine drinking

Culoteau, Gilles, 108–9

The Cult of the Nation in France (Bell), 9

Curnonsky, 162

Darton, Robert, 136

Daudet, Marthe Allard, 162

De Architectura (Vitruvius), 46–47

Debord, Guy, 155–56

Défense et illustration de la langue française (du Bellay), 22, 27–28, 31, 42, 168n39

degeneracy theories, 39–40, 48, 181n3

Déjeuner d'huîtres (de Tröy), 110, 111*fig.*

De lege agraria (Cicero), 171n13

De l'esprit des lois (Montesquieu), 115, 118, 124–25

Délices de la campagne (Bonnefons), 88–89

Les Délices de la France (Alquier), 91–92

Delille, Jacques, 143, 144–45, 184n22

De Maucroix, François, 112–13
Democritus, 85
Demosthenes, 57, 112–13
Dens, Jean-Pierre, 96
departments, France's division into, 134, 145–48, 149
De Re Cibaria (Bruyérin-Champier), 34–35, 149, 171n12
Descartes, René, 66, 82–84, 125, 177nn29,30. *See also* Cartesian rationalism
De Serres, Olivier, 48, 49*fig.*, 50, 76, 172n33. *See also Théâtre d'agriculture*
Detienne, Marcel, 115
Devis sur la vigne, vin et vendanges (Gohory), 29–32, 34
Devyver, André, 115
dialects. *See* regional language
Dictionnaire de l'Académie française, 2, 63, 173n6, 174n28
Dictionnaire universel (Furetière), 55–56, 59, 100, 179n22
Diderot, Denis de, 60, 108. *See also Encyclopédie*
Digression sur les Anciens et les Modernes (Fontenelle), 66–69, 84. *See also* Fontenelle, Bernard le Bovier de
Dion, Roger, 184n15
dirt and dirtiness, 35, 55, 61. *See also* earth; soils
Discours de la méthode (Descartes), 83–84, 177n41
disorder. *See* order/disorder
"Dissertation préliminaire sur la cuisine moderne" (Foncemagne), 129–32
La Distinction (Bourdieu), 8
Dive bouteille (Divine Bottle), 20–22, 61
diversity, 1, 3, 53; biological, 45, 86–87, 134–35, 136; culinary, 1, 3, 14–15; linguistic, 45–46, 53; literary, 158. *See also* regional *entries*
Domaine du Pradel, 49*fig.*
Donneau de Visé, Jean, 94, 178n4
Dougherty, Percy, 6
Douglas, Mary, 9, 55, 56, 72
droit du sol, 114
Dryden, John, 25

Du Bellay, Joachim, 22, 27–28, 29, 31, 42, 168n39. *See also* Pléiade poets
Du Bos, abbé (Jean-Baptiste), 12, 115, 118–23, 125, 182n23; influence on culinary perceptions of terroir, 127–30
Du Chastellet, M., 57
Du Vair, Guillaume, 174n14

earth and earthiness: terrestrial foods and wines, 98, 99, 100, 102, 128; under-ground places, 20, 61, 167n17; wine as revelatory of earth's secrets, 159–60. *See also* dirt; soils
education, 161, 186n19
Elias, Norbert, 9, 78
elitism: Boulainvilliers's biological elitism, 115–18, 119; in food choices, 8, 101–2. *See also* social status
Ellis, Harold, 116
Émile (Rousseau), 134–36, 144
Encyclopédie, ou dictionnaire raisonné des sciences, des arts, et des métiers (Diderot and D'Alembert), 60, 108, 138–40
English-style garden aesthetic, 143–45
environmental determinism, 1–2, 3, 8–9, 10; in ancient authors, 43, 46–47, 171n13; eighteenth-century views, 114–15, 119–26, 127, 134–36, 149, 181n3; and the mapping of France's depart-ments, 146; nineteenth-century views, 115, 119, 181n3; seventeenth-century views, 86–87, 90–92, 99–100, 104–7, 112, 180n41; sixteenth-century views, 33, 37, 41–46, 48, 52, 65–68, 171n16, 172n28; and twentieth-century literary regionalism, 156–59; in Vidal de la Blache, 160–61. *See also* human behav-ior and character; humans-as-plants metaphors; *specific authors*
Epicureanism, 82–83, 84–87, 90, 98, 100–101
Epicurus, 84, 85, 177n32
Espiard, François Ignace d', 175n43
Esprit des nations (d'Espiard), 175n43
Essai sur la noblesse (Boulainvilliers), 117–18, 181n10
Estienne, Charles, 32–34, 50, 51, 169–70n55, 178n1

"On the Vanity of Words" (Montaigne), 170n1
order/disorder, 55; culinary disorder, 71, 72, 103, 179n31; gardens as orderly landscapes, 73, 77–78
origin. *See* geographic origin
Ozouf-Marignier, Marie-Vic, 146

Paduanism, 60
painting, 126, 127
Pajot, Charles, 56
Palissy, Bernard, 171n16, 182n34
Pampille, 162
Pantagruel. See Rabelais, François
Paris: gastronomic supremacy of, 152; as locus of political and social power, 54, 72, 73, 76, 146, 148; and the mapping of France's departments, 146, 148; as neutral/objective terroir, 54, 69, 90, 98; as unfavorable terroir, 185–86n9; wine consumption and preferences in, 109, 138, 139*fig. See also* provinciality; regional *entries*
"Paris-Province" (Corbin), 148
Parmentier, Antoine Augustin, 140–41
The Pasteurization of France (Latour), 166n15
patavinité, 60
patriotism. *See* French national sentiment; nationalism
Peletier du Mans, Jacques, 22, 26, 29. *See also* Pléiade poets
Pellisson-Fontanier, Paul, 174n12
Perrault, Claude, 61–62, 85, 174n26
Perrault, Pierre, 61–62, 85, 174n26
Philip-Augustus (Philip II), King of France, 5
philosophy: philosophical references in sixteenth-century wine literature, 30; seventeenth-century Epicureanism, 82–83, 84–87, 90, 98, 100–101. *See also* Cartesian rationalism
physical characteristics, terroir and, 33, 34, 37, 41, 86–87, 120. *See also* environmental determinism
physicality: body/mind dualism, 66, 83–84, 85; in Epicurean philosophy, 85–86. *See also* sensation
physical labor, views of, 26, 27, 77, 117–18, 168n39

physiology: shift to physiological theories of medicine, 97, 128, 178–79n13; of taste, 85–86, 98, 101, 179n24; of wine digestion, 98–99, 101, 108
pigeons, 103, 179n34
Pinkard, Susan, 6
Pitte, Jean-Robert, 6, 186n19
Les Plaisirs rustiques, à Maurice de la Porte (Ronsard), 28–29
plants: natural limits for plant cultivation, 55, 67, 68, 75, 80, 81, 121; nutrient uptake by, 179n24. *See also* agriculture; gardens; humans-as-plants metaphors
Plato, 18, 19, 171n13
pleasure and hedonism: in Rabelais, 15–17, 19, 22; in Renaissance poetry, 23; in Renaissance wine literature, 30, 33, 34
Pléiade poets, 10, 13, 22–25, 31, 37, 48; affirmation of place in, 13, 24–25; agricultural metaphors in, 26, 27–29, 39, 168n39; bacchic imagery in, 10, 18, 22–25, 26–29; engagement with the French language, 22, 23, 24, 27–28, 29, 42; georgic imagery and influences, 18, 24, 26–28, 35–36
Pliny, 169–70n55
Pluche, abbé, 184n30
Le Poème des mois (Roucher), 143, 184n22
Le Poème des saisons (Saint-Lambert), 143, 184n22
Poètes du terroir (van Bever), 157–58
poetry: modern regional poets, 157–58; naturalness/naturalized mythology in, 23, 26, 168n36. *See also* Pléiade poets; *specific authors and works*
politeness, 56, 59–60, 72. *See also* sophistication/refinement
political identity. *See* French identity; French national sentiment
political theory and political terroir, 11–12, 114–32, 133; environmental determinism in, 43–48, 52, 114–15, 123–25, 181n3; mapping of France's departments, 134, 145–48, 149; seventeenth-century centralization of power and its implications, 54, 72, 76; *thèse royaliste/thèse nobiliaire* debate, 11–12, 114–15. *See also specific authors and works*

polygenetic theory, 116, 117, 118, 119, 182n21
potager du roi (Versailles), 79–81, 81*fig.*,
    144. *See also* Versailles gardens
Précellence du langage français (Estienne),
    58
La Promenade de Versailles (Scudéry),
    79–80
provinciality and the provinces: mapping of
    France's departments, 134, 145–48, 149;
    reflected in food choices, 104; viewed
    negatively, 58–59, 66, 69, 73, 76, 87, 90,
    134; viewed positively, 134, 135–36. *See
    also* Paris; regional *entries*; rusticity
psychogeography, 155–56, 185n4; terroir as,
    7–8, 155–59, 161, 162–63
Purity and Danger (Douglas), 9, 55, 72
purity/impurity: of climate, French
    national sentiment and, 91–92; cultural
    obsessions with, 55; purity as sophistica-
    tion, 11, 62, 65; racial purity in Boulain-
    villiers and Rousseau, 116, 117, 118,
    134–35, 136; of reason, 60–61, 65–66, 67,
    84; terroir as corrupting force, 48, 52,
    59, 60–61, 62, 81, 82; water as purity, 60,
    70, 82. *See also* culinary purity; linguis-
    tic purity

Quart livre (Rabelais), 22
Quellier, Florent, 5, 172n35
Quesnay, François, 141
Quintinie, Jean de la, 76, 79, 80–82, 144,
    176n27, 177n29, 179n24

rabbit, 103, 179n32
Rabelais, François, 9–10, 13–22, 154,
    169n47; bacchic imagery in, 10, 18–22,
    167–68n22; boundary transgression in,
    10, 13, 14–15, 16, 17, 20–22; conflation of
    people with food, 14, 166n3; excess in,
    15–17; reflected in sixteenth-century
    wine literature, 29–30, 169n47. *See also*
    Rabelais, François
race: in eighteenth-century writings, 116,
    117, 118, 121, 125, 134–36
Racine, 105–6, 127
Rapin, René, 144
rationalism, 11, 65–66, 68–69, 83; in culi-
    nary literature, 88–89, 90, 129, 177n41;

as Versailles ethos, 79–80, 83, 177n29.
    See also Cartesian rationalism
reason: associated with origin/terroir,
    60–61, 65–66, 67, 84; Descartes's views,
    83–84. *See also* Cartesian rationalism;
    rationalism
red wines: the Champagne–Burgundy
    debate, 107–12, 113, 128; wine-
    color preferences, 98–99, 101, 128,
    179n15
refinement. *See* sophistication/refinement
*Réflexions critiques sur la poésie et sur la
    peinture* (Du Bos), 115, 118–23
regional differences: agricultural moderni-
    zation's impact on, 186n12; and the
    mapping of France's departments,
    146–48, 149; reflected in gastronomic
    maps and guides, 148–53; viewed posi-
    tively, 134, 135–36, 158–59, 185–86n9,
    186n17. *See also* boundaries; environ-
    mental determinism; regional foods;
    regional identity; regional language
regional foods and wines, 148–53, 155*fig.*,
    161; AOCs, 2–3, 155, 157, 161; the Cham-
    pagne–Burgundy debate, 107–12, 113,
    128; gastronomic tourism and guides,
    148–53, 155–56, 162–63, 186n14; in
    modern cookbooks, 162–63. *See also*
    culinary connoisseurship; culinary
    terroir; wines and wine drinking
regional identity and pride: and the Cham-
    pagne–Burgundy debate, 108, 109;
    literary regionalism, 10, 156–60, 185n7,
    185–86n9; and the mapping of France's
    departments, 146; modern pride in
    regional foods, 161; in the Pléiade poets,
    10, 27, 29, 31; and the Revolutionary
    spirit, 145, 184n34
regional language and speech, 64*map*, 149;
    regional terms in de Serres, 52–53;
    viewed negatively or ambivalently, 54,
    57–58, 60, 63–64, 65, 72; viewed posi-
    tively, 158–59. *See also* language and
    linguistic terroir
Remarques sur la langue française (Vauge-
    las), 58–59
Repas ridicule (Boileau), 102–4
restaurants, 152, 183n53

Symposium (Plato), 18, 19
Syntagma philosophicum (Gassendi),
    177nn32,33

Tableau de la géographie de la France (Vidal
    de la Blache), 160–61, 186n17
Tacitus, 43
taste (discernment), 8, 101–2; associated
    with climate/origin, 104–5, 119–20; the
    Côteaux's tasting skill, 94–95; culinary,
    8, 87–90, 104, 109, 132; literary, 104. *See
    also* aesthetics; culinary connoisseur-
    ship; food choices and preferences;
    sophistication/refinement
taste (flavor): culinary uses/associations of
    the term *terroir*, 2, 56, 61–62, 173n6;
    natural/wild foods and flavors, 40,
    70–71, 95–96; physiology of, 85–86, 98,
    101, 179n24; of soils, 35, 82, 138–40,
    170n65, 172n35; taste descriptors, 7–8;
    tasters' expectations and, 3, 165n5. *See
    also goût de terroir*
*The Taste of Place: A Cultural Journey into
    Terroir* (Trubek), 6
territorium, 5
terroir, as concept: overviews, 3–7, 9–12;
    recent scholarship, 6–7; related terms,
    8–9. *See also* terroirlessness
terroir, as term, 2, 4–5, 57; agricultural
    usage, 50, 55–56, 77, 145; associated with
    language, 58–60, 174n14; associated
    with people, 47, 106, 173n6; circumlocu-
    tions and avoidance of, 8, 153; culinary
    uses and associations, 2, 56, 61–62,
    173n6; equivalents in other languages, 3,
    165n6; in garden literature, 77, 82,
    176n10, 176n27; origins and early defini-
    tions, 2, 4–5, 173nn3,6; in Rabelais, 14.
    See also goût de terroir and *goût du
    terroir*
Terroir (literary journal), 185n7
terroirlessness: Champagne as expression
    of, 109, 112; gardens as terroirless sites,
    81–82, 136. *See also* neutrality
Le Théâtre d'agriculture (de Serres), 10, 37,
    48–53, 49*fig.*, 74–78, 169n43; agricul-
    ture and agricultural practices in, 50,
    51–52, 74–76, 77; anthropomorphizing

language in, 52, 173n42; on Champagne
    wines, 178n1; chapter organization, 51;
    Christian and moral overtones in,
    51–52, 172n40; estate owner's role in,
    74, 75–76, 80; fall from favor, 76–78;
    literary aspects of, 50–53; mythological
    references in, 52, 173n43; nature and our
    relationship to nature in, 51–52, 74, 75;
    pleasure gardens in, 77; popularity and
    influence of, 48, 51; regional terms in,
    52–53; soils and terroir in, 48, 50, 51–53,
    55, 74–76, 79, 82, 172n35; upper classes
    as audience for, 50–51, 172n36
Théorie des jardins (Morel), 144
thèse royaliste/thèse nobiliaire debate, 11–12,
    114–15. *See also* Boulainvilliers; Du Bos;
    Montesquieu
Thrésor de la langue française (Nicot), 55
Tomasik, Timothy J., 166n4, 169n47
Traité du jardinage (Boyceau de la Barau-
    derie), 76–78, 176n12
*Traité théorique et practique sur la culture de
    la vigne* (Chaptal, Rozier, Parmentier,
    and d'Ussieux), 140–41
transplantation metaphors, 9, 42, 68, 121,
    122–23, 126
travel literature, 162–63, 186n14
Treatise on Wine and Cider (Le Paulmier),
    35, 170n65, 178nn1,6
Le Trésor de santé, 87
trinch, 21
Tröy, Jean-François de, 110, 111*fig.*
Trubek, Amy, 6
Turgot, Anne-Robert-Jacques, 141, 142

underground places, 20, 61, 167n17
Ussieux, Louis d', 140–41
utility/beauty dichotomy, 77, 78

Van Bever, Adolphe, 157–59, 186n12
Varro, 5, 75, 169–70n55
Vaudour, Emmanuelle, 6
Vaugelas, Claude Favre de, 10, 57, 58–59
Vegetius, 41, 171n13
Véron wine, 17, 167n12
Versailles, court of, 72, 78; and the Cham-
    pagne–Burgundy debate, 108–10,
    180n51. *See also* Paris; Versailles gardens

CALIFORNIA STUDIES IN FOOD AND CULTURE

Darra Goldstein, Editor

1. *Dangerous Tastes: The Story of Spices,* by Andrew Dalby

2. *Eating Right in the Renaissance,* by Ken Albala

3. *Food Politics: How the Food Industry Influences Nutrition and Health,* by Marion Nestle

4. *Camembert: A National Myth,* by Pierre Boisard

5. *Safe Food: The Politics of Food Safety,* by Marion Nestle

6. *Eating Apes,* by Dale Peterson

7. *Revolution at the Table: The Transformation of the American Diet,* by Harvey Levenstein

8. *Paradox of Plenty: A Social History of Eating in Modern America,* by Harvey Levenstein

9. *Encarnación's Kitchen: Mexican Recipes from Nineteenth-Century California: Selections from Encarnación Pinedo's* El cocinero español, by Encarnación Pinedo, edited and translated by Dan Strehl, with an essay by Victor Valle

10. *Zinfandel: A History of a Grape and Its Wine,* by Charles L. Sullivan, with a foreword by Paul Draper

11. *Tsukiji: The Fish Market at the Center of the World,* by Theodore C. Bestor

12. *Born Again Bodies: Flesh and Spirit in American Christianity,* by R. Marie Griffith

13. *Our Overweight Children: What Parents, Schools, and Communities Can Do to Control the Fatness Epidemic,* by Sharron Dalton

14. *The Art of Cooking: The First Modern Cookery Book,* by The Eminent Maestro Martino of Como, edited and with an introduction by Luigi Ballerini, translated and annotated by Jeremy Parzen, and with fifty modernized recipes by Stefania Barzini

15. *The Queen of Fats: Why Omega-3s Were Removed from the Western Diet and What We Can Do to Replace Them,* by Susan Allport

16. *Meals to Come: A History of the Future of Food,* by Warren Belasco

17. *The Spice Route: A History,* by John Keay